THE GREAT
WHITEWATER
FIASCO

*An American Tale of
Money, Power, and Politics*

Martin L. Gross

Ballantine Books • New York

All rights reserved under International and Pan-American Copyright Conventions. Published in the United States by Ballantine Books, a division of Random House, Inc., New York, and simultaneously in Canada by Random House of Canada Limited, Toronto.

Library of Congress Catalog Card Number: 94-96246

ISBN: 0-345-39354-6

Cover design by Richard Hasselberger
Cover photo © FPG International

Manufactured in the United States of America
First Edition: August 1994

10 9 8 7 6 5 4 3 2 1

To my wife, Anita

CONTENTS

CAST OF CHARACTERS
(In Order of Appearance)

William Jefferson Clinton, Attorney General of Arkansas, Governor of Arkansas, President of the United States.

Hillary Rodham Clinton, wife, right hand, and left hand, aide to and manager of Bill Clinton.

Robert B. Fiske, Jr., former Special Counsel, or as Janet Reno had mislabeled him, "Independent Counsel," who investigated the Whitewater phenomenon.

James Blair, counsel for Tyson Foods, large contributor to Clinton's campaigns, and tooth fairy for Hillary's $99,000 gain in cattle futures.

Robert "Red" Bone, broker who reportedly did, but didn't, handle Hillary's commodities coup.

Jeff Gerth, *New York Times* writer who broke the Whitewater story and who deserves, but probably won't get, the Pulitzer Prize.

James B. McDougal, owner of the Madison Guaranty Savings and Loan and the main protagonist, along with the Clintons, in this Shakespearean drama.

Hugh Rodham, Hillary's father, who influenced her toward Barry Goldwater politics, then was disappointed politically.

Professor Alan Schechter of Wellesley, an important influence in moving Hillary in the liberal-left direction.

John Robert Starr, former editor of the *Arkansas Democrat-Gazette*, whose criticism, then support, of the Clintons broke and made their early political career.

Senator William Fulbright of Arkansas, who has played an overwhelming role in Bill Clinton's ascendancy—as everything from employer, contributor, Oxford and draft facilitator.

Cliff Jackson, former Oxford classmate who inadvertently helped Clinton avoid the draft and is now the President's sworn enemy.

John Paul Hammerschmidt, Arkansas Republican Congressman, one of two men who has beaten Bill Clinton in an election.

Bernard Nussbaum, former counsel to President Clinton, who met Hillary when they both served on the House staff working to impeach President Nixon.

Jimmy Carter, for whom Hillary worked in Indiana, and who rewarded her with a federal patronage post when he became President.

Sam Heuer, McDougal's lawyer, who handled his 1990 case on federal fraud charges and saw his client acquitted.

Sheffield Nelson, Republican candidate for governor of Arkansas, who helped tip off the press to Whitewater and taperecorded an interview with Jim McDougal.

Jim Guy Tucker, current governor of Arkansas and a recipient of large loans from Madison.

Congressman Jim Leach of Iowa, ranking Republican member, and intellectual, on the House Banking Committee, who is skeptical of all things Whitewater and has pressed the investigation.

Frank White, jovial Republican Arkansan who beat Clinton for the governorship in 1980, then lost to him in 1982.

Harry Thomason and Linda Bloodworth-Thomason, Hollywood moguls with Arkansas roots who engineered the extraordinary physical transformation of Hillary Clinton.

Susan McDougal, the banker's wife and partner in Whitewater, who received a crucial and controversial $300,000 loan—that has defaulted at taxpayer expense.

Madison Guaranty Savings and Loan, the only nonhuman in the tale, but probably its most important character.

Webster L. "Webb" Hubbell, former Razorback football star,

Hillary's law partner at the Rose Law Firm, and (for a while) number three man in the Justice Department.

Seth Ward, father-in-law of Webb Hubbell, whose name crops up from time to time.

Vincent W. Foster, Jr., Hillary's former law partner and closest friend of the Clintons, who committed suicide while serving as deputy counsel to the President.

William H. Kennedy III, the fourth member of Rose Law Firm's "Famous Four," who served in a top position at the White House until he forgot to pay his nanny taxes.

C. Joseph Giroir, former head of Rose, who built the firm, then left, some say nudged out by Hillary, et al.

David Watkins, who made a small fortune for Hillary, then served in the White House until he helicoptered to his golf game.

Don Tyson, head of Tyson Foods, a generous contributor to Clinton and grateful recipient of the Governor's political largesse.

Beverly Bassett Schaffer, former head of the Arkansas Securities Department, which oversees S&Ls. She approved the Rose (Hillary's) plan to save Madison Guaranty, after which it lost more of the taxpayers' money.

Marlin D. Jackson, close friend, political appointee, and overly generous banker for the Clintons, he warned Bill of the coming debacle of Madison Guaranty.

Betsey Wright, longtime chief of staff to Governor Clinton, second most important woman in his political life, and now a Washington lobbyist with the best access to the White House.

David Hale, a convicted loan company operator who had been named a judge by Clinton; he helped piggyback the Arkansas "political family," allegedly including Whitewater.

Ken Peacock, a young Arkansas businessman whose name appeared on a $3,000 contribution to Bill Clinton—which he never made.

Roger Clinton, the President's half brother, who was convicted of selling narcotics.

Dan Lasater, a mystery man of the tale: millionaire (Ponderosa restaurants), big contributor to Clinton, favored Clinton bond dealer, and convicted cocaine user.

Roy Drew, who once handled Hillary's money and was destroyed financially when he opposed Clinton's state bond program.

Patsy Thomasson, who ran Lasater's business while he was in jail and is now administrative boss at the White House. She is reputedly one of the three who entered Foster's office the fateful night of his suicide.

Tom C. McCrae IV, opponent of Clinton in the 1990 race for governor, who became a victim of Hillary's ire and ingenuity.

Jackson Stephens (Mr. Jack) of Stephens, Inc., billionaire reputed to "own" Arkansas, who fought, then finally backed Clinton when he came to believe the Governor was invincible.

Winston Stephens (Mr. Witt), who owns the other half of the state.

Gennifer Flowers, attractive reputed mistress of Bill Clinton, whose announcement of their affair did not stop him from winning the presidency.

Curt Bradbury of the Worthen Bank in Little Rock, who financed Clinton—with a $3.5 million loan—when Bill looked like he was on his political back.

James Lyons, a lawyer, a close friend of Bill's, and an apparent political genius, who "cleared" Clinton of wrongdoing in Whitewater during the 1992 campaign.

Jerry Brown, candidate for President in 1992 who then futilely raised the question of Whitewater.

L. Jean Lewis, RTC criminal investigator in Kansas City, whistle-blower extraordinaire, patriot, and the woman who exposed one part of Whitewater.

Janet Reno, Attorney General of the United States, who refused to name a Special Counsel on Whitewater—until Congress screamed.

Paula Casey, former law school student of Bill Clinton's, and new U.S. Attorney for Little Rock. She decided that the criminal referral on Madison-Whitewater held "insufficient evidence."

President George Bush, who was afraid to use the criminal referral mentioning the Clintons in his inept 1992 campaign.

April Breslaw, RTC attorney in Washington, who traveled to Kansas City to tell investigator Jean Lewis that the "people at the top" would be "happy" with a soft report on Whitewater.

Roger C. Altman, former Deputy Secretary of the Treasury and former acting chief of the RTC, whose testimony at the Whitewater hearings was considered suspect by several members of the Senate.

Neil Eggleston, a White House counsel who ran from the hearing room when he heard Roger Altman deliver incomplete testimony.

Lloyd C. Bentsen, Secretary of the Treasury, who disclaims any knowledge of anything to do with it all.

Jean Hanson, chief counsel for Treasury, who first brought news of the criminal referrals to the White House and who now contradicts the stories of both her bosses.

David Kendall, the First Family's personal lawyer, who had the Whitewater papers in his possession for a while and who White House staffers thought should have a private briefing from the RTC on the Clintons' Whitewater problem.

Ellen Kulka, chief counsel of the RTC, feared by the White House as being "tough."

Henry Gonzalez, less-than-eloquent chairman of the House Banking Committee, whose gavel had a distinctly partisan ring.

Donald Riegle, the chairman of the Senate Whitewater hearings, who bent over backwards to ensure fair, nonpartisan hearings.

Harold Ickes, Deputy Chief of Staff to the President, who with

Stephanopoulos became incensed when Roger Altman suddenly
"recused" (excused) himself from the Whitewater affair.

Lloyd C. Cutler, the President's interim counsel, who provided
light entertainment at the House Whitewater hearings by insisting that his investigation was impartial.

Senator Alfonse D'Amato, feisty ranking minority leader on
the Senate Banking Committee, who brings charmlessness to his
well-researched attacks on Whitewater.

Joshua Steiner, chief of staff to Treasury Secretary Bentsen,
whose diary scribblings made him the Liz Smith of Whitewater.

George Stephanopoulos, son of a Greek Orthodox priest, forgot his political ethics when he went ballistic and discussed how
to fire a Republican investigator working for the RTC.

Emil Ludwig, Comptroller of Currency and close Clinton friend,
who was approached on the New Year's weekend to lend a little
expertise to the quandry.

Congressman Eric Fingerhut, the only Democratic member of
the House Banking Committee who is willing to admit that Whitewater even exists.

Bruce Lindsey, former law partner and senior advisor to the
President, who first told the President about the RTC investigation in early October 1993.

Margaret Williams, Hillary's chief of staff, who spirited the
Whitewater papers into the White House family quarter's safe the
night of Vince Foster's suicide. She is probably the most important staff person in the White House—bar none.

Kenneth W. Starr, who on August 5, 1994, was named Independent Counsel by a panel of three judges to replace Robert Fiske
as Whitewater investigator.

And now . . . to our tale.

THE GREAT
WHITEWATER
FIASCO

Chapter One

Whitewater, Hillarygate, and High Politics

Little Rock, Arkansas, is an undistinguished small city that spreads out on an almost table-top plain. Physically, it is a conglomeration of a handful of new buildings, like its tallest, the 38-story TCBY skyscraper, punctuated here and there among smaller, older structures, and all strangely broken up into a checkerboard of parking lots that seem to take up half the downtown.

The city had a small boom in the 1980s, which added such towers as the attractive glass one that houses the multi-billion-dollar Stephens investment firm—the nation's largest outside Wall Street. But the boomlet has since leveled off, even declined, giving Little Rock the appearance of a mundane community with scores of closed, empty stores in its downtown. On a business day, the place seems as sleepy as some others on a peaceful Sunday.

The city of 175,000 is enlivened mainly by its politics

3

and its two public buildings, the state capitol, which is a
near replica of the original in Washington, and the Old
State House, a tasteful Greek Revival structure where Bill
Clinton announced his run for the presidency in 1991. That
antique is close to the modern glass Excelsior Hotel,
which, with the beautifully renovated Victorian-style Capitol Hotel, is the center of local activity, and the purported
site of some of Mr. Clinton's personal adventures.

On the other side of town, western Little Rock, where
much of the economic action is moving, is an anonymous
four-story brick building with tinted windows at 10825 Financial Centre Parkway. This is the home of the interlopers from
Washington. Suite 134 was the home of the Office of Special
Counsel Robert B. Fiske, Jr., who had been named by the
Justice Department to investigate Mr. and Mrs. Clinton and
several others involved in a series of circumstances that have
been given the collective name of "WHITEWATER."

(The new Independent Counsel has taken occupancy
of the same quarters.)

The Special Counsel
That inquiry has been going on since January 1994, when
Mr. Fiske came to Little Rock and quickly swore in a special grand jury to add to the one operating in Washington.
He brought in a large staff, including eight prosecutors
and some twenty-five FBI agents, attorneys, and accountants, to conduct upwards of three hundred interviews to
help him uncover the secrets of one of the strangest cases
in American history. Mr. Starr has retained most of them
and added some staff of his own.

The government has taken a three-year lease on that

property (another example of waste?), but it's hoped that Starr will not try to best the record of Lawrence Walsh, the Independent Counsel in the Iran-Contra affair who took seven years to wrap up his business, and spent $38 million doing it.

Whitewater, with its convoluted maze—which we shall try to unravel in all its exquisite detail—is not *officially* related to another revelation. A sister to Whitewater, it is just as instructive in how politics and money are lovingly married in America.

That story involves one of the swiftest speculative successes in American financial history. It has been called Bullgate, and Cattlegate, but none of the names has stuck. (Whitewater had the value of the word "water" appearing in both this fiasco and Mr. Nixon's tragedy.) Probably, the closest tag that will stick is the somewhat euphonious "Hillarygate."

Both stories, Whitewater and Hillarygate, actually began sixteen years ago, within months of each other. It was between August and October 1978, a pregnant time for President Clinton and his wife, and perhaps equally vital in the short history of our times.

Their motives were quite human: to make a big buck. But there was one complication. It was just before the 1978 election for the governor of Arkansas.

One Party State

The real event, the Democratic primary in a generally one-party state, had already been held. Bill Clinton, the young attorney general of the state, elected less than two years before in his first successful race for office, had beaten

four competitors for the gubernatorial nomination with a
solid 55 percent of the total. Only five years out of Yale
Law School, he didn't even have to face a run-off for the
top Democratic spot.

He still had to run against the Republican nominee, A. Lynn Lowe, on November 7, but no one paid attention to that. The only Republican governor in Arkansas
since Reconstruction had been Winthrop Rockefeller, and
he was gone.

The polls showed Clinton ahead by almost two to one,
and barring some unforeseen political disaster, Bill Clinton, age thirty-two, and Hillary Rodham (she still used her
maiden name), age thirty-one, were about to become the
youngest First Family in the history of Arkansas, and the
second youngest in the history of the United States.

By January, Bill Clinton and his wife would enter
the rent-free governor's mansion, a large pinkish brick,
pseudo-Colonial home on Center Street, what was *once*
a good residential neighborhood, but had started to de-
teriorate like much in downtown Little Rock.

Having conquered the high plateau of Arkansas politics,
they now turned their attention to the gilded world of
money. Between them, the soon-to-be First Couple didn't
have a spare thousand. The Governor's job paid $35,000 a
year, but he had yet to get his first paycheck. Hillary had
been an attorney at the prestigious Rose Law Firm for only a
year and was still earning a limited salary of under $25,000.

But that was no handicap for surely the most dynamic
political couple of our time. As the powers-soon-to-be in
Arkansas, they had many chances to get rich—and many
people to help them. Unlike others in the Little Rock phone

book, the Clintons had access to deals with inside cachet, some tailor-made for a future governor and his wife. And they took full advantage of them.

They Had No Capital
The two "investments" came almost simultaneously. And best of all, they required almost no capital—for they had none. The first investment was to make them a quick fortune, at least by the standards of the time and place.

But the second, labeled Whitewater, failed. It was not only to lose money, but would drag the couple down into a morass of charges—some involving them and others tagged to their colleagues—from which the Clintons may never really extricate themselves.

The first investment, by Hillary, involved James Blair, a successful attorney who was then chief outside attorney for Tyson Foods (and is now their official counsel). A close friend of the Clintons, Blair was active in Democratic party affairs, and contributed and worked in Clinton's campaigns. In 1978, he was trading cattle futures with a brokerage firm called Refco, Inc., in Springdale, Arkansas, and making a great deal of money.

Cattle futures is a very risky business in which one bets which way the price will go and in which 80 percent of the investors lose money, even their shirts or chemises. They were then particularly active. Prices were gyrating wildly up and down, and millions were being made. At the same time, Blair's client, Tyson Foods, the world's largest poultry producer and dedicated backer of Bill Clinton, was also trading in three corporate accounts at Refco.

Blair approached the Arkansas First Lady-to-be and

suggested that she open an account at Refco and use his broker, Robert "Red" Bone. She didn't have to know the first thing about commodity trading. Blair was an expert, having done it for years, and evidenced by his enormous profits. He'd advise her on what to do.

A Wonderful Day

Hillary supposedly invested $1,000 and within a year had run it up to $99,537. The very first day, Hillary made $5,300 on the $1,000 investment, a statistical impossibility, say most experts in the field—*if* the rules of the trade were followed.

Commodity professionals quoted in the press indicate that Hillary would have had to put up $14,400 for twelve cattle future contracts for her to make $5,300 profit in one day. But of course she didn't. The most telling point about her good luck is that for some reason it has been an enormous embarrassment to the Clintons, who initially refused to release their 1977–1979 income tax returns for fear the commodities bonanza would be revealed.

In other hands, like those of a lottery winner, it would be loudly proclaimed. Instead, the Clintons, who have tried to present the image of "Log Cabin Democrats," as *Business Week* labeled them, have carefully kept the secret of this capitalist victory from the public and the media for sixteen years.

Unlike Whitewater, the cattle coup was known only to her husband and closest intimates, who faithfully kept her confidence all this time. Until a team of reporters headed by Jeff Gerth of the *New York Times* broke the story in March 1994, in an excellent piece of investigative journalism, it was an unknown fact.

Also unknown was Red Bone's early statement that he had never dealt with Mrs. Clinton in his life. Since Bone didn't have discretionary power, does that mean the trades were not truly made? Were the profits not legally hers? Does Hillary have to return the money? And to whom?

Initially, Mrs. Clinton developed a cover story that she had made all the trades herself by taking Blair's advice and by boning up on *The Wall Street Journal*.

Then, in typical White House fashion, she changed her story and confessed that Blair had made most of the trades for her. In fact, the White House finally confessed that Blair had made *thirty* of *thirty-two* trades for Hillary.

The reality is probably even less sanguine than that. The skeptical *Wall Street Journal* says that there is a "suspicion that someone cut a lot of corners to steer Bill and Hillary to nearly $100,000 in commodities gain."

They add: "Or maybe they weren't her trades at all," a theory that is growing in currency.

Short on Proof

The $1,000 was obviously less than sufficient for her trades. But equally important, there's no evidence that Hillary ever invested a nickel with Refco, let alone $1,000. When the White House was recently asked to produce the check, they answered with a straight face. They "could not find it."

A Columbia University Law School professor, one of four chosen by the White House to explain their 1977–79 taxes, which includes the commodities coup, believes that since there were no checks and no risk of *real* loss, the money could be considered a gift.

Mrs. Clinton has learned, the hard way, that there is no

zone of privacy when it comes to politics and money at the White House level. Though she is still "bewildered" by the public interest in their money affairs, she does seem to finally understand that the camouflage of local politics and cooperative Arkansas press that once protected them does not apply to New York, or Washington, or Los Angeles.

Reluctantly accepting that, she recently made an attempt to be forthcoming. Well dressed in a pink wool jacket, she positioned herself in an isolated single chair in the White House and bravely took questions from the press. In the netherworld that surrounds this mystery, her answers were the makings of history.

Why, she was asked, wasn't she bothered by margin calls, since she had not put up sufficient funds to cover her trades? (At one point, she was $117,500 short, perhaps ten times the family's net worth at the time.)

Perhaps she wasn't bothered by Refco, Mrs. Clinton offered, because either the back office was too busy, or because she was "too good a customer" to annoy. Good customer hardly describes someone who neither deposited, nor could deposit, the sums needed to play the risky game of cattle futures, which, in normal circumstances, could have bankrupted the young couple in a matter of hours.

When asked if she had received favorable advantage in her commodities trades because of who she was, Hillary gave her best lawyerly response: "There's really no evidence of that."

Flippant Response
The subject then moved to Whitewater, eliciting an answer that reporters who were present considered "amazing."

The question, to paraphrase it, was: "If you aren't putting money into the venture and you also know the venture isn't cash flowing, wouldn't you question the source of the funds being used for your benefit?"

"Well, shoulda, coulda, woulda," Mrs. Clinton responded. "We didn't."

The supposed losses on Whitewater are still in heated limbo, but we can ask what became of the cattle future gains. In 1979, while Bill Clinton was in the governor's mansion, $55,000 of it was invested in bonds. When he was abruptly defeated for reelection as governor in November 1979, they lost the use of the governor's mansion and went house hunting.

"Mrs. Clinton used $60,000 of the profit as a down payment on a house in Little Rock," explained Jeff Gerth when interviewed. "But during the 1992 campaign, I submitted written questions about her finances to her attorney. The answer to the question about where she got the money to buy the house was quite different. She said it came from 'our savings and a gift from my parents.' There was no mention of cattle futures."

The anomalies, complexities, and mysteries of that financial coup are as extraordinary as those surrounding Whitewater. As they unravel in shifting explanations, they dog, and will continue to confuse the image of Mrs. Clinton as someone ostensibly dedicated to the "politics of meaning." Skeptics might harshly retranslate that as the American "politics of money."

The portrayal of Hillary as "Saint Hillary," as a *Times* Sunday cover story once called her, clashes with the reality of a very sharp businesswoman and corporate lawyer

who has made her family rich. In the final analysis, Hillarygate may not overshadow its sister activity, Whitewater,
but it could add another giant dimension to a system of
money favors available to prominent American politicians—through their spouses.

The revelation of her commodity trading in the press
triggered still another announcement from the shell-
shocked White House, which has become expert at amend-
ing, confessing, and reamending anything related to these
affairs. In April 1994, they even surprised the skeptics
when Mrs. Clinton's office (she has a taxpayer-paid staff of
thirteen!) suddenly announced that she had made other
commodity trades in the same period, unknown to anyone
outside the closed circle.

A New Profit
This time it was with the Stephens, Inc. brokerage house,
and she had turned a $6,500 profit. The White House ex-
plained that a tax error (one of many to come) had been
made. Instead of reporting the $6,500 gain, Hillary had re-
ported a *loss of $1,009* to the Internal Revenue Service
on the Stephens trades. With back interest, but strangely
without penalties, the Clintons volunteered to pay the IRS
the $14,615 they owed.

This is no longer any strain on the Clintons. Recent financial disclosures show their net worth as being as high
as $1.6 million, most of it Hillary's. Picky skeptics wonder
whether ordinary taxpayers would be handled so gingerly.

Even her husband couldn't get his story on the cattle futures straight. At a town meeting, he declared that Hillary
had stopped trading during her pregnancy because of the

stress (which became the "operative" tale), and also because she got "cold feet" when the brokers gave her a margin call.

The White House quickly put out an updated operative story. No, she had never received a margin call, and Hillary had traded right up through the birth of Chelsea. In fact, in the very week of the birth, she had made three trades, raking in $10,000 more in profits!

The connection of her commodities mentor, James Blair, to Tyson and the Clintons has also raised eyebrows. This is especially true because that largest employer in Arkansas has been uncomfortably close to Bill Clinton and the recipient of many Arkansas favors during his term as Attorney General and Governor, and now in the White House.

Tyson counsel James Blair and the First Family are so close that the day Bill Clinton was inaugurated as President, Blair and his wife slept over in the White House. When the Clintons, who no longer own a home, visit Arkansas, they often stay at the Blairs' waterfront home.

The Clintons are not without gratitude. Diane Blair, James Blair's wife and good friend of Hillary's, has been named by President Clinton to the board of the Corporation for Public Broadcasting, which uses taxpayer funds to support public television and radio. She is only one of Hillary's old friends who have been rewarded with judgeships, U.S. Attorney positions, and other political plums.

(The *New York Times*, which generally backs the Clintons politically, has taken the lead in its attacks on Hillarygate, which they exposed. One *Times* columnist, William Safire, has even gone so far as to label the cattle trades an indirect form of political "bribery," a charge that was sharply contested by a Tyson executive.)

Sweetheart Deal

The other investment, Whitewater, is of course better known. It stands for the Whitewater Development Corporation which was first organized in August 1978 as Whitewater Estates, just months before Clinton's gubernatorial victory at the polls. There were four principals: James B. McDougal and Susan McDougal, corporate officers, and Bill and Hillary Clinton, shareholders. The Clintons put up either nothing or $500 in cash and received a 50 percent share in both the equity and the profits, in what skeptics have modestly labeled "a sweetheart deal."

The idea was a simple real estate development concept: to buy 230 acres of forested land in the Ozark Mountains and subdivide it into forty-two lots for vacation homes. If successful, the project would net at least $250,000 in profits, with no real investment. Before it was through, though, more input, output, and aggravation were attached to this simple deal than possibly any its size in financial history. And, of course, it's still going on.

The land was quite beautiful. It was in the Ozarks in northwestern Arkansas, on a bluff overlooking the White River. Bill and Hillary had already picked out a picturesque riverfront lot for their future vacation home, one that never materialized on the troubled site. Since the land price was a substantial $203,000 (more than twice that in today's dollars), some way had to be found to finance it.

James B. McDougal is several years older than the Clintons. He had been active in Democratic party politics, and had participated in several of Bill's campaigns. The two had become good friends over the years, as had Hillary and Susan McDougal, a real estate broker and marketing woman.

Bringing Bill Clinton, the next Governor of Arkansas, into Whitewater made good business sense. No one could predict when the power of the state would be useful to the project. Apparently, McDougal's political vision was good. On several occasions, as we shall see, the Arkansas state-house became quite handy, perhaps even the vehicle for Whitewater's survival when things got bad.

Conflict of Interest

The potential conflict of the Governor-to-be going into a land speculation in which he received half the equity for nothing, or almost nothing, didn't seem to trouble Bill Clinton— either because of naïvéte, indifference, or insensitivity. The only problem for the Clintons, who were pinching themselves, was how to finance the land.

Wheeler-dealer McDougal, who was known throughout the state, went to colleagues at a bank near Whitewater, the Citizens Bank and Trust Company of Flippin. The executives of the bank have since explained that the Clintons had few assets and no collateral. They couldn't be given such a substantial loan. Instead, the financing was based on McDougal's reputation as a developer. The bank would advance about a 90 percent mortgage. The relatively poor Clintons were riding on their friends, the McDougals.

But there was a hooker. A down payment of $20,000 was needed. The Clintons had nothing like that, and McDougal's money was tied up in other deals. Instead, the foursome borrowed the $20,000 from another bank, this one in Little Rock, as a personal loan and used it as the down payment on Whitewater. This is generally a no-no in the banking world, where buyers are supposed to have some *real* equity in the property.

Because it was a land purchase, the financing was all the more amazing. While homes are sometimes given a 90 percent, or even a 100 percent, mortgage, land deals are more speculative. Land is not a liquid asset, and cannot easily be sold by the bank in case of default.

"We never give more than a 50 percent loan on the appraised value of land," says a bank officer in Connecticut. "In fact, I don't think any bank would." But the banks in Arkansas were dealing with the next Governor of their state. The loan was made and title taken to Whitewater by the four partners.

Jubilant those days in October 1978, the Clintons dreamt not only of political power, which awaited them only three weeks hence, but of their seemingly victorious double play on the road to real riches. But on that glorious day they had little idea of its implications for the future of a president of the United States and his first lady sixteen years later.

The tortuous trial of Whitewater will unfold here, and with it the tribulations of how one little company designed to sell vacation sites could spiral so outward as to engulf not only a famous political family, but a nation as well.

Chapter Two

Politics as Usual

The Money Merry-Go-Round

Whitewater has sparked a whole spectrum of opinion, some of it quite angry— even vitriolic—from both sides of the political aisle.

Is it really a scandal of the dimensions of Watergate, or just a partisan sideshow full of sound and fury? If Watergate was originally called a "third-rate burglary" by its perpetrators, is Whitewater a fourth-rate real estate deal that's been blown out of proportion?

On the other hand, did Bill Clinton abuse his power as Governor of Arkansas for personal and political gain? Did Hillary exploit her position as First Lady of the State to enrich herself and her family? How did the once-poor couple become millionaires?

Has the White House been guilty of obfuscating a tangled case with seemingly endless tributaries? Apparently they encompass not only money, but such Greek tragedies as suicide and ruined reputations, even illegal arm-twisting by federal agencies, and now hazy, incomplete and contradictory testimony by several witnesses at the summer 1994 Congressional hearings.

The former Special Counsel had given a clean bill of health to White House personnel, but critics in Congress still believe there is a "cover-up" and made charges of RTC–Treasury–White House collusion during the hearings. And more important, they await the *real hearings*, covering the pre-White House days, which may— or may not— come in 1995 along with the new Independent Counsel's report on the curious goings on in Little Rock a decade and more ago.

Partisan View
Public opinion is divided, mainly along partisan lines. Democrats see Whitewater as a Republican vendetta, a mean-spirited attempt to embarrass the first Democratic president since 1980, a president, incidentally, with an agenda the Republicans despise.

To Republicans, Whitewater is the Rosetta stone to the President's character. They say that the man who avoided the draft and seems to have an unlimited libido has shown his inability to be straightforward about any personal blemish, no matter what. Now, these same critics trumpet, his wife—haltingly divulging the facts about her $100,000 commodity trades—may share that same weakness.

Could both views be accurate? Quite possibly. But for many reasons, the two sides miss the true significance of Whitewater. It is not, as some portray it, just a political aberration that surfaced in unsophisticated Arkansas. Neither is it merely the tale of a White House administration in trouble and under attack by the opposition and the media. In that arena, what's new? That sad story ranges from Democratic Deep Freezes to Republican Deep Throat.

Whitewater's true significance is the connection it makes between politics and money, the most powerful tale in contemporary American democracy. Actually, it is the perfect symbol of our ailing democratic system, one abused by Democrats and Republicans alike nationwide, in lock step to protect their privileged sanctuaries.

Much has been made of President Clinton's sexual pecadilloes. It's surely entertaining, perhaps even dismaying. But it's hardly instructive, except perhaps as a sign of character. In that arena, even if all the charges are true, he's still an amateur when compared to the late John F. Kennedy, his hero and an American icon.

Use and Abuse

But Whitewater *is* instructive. In fact, it's a computer chip schematic of how American politicians use and abuse money, the final corrupting influence in democracy. In 1992, we spent one *billion* dollars on our federal elections alone, making the traditional cozy partnership between cash and politicians even cozier.

A former governor of Arkansas (not Mr. Clinton) recently told me just that in Little Rock: "You know what's wrong with all American politics?" he asked rhetorically as he dipped into his pocket and took out a money clip stuffed with dollars. "This!"

Whitewater is significant not because it's peculiar to that state, or that period in time. It's important because it represents American politics *as usual*—a case of corruption, or near corruption, or conflict of interest, or abuse of ethics by a large number of people in public life. It is a story that characterizes the present American political scene, whether in Arkansas, New York, California, or Washington.

Of course, the story is heightened because two of the players in this convoluted tale are the sitting President of the United States and his active wife, dominating a cast of many. The law has either been broken or bent by someone—as the Independent Counsel will determine—or everyone has operated quite legally, if possibly unethically.

In the final analysis, it makes little difference. The facts as unraveled here will show how the traditional use of public and private money in American politics distorts democracy.

Whitewater is only the latest in a chain of stories involving influence peddling, cover-ups, and simple lying. Much of it seems to involve presidential administrations of both parties.

We can go back as far as Teapot Dome in the days of Republican Warren Harding in the mid-1920s, when the Interior Secretary took bribes to allow oil companies to dip into government reserves. Even before that there was the administration of Ulysses S. Grant, in which two Vice Presidents were brought down for being involved in a bribery scheme to help the railroads.

The Famous "Checkers"

More recently, we've had the "Checkers" scandal of Vice President Nixon in 1952, who was accused of having an expense slush fund provided by rich Californians. He brought the nation to tears by refusing to return his cocker spaniel

"Checkers" to his benefactors. (Notice that those who "fess up" tend to get out of it?)

We've seen Ike's chief of staff Sherman Adams shot down for a single vicuña coat; Jimmy Carter escaping brother Billy's strange ties with the Libyan government; the endless investigation of Iran-Contra, which finally fizzled. The daddy of them all, naturally, was the Watergate cover-up, which earned the *Washington Post* a Pulitzer and brought down Richard Nixon.

In the non-presidential department, we've had our share of erring politicians as well. Some of the charges were serious, some less so, but all celebrated. Jim Wright, former Speaker of the House (who's still receiving some $250,000 a year in federal funds for an office and staff) left after a hazy brouhaha that seemed to involve an unethical book deal. Former House Ways and Means Chairman Dan Rostenkowski ostensibly hit all the bases, according to a seventeen-point indictment—from stamps converted to money to crystal bowls stored in his basement—which the Justice Department will eventually try in court.

The variety of charges and stories is incredibly varied, and no one seems able to predict the next political twist of power, influence, and sin. Wilbur Mills, former chairman of the same Ways and Means Committee (maybe handling too much of the public's money distorts their values) was bounced in the 1950s when he was found putting a stripper who couldn't type on his payroll.

There is sometimes smoke without much fire. The Keating Five, senators who ostensibly took large campaign contributions from the convicted Savings and Loan (S&L) operator, Robert Keating, and sought to help him with the regulators, escaped without even a gentle wrist tap, except for Alan Cranston, who was reprimanded. A former chairman of the House Banking Committee was attacked publicly for getting a $1,000,000 loan from an overly-friendly bank, but he was reelected the first time out.

Tony Coelho of California, a former House whip, was not charged with anything. But he did quit under pressure when it was disclosed that he had purchased $100,000 in junk bonds, financed in part with a loan from a troubled California S&L. (Mr. Coelho has since returned to politics as the National Chairman of the Democratic Party.)

Profitable Celebrityhood
Still others learn how to cash in on their political celebrity without breaking any laws, generally proclaiming their love of the free market along the way. Speaker Tom Foley legally gained $100,000 profit in new stock issue trades recently from a generous Boston firm. He didn't broadcast it to the world, but it was uncovered by an intrepid reporter. And now Republican Alfonse D'Amato is shown to have beaten Foley's record by making $37,000 in a single day on an Initial Public Offering offered to the well-placed.

And fifteen years earlier, a future First Lady magically turned a $1,000 investment into $99,537 from cattle futures, a subject she knew nothing about. Nor should we forget a son of Republican President Bush, whose name power enabled him to benefit from a giant S&L debacle.

The newest cause célèbre is Whitewater. Was anything done that is illegal? Or unethical? Should anyone go to jail? What will be the final result?

No one yet knows the judicial bottom line, but it is becoming clear that Whitewater (and its parallel tales) is perhaps the most instructive case in the juxtaposition of money, power, hubris, and politics in recent times.

As it unfolds, we'll see the tale encompass almost every possibility for mayhem in our political system, including serious allegations of:

- Bank loans made without collateral
- Campaign contributions and loans paid off with political favors
- Unwarranted appointment of cronies in top positions
- Misuse and theft of federally guaranteed funds
- Deals with powerful lobbies against the public interest
- Conflicts-of-interests galore in legal and banking practices
- Unethical behavior by government agencies
- Slush funds and other financial shenanigans
- Attempt to stifle investigations that touched on Whitewater
- Abuse of banking laws
- White House cover-ups

Whitewater is also important because it exposes the use of legalism to *pretend* that an immoral system is moral. Too often, American politics so disastrously mixes cash with power that it creates an explosive philosophical concoction that risks everything decent in our democracy.

The Money-Go-Round

Money, money, money. It makes American politics go round. But at least the Whitewater case is bipartisan. The mainly

Democratic players found a financial home in a system of
Republican-spawned S&Ls, and Small Business Administration millions floated around by a Republican administration.

In my two previous books, *The Government Racket*
and *A Call for Revolution*, I showed the poisoning effects
of money in politics and offered remedies. I will do that
again, this time more comprehensively by offering changes
in our election laws, campaign fund-raising, conflicts of interest, banking, and government agency operations at all
levels to make another Whitewater impossible, or at least
more difficult.

That's the theme of this book: not so much to place
blame as to explain the details of what may now be legal
and usual, but is actually morally corrupt.

In the process, I will not excuse Whitewater. Quite the
opposite. But I will show that in the main, it's been an expert manipulation of the present lax rules.

What's the result of this and other scandals? Simply
raging distrust of government. It's no accident that only 15
percent of the public now trust the federal government—
down from 75 percent approval some thirty years ago.
When someone announces for public office, most often the
question is not what he believes in, but "How much money
can you raise?" No one could say it better.

The President and his wife are not the only players
in this piece of Americana. There's a supporting cast of
Arkansans who had gained wealth and power in their
home state, several of whom then emigrated to Washington with their leader, only to find the glare of the Capitol
spotlight too harsh, even for minor pecadilloes and ex-
cesses.

The New Morality
There is also a second, less vocalized, reason for the potency of the Whitewater tale. Those who profited, financially and politically, are mainly members of a generation that has loudly proclaimed their special sensibility and "new morality."

It was an ethic born of the American Cultural Revolution of the 1960s, one that defined differences from the parent generation of World War II— differences loudly announced on college steps or at the family dinner table.

It is an ideological split between the World War II and Korean War generation and many of the child-elite of the 1960s—symbolized in the persons of the President and Hillary Rodham Clinton.

They claim that their idealism is superior to those who survived the Depression, won World War II, then succeeded in the postwar years. To the elders, it was a matter of pride. To their youthful critics, it was often a case of smugness. That era of 1930s to 1960s lacked a true moral base, these boomers claim. Sure, it included the "last good war," but it failed *theologically* by not inviting the poor and the members of racial minorities into the American dream.

Those who led the 1960s movement saw themselves as more altruistic, more sacrificial, more intuitive about the needs of the left out. Emerging from their secure pink and blue suburban nurseries, they have now matured into this imperfect world. Like the Clintons, they've already taken much of the power, but they still scream loudly about the injustices, frustrated by their inability to do much, if anything, about it.

They had been born into the Good Society of the

1940s and 1950s and part of the 1960s. From the 1960s and onward, they sought to make it into the Perfect Society. A quarter of a century later, an observer would have to conclude that not only didn't they achieve their goal, but they might have lost the original Good Society in the process.

Why, then, is Whitewater important in that argument?

It is important because the New Morality proclaimed by the 1960s generation too often conflicts with their actions, which seem to bear a startling resemblance to those of their fathers and mothers. Whitewater is just one more piece of evidence that the new generation is no better than the one that preceded it, if somewhat more hypocritical. In truth, the boomers seem no different at all when it comes to morality. Political corruption as a way of life remains the American standard.

The Perfect Example
Whitewater, then, is the intersection of two tales. One is that of a moral revolution that has failed its own ideals. The other is the story of American politics as usual, the marriage of money and power. It has always been around, but it has now overwhelmed us. If Whitewater had not come along to provide the example for this unhappy partnership, we'd have had to search elsewhere to make the point.

But Whitewater is right here, waiting to be explained, then analyzed, as to what went wrong.

To research this book, I've called upon numerous sources: hundreds of official and personal documents (including Jim McDougal's 2,000 pages on Whitewater purchased for $1,000); scores of interviews in Little Rock,

Washington, and elsewhere; help from such federal agencies as the Resolution Trust Corporation, the Small Business Administration, the FDIC, the General Accounting Office, and the personal cooperation of several members of Congress and their committee staffs.

We've seen the truncated Congressional hearings, held at the end of July 1994, which revealed the bumblings and interference of the White House and its highest-level staff in the mishandling of the Whitewater investigation—but apparently all quite legal. And we still await more comprehensive Congressional hearings (if they come) and the final report of the new Independent Counsel, which *may* address many of the points raised here.

We've also gone back to the 1960s and 1970s to study the Clintons, searching for clues to ideas, motives, and character that made Whitewater possible. We've tried to trace the story from its infancy to its present, if not yet complete, fruition, and to simplify what sometimes seems mystifying and overly complex.

It's a tale that bears studying as a case history in American politics with warnings for the future—for us all.

Chapter Three

The Making of the Clintons

The 1960s Redux

I. HILLARY RODHAM

Hillary Rodham Clinton has been called a number of things, but no one ever said that she was bashful.

At the 1969 Wellesley commencement, she approached the lectern of that prestigious women's college wearing an oversize cap and gown that made her look smaller than she really was. Hillary was not the valedictorian, but as the acknowledged leader of campus protests, she had convinced President Ruth Adams to let her deliver the first student address in the college's history.

The administration had checked the script beforehand, but Hillary quickly dispensed with it, Peering through oversize granny glasses, she delivered a warning—or a promise—that things would never again be the same.

Ms. Rodham began by insulting the featured speaker, liberal Republican Edward Brooke, the first black senator since Reconstruction. Calling his commencement remarks "irrelevant," she went on to boast that the "New Left" protests were "a unique American experience" and a "great adventure."

Hillary's rhetoric shocked many as being rude. "She really trashed Senator Brooke," recalls a Wellesley professor. But she also promised that the life of her classmates would be different from that of their parents, and the graduates cheered.

"The prevailing, acquisitive, and competitive corporate life . . . is not the way of life for us. We're searching for more immediate, ecstatic, and penetrating modes of living," Hillary assured everyone, unaware that twenty years later she would be one of the highest paid corporate lawyers in Arkansas.

A True Suburbanite

But on that commencement day she vowed to follow a different path, one that began conventionally in Park Ridge, Illinois, a Chicago upper-middle-class suburb where her father, Hugh Rodham, a textile entrepreneur, had provided a neo-Colonial brick home and the amenities of the good life for Hillary, her two brothers, and her mother, Dorothy.

A Methodist and Goldwater Republican, Rodham hoped his daughter would follow in his footsteps. And for a while she did. In 1964, at the age of seventeen, she became active in the Goldwater-for-President campaign, proudly hanging the Arizonan's poster in her high school.

Hillary was an early political junkie, and was elected to the student council, then as vice president of her class. She loved to argue, quite aggressively, on virtually any subject, a classmate commented. Considered cool and steely confident, she was nicknamed "Sister Frigidaire."

A classic achiever, Hillary graduated with A's, was named to the National Honor Society, worked on the school newspaper, and was in the debating group. Ever the tomboy, she became a school gym leader.

Her early ambition—which proved somewhat prophetic—was revealed in a high school essay. She confessed that she wanted to marry a senator and settle in Georgetown. Shades of the late Jackie Kennedy, but with a sharp difference. Hillary was interested in politics, not in art and fashion.

After graduation, where she walked away with prizes, the Goldwater Girl chose Wellesley and arrived on the beautiful Massachusetts campus with her bobby socks and a solid Republican bias. In no time, she was elected president of the Young Republican Club.

But there was a chink in her conservative psyche, one cut back in Park Ridge. In 1960, when Hillary was only thirteen, Methodist Reverend Don Jones, a young navy veteran and an "existentialist," as he called himself, became Youth Minister at the Park Ridge church.

He introduced Hillary to the fashionable intellect of the day—the works of J. D. Salinger, Picasso, e. e. cummings, film director Francois Truffaut, the lyrics of Bob Dylan, and Beat poetry. He arranged a trip to a Chicago ghetto where they met black youths, an experience that triggered Hillary's guilt. "It just kind of opened my mind," the protected young woman later explained.

When Hillary was fifteen, Jones shepherded his young flock to hear Martin Luther King in Chicago. His inspirational words mesmerized Hillary, who shook his hand and was later to become wedded to racial issues.

The Wellesley Shift

Jones's teaching registered but did not bloom until Hillary arrived at Wellesley. She was still a Republican, but the school was the site of a dramatic transformation. During her four years, she metamorphosed from a Goldwater Girl, to a liberal Rockefeller Republican, to a Democrat, to a left-wing Democrat, to a dedicated radical leading every college movement in the heady revolutionary days of the late 1960s.

"Hillary was known to everyone on campus," explained Dr. Alan Schechter, a mild-mannered Brooklyn-born political scientist, when interviewed at Wellesley. "Not only was she one of the best students I've ever had, but she was good on her feet, speaking eloquently without notes. Eventually, she became president of the student government."

A reading of the school newspaper, *Wellesley News*, for 1968–1969 regularly brings up Hillary's name. Whatever the cause—black enrollment, open dorm rights, student control of curriculum, and anti-war protests—Hillary was there, front and center, and never with self-doubt.

Quickly, she adopted the protest clichés of the time, including "relevance." But Hillary didn't just mouth it. She led the successful movement to have the college eliminate its strict academic requirements, replacing them with student electives. Traditional courses were no longer "relevant" to the crisis, she said, aping the anti-intellectual crusade of the time.

She also opposed grades, opting for a "pass-fail" system, another cliché of the movement. As the war in Vietnam became inflamed, she took up that protest as well.

The Big Challenge

"My classmates and I . . . challenged the college from the moment we entered," she later boasted. One challenge involved campus living rules, which were then controlled by the college—*in loco parentis*, in place of parents. Students pledged that they would obey the *College Government Handbook*, known ominously as the "Grey Book."

"Get out your BREAK THE VOW buttons," Hillary pressed her fellow students, the college newspaper reported. She became the leader of the fight against curfews and won, eventually giving students the right to come and go as they pleased, and entertain whomever, whenever.

(Today, says a Wellesley source, men freely cohabit in the dorms of what is still an all-women's school. The males sleep in the women's beds and stay there until "we try to kick them out after a few days," the source says.)

Hillary was soon the acknowledged campus leader. In tune with the times, she even adopted a fashionable Hippie pose, painting a flower on her arm. Hillary wore the 1960s outfit of ill-fitting sweaters, large skirts, and oversize granny glasses. Her hair was clipped short and stringy. "She was not physically attractive," one Wellesley source confessed.

But she never relied on beauty, or charm, or even popularity. (She did have several close political friends, who are now being rewarded by the First Lady. At least two of her Wellesley classmates have been named to federal

posts, one as a U.S. Attorney in Oregon, and the other as
the U.S. Representative to the World Bank.)

Working Within

Hillary's secret was that she never appeared to be a radical—even when espousing radical causes. She worked
within the system, sensing where the power lay, and how
to play to it. And finally, how to seize it. But her pragmatism never dampened her ideological power, which many
believe is truly radical and deep-seated. More so, in fact,
than that of her husband, the President.

In addition to Don Jones, another mentor who shaped
her ideas was Dr. Alan Schechter, who taught constitutional law and has helped 700 women students like Hillary
go on to become attorneys.

Schechter recalls Hillary vividly. "She wasn't warm
or charming," he explained. "She was more restrained—
always her own person. She was very smart, straightforward, and pragmatic. She could even cut someone up if she
wanted to. I knew she would succeed at whatever she did."

He does take some credit (or blame) for moving Hillary
leftward. But *if* she became a radical, he says that he believes
it was more the influence of Reverend Don Jones and Saul
Alinsky, then a well-known radical philosopher who had theories about how to cure poverty. She met him in Chicago, and
he became the subject of her senior paper. The new Hillary,
said Schechter, was also a product of the times—the 1960s.

Teach-Ins

By 1968, Hillary had moved into the left wing of the Democratic Party and campaigned for Eugene McCarthy for

President. On campus, she ran for the presidency of the student government, and won. Afterwards, she hosted a series of teach-ins against the war, generally in the school chapel.

Schechter says that he lost touch with her after she graduated in 1969. "But we met again at a Wellesley reunion in 1989 when she was the wife of the Arkansas governor," he recalls. "We spoke for an hour, and we've been in touch, off and on, ever since."

As proof of his point, the White House called during the interview to discuss the Wellesley students who would spend the summer as presidential interns. In fact, the night Bill Clinton announced for the presidency, Hillary wrote Schechter that she was embarked on that "great adventure."

On to Yale

Hillary graduated near the top of her class, and entered Yale Law School. She told friends that she "was not interested in corporate law," and was quoted as saying that "life is too short to spend it making money for some big anonymous firm." Of course, in less than a decade, Hillary had become an attorney, then a director, for some of the nation's largest, most "anonymous" firms, including Wal-Mart and TCBY.

Yale was her choice, and things moved quickly there, in the same radical direction as at Wellesley. A close reading of the *Yale Daily News* for 1969–1970, Hillary's freshman year, reveals a campus in torment. Tents sprouted as students, including Hillary, cut classes and attended a week long anti-Vietnam teach-in.

By the spring of 1970, New Haven was figuratively aflame, forcing merchants to board up their stores. The ruckus was over the Black Panthers, several of whom were being charged for the murder of one of their own. The trial was to be held in the federal courthouse right across from the college green. Black Panther leaders on campus shouted "kill the pigs," insisting that the charges against the Panthers be dropped. The student senate came out against violence, but voted to strike in sympathy and demanded that Yale donate $500,000 to the Panther defense fund.

In the Lead

Throughout the melee, Hillary Rodham, a first-year law student, was in the forefront—as leader, compromiser, agitator, counselor. When interviewed, Professor Abraham Goldstein of the law school recalled standing in the back of an oversize lecture hall and watching, impressed, as Hillary ran the school's largest protest meeting.

The students overflowed into the aisles as Hillary, seated on the edge of the stage in blue jeans, skillfully directed the arguments. Soon she was named to negotiate with the administration.

Student protests also flamed on the green, just across from the courthouse. According to one source, Hillary was in the forefront again, walking among the angry students, checking with the young marshals, trying to keep order so that the protestors wouldn't be gassed by the National Guard.

Hillary could only play the leadership role at Yale so early because she had already gained celebrity status. *Life* magazine had run a story about her angry Wellesley commencement speech, and the young pundit was often the center of attention, holding informal court in the lunchroom.

In the midst of the Panther trial, she helped organize students, who with her took turns monitoring the courtroom proceedings and reporting back to the American Civil Liberties Union. According to one friendly report, she regularly moved in and out of Black Panther headquarters.

The New Hillary
This was no longer the little girl from Park Ridge, Illinois. Hillary Rodham was now an accomplished student radical working on the front line of campus protest—the hallmark of the 1960s and early 1970s. And always with her trademark: a careful blend of coolness and pragmatism.

In May of that year, she addressed the League of Women Voters in Washington. Hillary now demanded not just reform but basic political and economic change in the American system. "Our social indictment has broadened," she said. "Where once we advocated civil rights, now we advocate a realignment of political and economic power. . . . how much longer can we let corporations run us?"

(Not long after, of course, Hillary was helping to run several corporations, earning enormous fees in the process.)

That summer she worked for Senator Mondale's subcommittee on migrant labor, and also met Marian Wright Edelman, head of the Children's Defense Fund. Hillary became interested in children's civil rights, out of which came a controversial article by her interpreted to mean that children could sue their parents—something that was later to set conservative Arkansas on its ears.

Hillary had dated off and on at Wellesley and Yale, but had not clicked romantically with the man of her dreams. Then in early 1971, in the Yale library, she met a gregarious southerner who she later said was "so smart and so human at the same time."

No one was there when the southerner, a fellow law student one year behind her, told Hillary that he expected to become President of the United States. That exceeded even her fantasy of marrying a senator. And besides, the young man shared virtually all her views of American society and the need to change them—in their own image.

His name, of course, was Bill Clinton.

II. WILLIAM JEFFERSON CLINTON

Bill Clinton is not Hillary Rodham. Far from it.

Gregarious, cuddly, adolescently friendly, he comes at everything from the opposing pole of Hillary's academic dissection. In the current lingua franca, he is a "schmoozer" rather than a pedant. He's a smart but emotional person. Even though he may be privately arrogant, he goes out of his way not to argue or appear closed-minded. In fact, he goes through paroxysms of picking everyone's mind before he makes up his own, a world away from super-sure Hillary.

What Bill and Hillary do share is a sense of extreme righteousness. Some others see it as hypocrisy—a "holier than thou" attitude that critics believe may be at the core of their problems, whether Whitewater or managing the White House.

But at their first meeting, Hillary saw not only a bright young man, but one with warmth, charm, and an easy non-threatening manner, all factors she lacked. She also saw a future political leader to whom she could hitch her own bright star. It was a match made in the cosmos of those exciting times.

The Ones to Fix It

They were also political soul mates, convinced their new vision was mankind's best hope. What was the vision? It can be complex, but there were two simple criteria at the time: the Cold War was too Cold and America's poor and minority citizens who had been left behind should matter more than the working middle class, who supposedly could take care of themselves. And most important, they were convinced they were the ones to fix it all.

They agreed entirely on the racial problem—that the plight of American blacks was the product of American white racism. Both identified with minorities, a cause that had come to Hillary in her wealthy segregated enclave through intellectual examination and elitist guilt. Bill, however, felt it in his gut, having grown up with black children near his grandfather's store.

There was one interesting difference. Hillary, who railed against corporations, seemed to love money and comfort, while Bill was indifferent. Says John Robert Starr, former editor of the *Arkansas Democrat-Gazette*, "Bill Clinton never gave a damn about money." (Except, of course, to fuel his many campaigns.)

Clinton was an early boomer, born in 1946, a year before Hillary, and only months prior to his father's death in a car crash. He was named William Jefferson Blythe IV after his father, who had been a World War II Army veteran. When Bill was two, his mother, Virginia Cassidy, left him with his grandparents in rural Hope, Arkansas, to go to Louisiana and study to become a nurse anesthetist.

Middle Class Existence

On her return, she married Roger Clinton. Bill was never poor, even though his grandparents' home had no indoor plumbing, and for two years as a child he lived on a farm. But later in Hot Springs, his stepfather, Roger Clinton, who sold Buicks, and his working mother, provided a comfortable middle-class life. As a young man, Bill even drove a racy Mustang.

Bill's trauma was not financial but emotional. Roger Clinton was an alcoholic. Normally decent, he became violent when drunk and would beat his wife, Bill's mother. When Bill was fourteen, the couple were divorced, and then over the young son's objections, remarried. To make his mother happy, Bill legally changed his name from Blythe to Clinton. Later on, when his stepfather contracted cancer, the violence and bitterness stopped.

Like Hillary, Bill showed leadership qualities early on. A natural, even obsessed, politician, he was elected to the student council in the tenth grade at Hot Springs High. If not the top student, he was a National Merit semifinalist and president of the Beta Club, an academic honor society. He played saxophone in the school band, was the band major, had the lead in *Arsenic and Old Lace*. Among several civic prizes, he received the Youth Leadership Award from the Elks.

Young Bill Clinton was Mr. Responsible, Mr. Popularity, Mr. Helpful, the seemingly perfect archetype of an American adolescent—and without the chilly intellect of Hillary. No one in Hot Springs could then imagine that thirty years later, the former *Arkansas Democrat-Gazette* editor would ever label Bill Clinton "that lying son of a bitch."

In 1963, at age sixteen, Bill was named a delegate to the Boy's Nation convention and came triumphantly to Washington, where he lunched with Arkansas Senator William Fulbright. Then, in a defining moment, Bill shook hands with President John F. Kennedy. The effect was personally electrifying.

By age seventeen, Clinton had a daydream, which he later shared with Hillary. He wanted to be—and expected to become—President of the United States.

He attended Georgetown University in Washington, and within days had run for student office, and was elected without opposition. It was 1964, a year of decisions. We had entered the Vietnam War, the first civil rights bill had just been passed, and Lyndon Johnson had begun his war on poverty. Bill agreed that government could do the job, and set a goal to return to Arkansas, gain political office and get it done. Meanwhile, he worked part-time in Senator Fulbright's office.

The Rhodes Scholar
A new challenge faced him. A finalist in the Rhodes scholarship contest for Oxford suggested that Clinton try out.

Bill didn't think he had a chance—unaware he was at the right place at the right time, which has been part of his phenomenal success. Fulbright, a Rhodes scholar from Arkansas himself, highly recommended Bill, who was accepted.

Unlike Hillary, Clinton showed no interest in radical causes at Georgetown. His student campaigns involved such banal campus staples as better food, but his concerns rose when two of his champions, Martin Luther King and Bobby Kennedy, were assassinated in 1968, his senior year.

Their deaths alienated him, but it was a different issue—the Vietnam War—that eventually radicalized Bill Clinton.

Although many at Georgetown had gone off to Vietnam, Bill Clinton only wanted to join the antiwar protest. As a Rhodes scholar-to-be, he was suddenly taken seriously in the movement. After graduating from Georgetown, he was invited to a conference on Martha's Vineyard for young anti-Vietnam activists attended by Larry Rockefeller and fellow Rhodes scholar Strobe Talbott. (Clinton has since named Talbott as the State Department's number two man.)

That fall, Clinton was on his way to Oxford, a vital step in his metamorphosis from Arkansas "bubba" to sophisticated young scholar. There, he continued to make friends. In fact, people at Oxford were finding it almost impossible not to like the tall, teddy-bear-like American.

(Some people regret falling for Clinton's charm. "He was irresistible as a person, one-on-one," recalls John Robert Starr, the Little Rock editor. "Many is the time he's used his charm to con me. In 1990, he swore that if my paper supported him for reelection for governor one more time, he wouldn't run for President in 1992. We supported him, but it turned out that he was lying.")

Only one thing disturbed Clinton's carefree year at Oxford. He was deathly worried about the draft.

LBJ had eliminated deferments for graduate school, and it was a near miracle that Clinton had reached Oxford. He was 1-A—draft bait—at the local board in Hot Springs, but his uncle, Raymond Clinton, a GM dealer, had helped persuade the naval reserve commander to take Bill in and grant him a 1-D deferment. However, Clinton never showed for the physical. Instead, Raymond Clinton's lobbying plus strong appeals from Fulbright's office allowed him to get to Oxford.

The draft board's executive secretary was quoted as saying:

"We were proud to have a Hot Springs boy with a Rhodes scholarship. . . . The board was very lenient with him. . . . We gave him more than he was entitled to."

Induction Notice

But they could only bend the law so far. In April, he received news at Oxford that he was to be inducted in June. Somehow, his friends managed to have the induction notice postponed to July 28, 1969, but that was the final date of his freedom.

Clinton called on his ingenuity, which has always been matched by near-magical luck. He thought of Oxford classmate Cliff Jackson, the only other one from Arkansas— and surprisingly a Republican. Normally, a Republican in Arkansas isn't worth a penny of sunflower seeds. But for

the first time since Reconstruction, a Republican, Winthrop
Rockefeller, had won the governership.

The summer before, Cliff Jackson, who had graduated
first in his class at Arkansas College, had worked with the
Rockefeller team, then had gone on to Oxford as a Fulbright scholar. Clinton became friendly with him.

Could Jackson use his influence with the Republican
administration in Arkansas to quash the July draft notice?
Clinton boldly asked.

"Bill didn't want to go to Vietnam in the worst way,"
Jackson, a tall spare litigation attorney, recalled over dinner in Little Rock. "We met at Oxford, and played together
on the 'B' basketball team. I found Bill fun to be around,
but obsessed with power."

"What about the draft?" I asked. "Did he really avoid it?"

"I was a 1-Y for medical reasons, but Bill was in good
physical shape," Jackson explained. "I knew someone
who could help him. Colonel Willard 'Lefty' Hawkins had
been named by Rockefeller to head Selective Service in
Arkansas. He had the power to quash a draft notice."

Jackson stopped for a moment to cogitate, weighing
the importance of what had happened.

The Man Who Did It

"I suppose I'm the one who got him off the hook," he said
almost sadly. "I contacted Colonel Hawkins and arranged a
meeting with Clinton and his mother. Hawkins then sent
him to Colonel Eugene Holmes, head of the Reserve Officers Training Corps (ROTC) at the University of Arkansas.
Clinton signed a binding letter that he'd enroll in the law
school there, then join the ROTC. With that, Colonel

Holmes gave him a 1-D deferment, and the July 28 induction notice was voided. But after only a few weeks, Clinton started to wiggle out of his pledge."

It turns out, relates Jackson, that there was no ROTC slot available until the spring of 1970.

"Rather than enroll in the law school and wait, Clinton broke his agreement and left the country," Jackson remembered. "He had no intention of joining the ROTC. It was just a ploy to gain time." Then, in October, 1969, when there was little danger of being drafted, he notified his draft board to reenter his name in the lottery. He got a high number, and was safe from the draft.

"What then was the problem," I asked Jackson, "if he received a high lottery number?"

"First, he pulled strings to get to Oxford without a deferment. He must have been breaking the law," Jackson explained. "Then he managed to get the June induction notice pushed back. After that, he lied about the facts to get me and Colonel Holmes to help him. He made an agreement to serve in the ROTC, but not only didn't he join, he never enrolled in the law school where the unit was."

"Why the silence by you all these years?" I asked Jackson.

He thought for a moment.

"The whole story came back to me when the *Los Angeles Times* asked for a letter from Clinton so that they could verify his signature. I found one which mentioned that Clinton had already received an induction notice at the time I helped him. I had completely forgotten. I was horrified and that's why I went public. On all counts, Clinton had manipulated me and the two colonels to get out of serving."

The Letter

During the 1992 campaign, Colonel Holmes's assistant—
after holding it for twenty-three years—released a letter
from Clinton to the Colonel. In it, Bill said that he
"loathed" the military, and that the draft was "immoral."
He said he wouldn't be joining the ROTC, which he no
longer needed, and had gone back into the draft to maintain his "political viability."

The letter is an extraordinary confession:

"I had no interest in the ROTC program in itself and all
I seem to have done is protect myself from physical harm,"
Clinton wrote. "Also I began to think I had deceived you
. . . by failing to tell you all the things I'm writing now."
Clinton proceeded to tell Holmes that he had lost his self-
respect, and couldn't sleep for weeks. The shame was
such, he said, that he had written his draft board asking
that they take away his 1-D deferment and put him into the
draft. *But, adds Clinton, he never mailed that letter.*

"Do you regret having helped Clinton in the draft matter?" I asked Jackson.

"Yes, I do. Even though many young people were getting preferential treatment at the time, I wouldn't do it
again. It wasn't right in retrospect."

Jackson is now the attorney for the state troopers who
claim they helped Clinton with his sexual affairs. He even
assisted Paula Corbin Jones in announcing her lawsuit
against Clinton for sexual harassment.

"I saw signs of his inability to be faithful to anyone or
anything early on," Jackson relates. "At Oxford, he introduced me to a young woman. She was a real beauty. He said
she was the woman he loved, and the future mother of his

children. I never saw her again. Then a few years later, when Clinton was running for Congress, I met a young woman— the daughter of a prominent Arkansas politician—who told me she was Bill Clinton's fiancée. Of course, Clinton had lied to her. He was then living with Hillary."

Local people are split about Jackson himself. Some consider him the fountainhead of truth. Others are skeptical.

"Cliff Jackson is just plain jealous of Bill Clinton's success," Max Brantley, editor of the *Arkansas Times*, a liberal weekly in Little Rock, recounts. "Jackson thinks he's more intellectual and moral than Clinton. I don't know about that. But they started out together at Oxford and Jackson is just a litigation lawyer who was defeated for prosecuting attorney in Little Rock. Meanwhile, his Oxford buddy Bill Clinton is President of the United States."

Activism Begins

In his first year at Oxford, Clinton was easygoing, but in his second year, he became an important antiwar activist. The summer before he had worked in the Vietnam Moratorium Office in Washington, and back in England, he threw himself into the cause.

During the 1992 presidential campaign, Clinton claimed that he had only been an "observer" in the antiwar protests. But on December 3, 1969, he revealed the truth in that letter to Colonel Holmes.

"I have written and spoken and marched against the war," Clinton wrote. "After I left Arkansas last summer, I went to work in the national headquarters of the Moratorium, then to England to organize the Americans . . . for demonstrations October 15 and November 16."

Obviously, he had been an anti–war activist, not the "observer" he had claimed to be. These demonstrations, held in front of the American Embassy, were only part of Clinton's antiwar activities. More startling was his trip from England to Moscow for an international Vietnam conference, an expensive Intourist journey for a student with no real income.

On to Law School
Freed of the draft, Clinton decided not to study law at Arkansas, but to go on to bigger things. He enrolled in the Yale Law School in the fall of 1970, one year after Hillary Rodham, a woman he had never met.

At Yale, Bill, who has never been accused of sloth, took three jobs—teaching at a community college, and assisting a city councilman and a New Haven attorney. It was during that first year that he met Hillary Rodham. Bill had just come off a failed love affair and wasn't looking for another. But he had noticed Hillary in class, and she had seen the affable young man, and heard him brag about Arkansas, even about the size of its watermelons. One day, they met in the library and Hillary took the lead and introduced herself. Soon, she was spending time at the beach house where Bill lived.

(Years later she told *Vanity Fair* that she liked the idea that the big Arkansan wasn't afraid of her.)

Clinton was not a bad law student, but some classmates believe that only Hillary's tutoring got him through with a reasonable record, the first example of the partnership that has sustained him for many years.

The year 1972 was ostensibly Hillary's last at Yale. It

was also the year Senator George McGovern was running
against Nixon. Gary Hart, McGovern's manager, asked
Clinton to run the Texas campaign, and the couple left Yale
for a few months. (Hart surely looks back nostalgically on
how poorly he handled *his* own amorous inclinations.)
They returned to Yale in November, in time to pass their final exams.

Physically, the couple didn't seem a match. Clinton
was a lumbering giant, with a quick smile and an enthusiastic handshake. He tended toward pudginess, but was attractive to women. Hillary was almost a foot shorter than
he, dressed unattractively, resolutely wore no makeup, and
hid her eyes with large-rimmed glasses.

But spiritually and politically, they were a matched
pair. In their confident hearts, they believed they held *the*
message for the future. Hillary decided to stay over at Yale
and graduate with Bill in 1973. Destiny had brought them
together. They had no money and no jobs, but they had a
vision for a New America, and were eager to begin to make
it a reality.

All they needed was the power.

Chapter Four

The Search for Power

Prelude to Whitewater

"BILL CLINTON FOR CONGRESS."

The poster said it all. Just six months after leaving Yale, William Jefferson Clinton paid his $800 filing fee and entered the 1974 Democratic primary from the Fourth District of Arkansas seeking a seat in the U.S. House of Representatives.

He didn't expect to win, for the Fourth was the *only* Republican district in the state. Covering the northern and western corners of Arkansas, the district has almost no minority population, is old Anglo-Saxon in lineage, and boasts of Ozark mountain types with a strong distrust of government. The incumbent, John Paul Hammerschmidt, the first Republican elected to Congress since Reconstruction, was popular.

Hammerschmidt smiled at reelection time in 1974, worried only about the effect of Watergate. His opponent, Bill Clinton, seemed like a token Democratic loser.

Clinton had come back to Arkansas hoping to open a law practice and smell around the political front. But he was sidetracked by an opening teaching law at the University of Arkansas in Fayetteville. He grabbed it, and although students considered him an easy marker and really one of them—he was only twenty-seven—he enjoyed teaching criminal law.

But, as everyone now knows, political campaigning is what Bill Clinton does (even after being elected) and has always done, as far back as the tenth grade. He decided to teach only part-time, and try his hand.

The Primary Race

His first challenge was to win the Democratic primary against three contenders. He ran a classically liberal campaign, lining up labor and teacher union support, and railed against Watergate, the "military-industrial" complex and its "obscene profits." He adopted an antibusiness stance, and with his somewhat long hair, Bill projected an antiestablishment stance.

Hammerschmidt was surprised. What good was such an approach in the state's only Republican district? And who in hell was this twenty-seven-year-old law professor anyway?

To understand what was going on, one has to understand Arkansas. It had come into the Union in 1836 as a slave state, and was basically agricultural and backward. Much of the wealth was—and is—in a few hands. Arkansas has always been forty-ninth in income and education, as it is still today. "Thank God for Mississippi" was the rallying cry and lament, especially for those who wanted to change it. Enter Bill Clinton.

Not an ideological state, it's a little Republican in the north, but absolutely Democratic elsewhere, especially in the southern delta, the poorest part with the largest black population. But unknown to most, the state has fewer blacks— only 17 percent—than any southern state. Poverty there is heavily white.

Arkansans like to think they vote for the person. If a man "showed good," he had a chance no matter what he believed. The same state that elected the extreme segregationist governor, Orval Faubus, named liberal William Fulbright to the Senate several times, and in 1968, voted for George Wallace for President over both Humphrey and Nixon.

Bill Clinton, a smiling big good ol' boy (or at least he looked like one), showed real good. He was articulate, and his schooling at Georgetown, Oxford, and Yale impressed the locals.

Clinton began with a whirlwind of energy, still his trademark. Getting into his 1970 AMC Gremlin miniature car, he traveled the back roads, thrilled to press the flesh of every voter in the district.

James Slocum, a Ph.D. in agriculture from Cornell who taught college and is now a chicken farmer, was one of those challenging Clinton in the primary.

"Bill Clinton is charismatic, a genius at interpersonal chemistry," said Slocum, a friend of Bill and Hillary's, when interviewed. "When he looks you in the eye and shakes your hand, you'll never forget it."

The big press down in Little Rock now sent reporters to cover this new political phenomenon. "Clinton runs—literally, physically runs—from place to place," said the

Arkansas Democrat. "He strives to personally meet as many of the district's eligible voters as possible."

An Impressive Performer

The night before the primary election, at a rally of Democratic candidates, each one was given three minutes. David Pryor, then running for governor, and now an Arkansas senator, was stunned, calling Clinton's speech a "brilliant" performance that brought the crowd to its feet. As far as the party powerful were concerned, he was the front-runner.

The next day, Clinton came out first in the primary election, then went on to win the runoff with 69 percent. Now Clinton had to face the Republican, John Paul Hammerschmidt.

He had only two problems: He had never raised money and the campaign was hopelessly disorganized. The money came from labor, but it was not enough. "We could have raised more," said Dave Matthews, a campaign staffer, when interviewed, "but Bill turned down a lot because there were strings attached."

(Within four years, Bill Clinton had become the champion money raiser in the history of Arkansas politics.)

One of his competitors in the 1974 race is sure that money called the tune. "Even though none of us raised much, I could still draw a graph of the votes each candidate received against the money each of us spent," says the Ph.D. chicken farmer, who figures he raised only $12,000, one-fourth as much as Clinton. "It would be almost a straight line."

The other problem Clinton faced was disorganization.

His mind and operations are mainly instinctual, and somewhat manic, making it difficult for him to focus on only one process at a time. As the campaign progressed, friends say he would leave important index cards unattended on a desk.

Enter Hillary

The person he needed was one of the best organized political workers extant: Hillary Rodham.

When they graduated Yale in the summer of 1973, the young couple seemed to have an irreconcilable difference. Bill Clinton pined for Arkansas. His dream of becoming president included first becoming governor. But he would have loved to have Hillary join him. She could practice law there and do very nicely.

Arkansas? The thought was repellent to the young Illinois suburbanite, who had tasted of Boston and New Haven. To her, Arkansas seemed the reincarnation of L'il Abner caricatures. She kissed Bill good-bye and moved to Boston to begin work at the Children's Defense Fund.

By January 1974, things changed abruptly for Hillary. She received a phone call from John Doar in Washington. A liberal Republican who had served in the Kennedy and Johnson administrations, Doar had just been named chief counsel for the impeachment hearings of President Nixon being held by the House Judiciary Committee. "Would you care to work for me?" he asked Hillary.

Bill Clinton had already turned him down, but had convinced Doar of Hillary's ability. Despite her dislike of Nixon and her work for McGovern (or because of it?), Doar took her on as one of his staff of forty-three lawyers, only three of whom were women.

On to the Nixon Impeachment

She moved to Washington, and spent the next eight months working seven days a week, fourteen hours a day, in an old hotel near the Hill, in complete secrecy, listening endlessly to Nixon's voice drone on the tapes.

On the Watergate staff she met Bernard Nussbaum, Senior Associate Special Counsel. Nussbaum was a New York lawyer who had the reputation of being a fighting liberal. They worked closely together and became good friends, personally and ideologically. After work, late at night, Nussbaum would often accompany Hillary to her apartment in southwestern Washington, not a particularly safe neighborhood.

(Neither one could guess that twenty years later, Hillary would get Nussbaum named as President Clinton's chief counsel. Or that his Washington career would end because of his un-Beltway handling of the Whitewater problem, an ironic twist for a man who had worked so assiduously to impeach Nixon. It is equally ironic that Hillary, now under attack in the White House, was also helpful in evicting Nixon from what is now her home.)

Hillary was confident that the three impeachment articles would be approved by the full House. But on August 9, 1974, President Nixon abruptly resigned, leaving the nation with a new President, Gerald Ford. And Hillary Rodham without a job.

Bill had already visited Hillary in Washington, telling her of his run for Congress and asking her to come to Arkansas with him. She could get a job teaching law school. Hillary had resisted, but when the impeachment job vanished, she thought of it again.

"You're crazy," her friends told her, to leave the East for such a backwater state as Arkansas.

But Hillary decided on the challenge, and went to Arkansas in the summer of 1974, right in the middle of Bill's congressional campaign. She took the teaching job, then quickly adopted the role she has played for twenty years—Bill's unofficial campaign manager and chief of staff, a position she has never relinquished.

The Powerhouse Partnership

The congressional campaign was the launching point for a political partnership in which Bill provided the raw energy and hand-to-hand political skills, and Hillary the organizational talent and policy wonking. Quickly, she filed the index cards and cleaned up the disorganization, and more.

At first, Hammerschmidt stayed in Washington, confidently issuing a barrage of attacks, calling Clinton a man with a "radical left-wing philosophy." Besides, he said, Clinton had run the Texas campaign for McGovern, a man rejected by the American people for his left-wing tendencies.

(Hammerschmidt, now retired, still believes that. "My district, like all of Arkansas, is mainly Democratic," the former Congressman explained when interviewed. "But these Democrats are ordinary folk who loved FDR, and who still voted for me. But Bill Clinton is different. He's a clever talker, but underneath I'm convinced that he's a real socialist. And so is Hillary.")

Rumors also floated around about Clinton's draft status, but those who knew the facts kept mute. There was also a putative scandal that turned out to be nonsense. A war protestor at the University of Arkansas had climbed a tree, refusing to come down until the war was over. A rumor spread that "The Man In The Tree" was none other than Bill Clinton.

But of course the rumor was false. At the time, April 1969, Clinton was in Oxford. Yet to this day, some people still believe it.

Despite it all, the Republican criticisms didn't create much controversy. Why? Most people believe that Clinton's manner refuted any possibility that he was a radical. Mothers took to him as if he were their own son. Radical? Nonsense, they say. To this day, Clinton's down-home quality is his best defense against such charges, even when his programs, his past, or his political appointments lend it some credence.

Lucky Lose

When the election was held, Hammerschmidt won, but by the scariest of margins. Clinton received 48.2 percent of the vote, the most ever gained against that Republican. A star was born. The *Arkansas Gazette* called him "the man to watch—the rising star."

"Best campaign I ever ran," Clinton said, not realizing that in a way he had been lucky to lose. Had he been elected to Congress some twenty years ago, the overexposure in that jaded body surely would have made him a less attractive figure by 1992, when he was a fresh face on the national scene.

After the 1974 campaign, Bill and Hillary had to examine their relationship. They were lovers, but they couldn't

live together in Fayetteville because of local mores. They
were finally married the following October and moved into
a miniature bungalow Clinton had bought. The wedding
was small, but there was also a reception for 200 politicos
at a local hotel, a reminder that Bill Clinton intended to go
places.

There was a unique touch to the wedding. The bride
retained her maiden name, Hillary Rodham. It didn't
trouble Clinton, but it was later to become a political
scandal.

At the law school, Hillary was a celebrity. Not only because she was Clinton's wife, but because of her work on
the Nixon impeachment and her innovations on campus,
including a rape crisis center. She was gaining a reputation
as an outspoken liberal and feminist. Her clothes and her
appearance, unchanged since Yale, were generally described as "hippie" and "sloppy" by bemused, and annoyed,
Arkansans.

Hillary came from a well-to-do family and wanted not
only the reputation as a reformer, but the good life as well.
(That dichotomy—which sometimes bears the label "lim-
ousine liberal"—seems to be her particular bane, a philosophical equation the wealthy presidential wife has yet to
tackle.)

That required money, which required more work,
something that comes naturally to both of them. They took
extra jobs. Hillary received a government contract to provide legal services for the poor, a job that was later to become a bone of contention. Bill took over the law practice
of a deceased lawyer who specialized in claims for Ozark
miners.

The Next Race

Together, they planned Bill's next political move. He could run again against Hammerschmidt, but they feared another loss. (Hammerschmidt stayed in Washington until he retired in 1992, and his place was taken by another Republican.) A race for the governor's seat in 1976 would be premature. The answer was the attorney general slot, which was being vacated by Jim Guy Tucker, the present governor, who was then running for Congress.

(In Arkansas the jobs seem to rotate within the Democratic party, as when another governor, Dale Bumpers, ran for the Senate in 1974, where he now is, and David Pryor took over the statehouse, only to gain a Senate seat in 1978, leaving the statehouse to Clinton, who then turned it over to former Congressman Jim Guy Tucker when Clinton ran for President.)

Clarence Cash, then deputy attorney general, who ran against Clinton in the primary for the attorney general's spot, clearly remembers that 1976 race.

"Clinton was the darling of the Democratic party," Cash recalled when interviewed. "He was a phenomenon from the beginning in Arkansas. He had enormous charisma—a kind of magic with the people. We other candidates didn't know what hit us."

Clinton won the Democratic primary with 55 percent, and the Republicans didn't even run anyone against him.

Hillary was equally a phenomenon, Cash says, but behind the scenes. "She looked like a hippie with her thick glasses and unfashionable clothes, but she was a great pusher and mover. Before Clinton arrived at a rally, Hillary would get there and make sure that there were plenty of flags. She also had a trick of spreading his supporters throughout the crowd. It looked like everyone was with Clinton. By the time he arrived, she had set things up for him perfectly."

By coincidence, Cash had worked with Clinton years before in Senator Fulbright's office in Washington. Clinton was a student at Georgetown, and Cash, who had graduated from Arkansas College, was working there for the summer. His view of Clinton contradicts some of the popular conventional wisdom.

Clinton Miffed

"People say Clinton is brilliant, but I heard from people at Georgetown that he was not an outstanding student—more absentminded," Cash reminisced. "But like everywhere, he was well-liked among the Fulbright people. On our résumés, it said we served on the Foreign Relations staff. Actually we worked in the mail room. One day I was asked to deliver an invitation for the Soviet Foreign Minister to the Russian Embassy on 16th Street. I got in a cab and delivered it, then came back and was bragging about it. Clinton heard me and got really "piffed" because he didn't get to do it. He had been out to lunch and was angry he had missed the chance."

What does he think of Clinton personally?

"Well, in public he plays the friendly populist, but I found him different in private. He was always sucking up to the important people on Fulbright's staff. I was just a country boy from Washington County and he slighted me. Clinton didn't think I was important enough to bother with."

A New Life

Clinton defeated Cash and another candidate, and his election as attorney general changed the couple's lives. Once Clinton won the AG spot, people who had ignored Hillary the Hippie, now found Hillary the Political Spouse quite valuable. In a short time, she became a money machine for herself and Bill.

In February 1977, a month after Bill was sworn in as attorney general, Hillary was hired as an attorney—its very first woman—by the prestigious Rose Law Firm. (No one doubts her ability, but as we shall see, she was paid heavily for light work.) Other perks and windfalls came rapidly her way. Hillary Rodham, still using her maiden name, was surprisingly named staff attorney for the Little Rock Airport Commission.

John Harmon, the former City Attorney of North Little Rock, who almost ran against Clinton for governor, questioned the appointment.

"If her husband had not been attorney general, she wouldn't even have been being considered for that job." Harmon explained when interviewed. "At the time, she had not established any legal credentials."

This windfall, among others, set up the whole question of conflict of interest involving the spouse of a powerful politician. That problem accelerated for Hillary as time went on and is still with us. Why were people doing things for her? Was it solely because of her considerable skill? Or was she also a convenient vehicle for influencing her influential husband?

(We'll face this entire, growing problem of spousehood of prominent politicians in our conclusion, "The Lessons of Whitewater.")

Clinton's political foes kept reminding the public of these conflicts. One pointed out that her airport attorney job was approved by Commissioner Seth Ward, whose son-in-law was Webster Hubbell, one of Hillary's colleagues at the Rose firm. (Hubbell later became a White House aide before he was forced to leave.)

Another claimed that as attorney general, Clinton did little to stop a rate hike by the Arkansas-Louisiana Gas Company (ARKLA), then controlled by the powerful Stephens family, who was also a client of the Rose firm.

Hillary's Fortunes

In a short period, not only had Hillary been named to the Rose Law Firm, then to her job at the Airport Commission, but she also had that government legal services contract for the poor. One Clinton foe claimed it would pay her up to $54,000, but Clinton said it was closer to $8,000. The Legal Services Corporation in Washington, which handles these programs at a taxpayer cost of $400 million a year, says it no longer has any record of what Hillary actually made.

Then in 1977, Hillary received a patronage appointment from the White House. Jimmy Carter had just been elected President, and he named Hillary to the board of the Legal Services Corporation. Later, Carter made her its chairwoman. This was not just a prestige appointment. The new job, which she handled while working at the Rose firm, came with a federal stipend.

Hillary's new part-timer was actually a payoff for work in the Carter campaign in the fall of 1976, when she traveled to Indianapolis to help the Carter campaign there. Her White House appointment came soon afterward.

Hillary had taught some criminal law, but couldn't practice it at Rose. Instead, she set up another business, as an associate of William Wilson, a prominent Little Rock defense attorney, on the side. She handled several criminal cases, and in one instance, she got a man off who was accused of beating his girlfriend.

"Hillary has a steel trap mind," Wilson said when interviewed. "She worked on a half dozen cases with me and I found her highly competent, in fact outstanding."

"Was she paid?" I asked. Wilson laughed. "Well, she wasn't working for nothing." (Recently, Wilson was named a federal district judge by President Clinton.)

Once again, Hillary's activities became a bone of contention. Opponents pointed out that her criminal work could be a conflict. As attorney general, Bill might have to rule on cases she handled. Would he rule against his wife?

Carpe Diem

By 1978, Clinton knew he'd be seeking higher office, either the Senate or the governor's seat. When then-Governor Pryor announced he would seek election to the Senate, that left the statehouse open and Clinton seized the day.

In no time, he raised a large campaign chest from the corporations, utilities, and banks he had once spurned, amassing a staff of fifteen, along with a chartered plane. Gone was his prissiness about taking in vast amounts of money. Gone too was the 1970 Gremlin.

Hillary moved into the front ranks of the campaign. As the *Arkansas Gazette* said, "She intends to be actively involved in policy making if Clinton is named governor." Clinton himself was not bashful about his wife's participation. "Buy one, get one free," he smiled, adding that she would be his key adviser.

Hillary herself became a major campaign issue. First, she was attacked for her conflicts as a lawyer-plus. Perhaps more important was her deviation from the norm for an Arkansas political spouse. She had that distinctly bohemian, unfeminine intellectual look, which was not much in favor in the state. Her outspokenness—like the time she insulted the local television station for not running David Frost's interview with Nixon—shocked still others.

Her legal attitude toward children, outlined in her article in the *Harvard Educational Review* in 1974, raised other eyebrows. Hillary had gone overboard, comparing the inadequate legal rights of children today to those of blacks, women, and Native Americans historically, asking for more freedom for children in such areas as schooling, motherhood, abortion, etc. It stimulated speculation that Hillary wanted children to have the right to sue their parents, an idea that continues to this day.

But perhaps the strongest anti-Hillary feelings were generated by a simpler fact: her name. She continued to use her maiden name. At one meeting, a fellow Democrat looked at her name tag: "HILLARY RODHAM!" he exclaimed. "THAT'S NOT YOUR NAME. IT'S HILLARY CLINTON!"

Failed Issue

"I made that a campaign issue," says Frank Lady, one of those who unsuccessfully contested Clinton. "People didn't like the idea of her not using her married name and I brought it up. There was a lot of talk about it, but it ended up having no effect at the ballot box. If I had to do it over again, I wouldn't do it."

Lady does think there was a continuing conflict in Hillary's role as the Governor's wife and an attorney for a law firm handling clients doing business with the state. "Her presence in the Rose Law Firm gave them a front door to the Governor's office," he charges.

Lady is awed by Bill Clinton's political skills, but as he says, "I'm not one of his fans. He's not reliable. In the governor's race, he posed as a champion of the little people and said he made several lawsuits against the utilities to keep rates down. Actually, he made only one. I believe the gas companies and the utilities had him in their hip pocket."

Whatever the carping, it was all useless against Clinton's charismatic presence.

"There was a kind of adoration of Bill Clinton," says John Harmon, a putative primary candidate in the 1978 race for governor. "I had grass roots support, but when I traveled around the state, people said they would support me, but first they had to find out what Billy Clinton is doing. If he runs for the Senate, I'll support you, they said. But when he announced for governor, I dropped out of the race before the filing date."

Like others, Harmon felt the sense of Clinton's invincibility.

"The newspapers were enamored of this young man, an attractive bright young star," he says. "He also had the support of the 'Good Suit Club,' a group of 100 powerful businessmen who met at the Excelsior or Capitol Hotel in Little Rock. They were key contributors. Now, nothing could stop him."

Explaining Bill

I asked Harmon if he could explain the Clinton phenomenon. Since the state is more conservative than Clinton, why
the enormous popularity, almost adoration?

"I think I know the reason why," Harmon speculated.
"Arkansas has had trouble finding things to be proud of. Now
here comes along Bill Clinton. He was good-looking, very
well spoken, well educated. As we say down here, 'he
showed good.' He was the hope of people who thought that
here's a young man who can present an image better than the
one we're stuck with—forty-eighth and forty-ninth in everything."

"Did his lack of military service come up?" I asked
Harmon, a tall bulky man with a pleasant Arkansas drawl.

"There were rumors that he had been a war protestor,
and his lack of military service was at the periphery of the
campaign. But no one had the facts. Cliff Jackson had the
incriminating letter about his draft status. If that had surfaced in 1978, I don't think he would have been elected
governor."

But it didn't surface. Clinton beat his opponents handily, taking over 60 percent of the primary vote. The general
election against the Republican, A. Lynn Lowe, was the
usual walkover, with Clinton getting 63.4 percent. Even
Clinton's opposition to an initiative that would have saved
taxpayers $60 million in sales taxes made no difference.

The election was on November 7, 1978. But just prior
to Clinton's sure victory, the couple had already added to
the financial perks that come with being politically powerful in America.

That, of course, was Whitewater.

Chapter Five

The Whitewater Debacle

The Swamp on the Hill

The lives of William Jefferson Clinton and James B. Mc-Dougal have come together over the last twenty-five years in friendship and political camaraderie—and also in the clash of a massive headache known collectively as "Whitewater," one which still bedevils them both.

Fate has treated them very differently. Mr. Clinton, as we know, is President of the United States. Mr. McDougal, on the other hand, has been struck by a series of indignities, all related to his Madison Guaranty Savings and Loan debacle in general, and his partnership with the Clintons in Whitewater in particular.

McDougal has gone through bankruptcy, a temporary mental ailment, loss of his income and property, a federal fraud trial, and a divorce. Until recently, he lived in a trailer near Arkadelphia, Arkansas, subsisting on a $723 monthly disability check from Social Security.

The President has reached the pinnacle of American society, but McDougal's financial and emotional trials are now beginning to rub off on his former friend as well. No one knows the final scenario, but having a full insight into Whitewater—as we'll lay it out—will perhaps lend a clue.

The gap between the two men wasn't always so cosmic. Long before Whitewater, back in 1968, it was McDougal who was the mentor to a young college senior named Bill Clinton. McDougal was running Senator J. William Fulbright's office in Little Rock, and Bill Clinton arrived there in the summer of 1968 after his graduation from Georgetown to help in Fulbright's successful reelection campaign.

As McDougal took him under his wing, even entertained him with deadpan imitations of FDR, Clinton quickly saw that the shrewd political operative exuded a natural intelligence "Only a notch below that of Clinton himself," says Sam Heuer, McDougal's lawyer. The two became fast friends.

The Real McDougal
The press has sometimes tried to caricature McDougal as an Arkansas "rube," but the reality is quite different. Once considered one of the best speechwriters on the Hill, he had also taught political science at his alma mater, a small Baptist college. (His ex-wife, Susan, another Whitewater player, was his student.)

McDougal is a fervid political liberal and proud of it. In that vein, he's a close twin of the President, if more emotional. In anger, McDougal recently called Congressman Jim Leach, a leading Whitewater critic, a "fascist," adding that he despised the Republican party for "starving the country for the last 100 years."

Both McDougal and Clinton had political ambitions, but even in 1968, it was obvious that the twenty-two-year-old Clinton was the natural. Over the years, McDougal hitched his star to Bill's, working in his campaigns, raising money, doing whatever was necessary for his "political family," with Clinton rising rapidly in that genealogy. (Does McDougal, we might ask, regret it all in retrospect?)

McDougal's political ambitions were mainly sublimated in Bill Clinton, but occasionally the longing would break out. This past spring of 1994, McDougal ran a quixotic race for the Democratic nomination for Congress, hoping to bring back the glorious pre-Whitewater days. But bedeviled by bad publicity and a worn-out image, he came out a poor last.

Political historians have forgotten that in 1982, at the same time Clinton was fighting to regain his lost governor's seat, McDougal was the Democratic nominee for Congress against Clinton's old nemesis, John Paul Hammerschmidt, in northern Arkansas. Like Clinton, McDougal lost to the powerful Republican.

McDougal has been blamed for Clinton's present Whitewater aggravation—as if the Clintons were naifs—but back in 1968, the meeting of the two men was a boon for the aspiring young Clinton. As we've seen, McDougal's boss, Senator William Fulbright, was instrumental in gaining a Rhodes scholar spot for Clinton, then performing lobbying handsprings to help keep him out of the draft.

As years went on, McDougal was an invaluable member of the tightly knit Arkansas "political family," as he calls it, doing what favors he could for the Democratic party, helping Clinton when each dollar raised was another brick on the road to the White House.

The two men have been estranged. The last word between them, according to McDougal's current lawyer, Sam Heuer, was in 1990, when then-Governor Clinton called McDougal to congratulate him on his acquittal on federal fraud charges.

The Nelson Tapes

In 1992, McDougal went to see Sheffield Nelson, who ran against Clinton in 1990 and is the 1994 Republican candidate for governor of Arkansas, for some legal advice. In a tape-recorded interview, McDougal let down his hair, and let out his heart. He showed his bitterness at Clinton—a reaction surely triggered by the feeling that the President had deserted him. After the debacle, when McDougal was kicked out of Madison Guaranty and went into bankruptcy, Clinton never offered him a job, or even the time of day.

McDougal was so bitter at his ex-partner, whom fate had rewarded so differently, that in the interview with Sheffield Nelson, he tore into the President.

Speaking about the Clintons' supposed loss on Whitewater of almost $69,000—since scaled down to $47,000 by the White House—McDougal, who apparently made all the mortgage payments on Whitewater, let the President have it.

"I saw that article in the *Post* where some guy just accepted the Clintons' $68,000 loss," said McDougal angrily.

"I could sink it (the estimate) quicker than they could lie about it if I could get in a position so that I wouldn't have my head beaten off, and Bill knows that."

(Later, we'll dissect the Clinton estimates of supposed loss, and perhaps do some more scaling down ourselves, which would agree with McDougal's original skepticism.)

But today, McDougal's anger has suddenly cooled or has been miraculously appeased. The "new McDougal," as one federal researcher calls him, has dramatically changed his tune. He has become very supportive of the President and insists on his former friend's total innocence in the Whitewater affair, on all counts. (He's a little more hesitant about Hillary.) McDougal's final attitude, one presumes, depends on whether he is indicted again by the new Independent Counsel, or given the same clean bill recently extended to the White House meddlers by Robert Fiske.

McDougal's lawyer, Sam Heuer, thinks his client is now home free. "I don't think Jim will be indicted," he said when interviewed in Little Rock. "He's already been acquitted by a federal court in connection with Madison Guaranty. To indict him again would be double jeopardy."

Back in the old days, McDougal stayed with Fulbright until 1974, when the Senator was defeated in a Democratic primary by Dale Bumpers, then governor and player in the state's game of political musical chairs. McDougal then left for a career in real estate and to help Clinton in his failed 1974 race for Congress. He was successful in business, investing and making money for friends and grateful politicians, including Senator Fulbright himself.

Once Hillary Rodham moved to Arkansas in 1974, the two families—Bill and Hillary and Jim and his wife Susan—became fast friends and built what Susan called an "unbelievable relationship." The McDougals lent a hand in all of Clinton's campaigns, especially the winning gubernatorial election of 1978.

Whitewater Begins

It was during that campaign that they started the fateful business known as Whitewater.

"I wanted to make some money for Bill Clinton," McDougal has said, and Whitewater was his instrument. The land in northwestern Arkansas was part of a larger parcel that had just come out of bankruptcy and was put on the market. The "101 River Development" company owned some 3,200 acres in the area, and sold the Mc-Dougals and Clintons 230 acres of it, mainly overlooking the White River, site of some of the best fishing in the state.

The price was $880 an acre, double the original price paid per acre just weeks before. Most people were surprised that they overpaid. The secretary of the selling company, "101," was also the president of the Citizens Bank Trust, the bank in Flippin that provided $182,611.20 of the $203,000 needed as a mortgage loan. The remaining $20,000 down payment was obtained from the Union Bank of Little Rock.

There are two schools of thought about how much cash the Clintons invested in Whitewater. Some say it was $500, but there appears to be no proof of that. The latest theory is that they invested only their name—which was apparently a bankable commodity since Clinton was about to become Governor of Arkansas.

Impressionable Bankers

The power of politics is seen in how easily even bankers can be mesmerized by celebrity. Frank Burge, the senior vice president of the Citizens Bank who attended the closing, seemed to have assumed that the $20,000 "down payment" came out of the collective pockets of Clinton, et al. He was "surprised" to learn—from the newspapers during the 1992 campaign—that even that was borrowed money, and that they had financed the entire Whitewater package.

As one of the Citizens Bank directors was quoted as saying about accommodating politicians for their publicity value: "You bring in one of these politicians just to use their name. You say, 'Oh, the governor's involved in this deal.' "

The deal included a prime piece of land, Tract 7, which seems to have been reserved for the Clintons. It was a gorgeous lot of twenty-seven acres of hardwood trees, sitting on a bluff at the confluence of the White River and Crooked Creek, with a direct view of the water. It might, Clinton confided to Chris Wade, the rental agent, be a perfect place to retire after his career in politics. But it was too good to use personally and was one of the first lots sold, for $35,000. Besides, the Clintons would hardly consider retiring on what is for them an accursed spot of earth.

Initially called Whitewater Estates, the development was made ready for business when McDougal put up $47,000 more for roads and improvements. A corporation

valued at $250,000, the Whitewater Development Corpo-
ration, Inc., was later formed, with the McDougals as officers and the Clintons as equal shareholders, even though
they had put up only their future political influence for
half the land.

(Of course, the Clintons did obligate themselves by
signing the mortgage, but it proved of no consequence for
they never had to make a principal payment on the land.)

Good Prospects

The chance for solid vacation home sales at first seemed
glorious, what with publicity about the Sun Belt, and people from the upper Midwest retiring southward. McDougal
was convinced it was a sweet deal for both families. The
lots sold well initially, but the high interest rates, which
rose to over 20 percent, dried up sales and hurt Whitewater's loan repayments to the banks.

Something was needed to stimulate sales at Whitewater.

The answer was a model home. The problem was
$30,000, the price of the house. By this time, in December
1980, McDougal had decided banking was more profitable
than real estate. With partners, including Jim Guy Tucker,
the present governor of Arkansas, he bought control of
the Bank of Kingston, a small institution in the northern
part of the state, but still rich enough to handle a $30,000
loan. But there was a hooker. As the controlling board
member of the bank, McDougal could not lend Whitewater the money, for he was an officer of the land company as well.

A way had to be found to circumvent the banking

laws. The answer was Hillary Clinton, an accomplished attorney then working for the Rose Law Firm in Little Rock. She was a shareholder in Whitewater, but not an officer. She volunteered to become the center of the ingenious scheme. McDougal's Bank of Kingston lent Hillary the $30,000 on December 16, 1980.

"Passive" Investors

The Clinton claim to innocence in Whitewater and its involved tributaries is that they were "passive" investors—putting up mainly their name and hoping for manna. But the tale of Lot 13, a three-acre piece of land on which the model home was built, tells a different story.

If Hillary had been any more passive, she would have been frenetic. The tale is one of *active* personal involvement by Hillary, and later Bill, that sets up legal and financial complications that have not yet been fully unraveled, even by astute federal investigators.

But from what we do know from the government, other sources, and our own investigation, most of the story of Lot 13 can be pieced together. It seems a surprising lapse of legal and/or ethical values by attorney Hillary Clinton, then wife of the Governor, with accounting, corporate, and tax ramifications of enormous consequences.

Considering her academic skills, Hillary Rodham Clinton should have known better. That transaction finally dragged the Governor as well into something in which they should never have been involved.

The story, which covers the 1980–1982 time frame, but also takes us, flash forward, a few years, is a convoluted tale.

It goes as follows:

1. The Whitewater Development Corporation couldn't borrow $30,000 from the Bank of Kingston for the model house because Jim Mc-Dougal was in operative control of both, and that would violate Arkansas banking laws.

2. Hillary Clinton—a shareholder but not a corporate officer of Whitewater—volunteered to do it personally.

3. The bank holding the Whitewater mortgage released Lot 13 from its indebtedness.

4. Whitewater Development transferred Lot 13 to Hillary Clinton, apparently without any cost to her. There are no tax stamps attached to the deed documents, which indicates a non-transfer of funds.

5. Hillary used the land as collateral to get the $30,000 loan, which was granted to her by Mc-Dougal's bank. There is still some doubt, says one government source, whether the land was transferred in time to make the collateral legal, or whether she received the loan without collateral before the land was transferred, which would be unethical, even possibly illegal, says the source.

6. She probably turned the $30,000 loan proceeds over to Whitewater because a check for that amount, not noted as to its source, was deposited into the Whitewater account during this period in 1980.

7. A modular home was purchased by Whitewater and placed on Hillary's Lot 13.

8. Hillary, personally, not Whitewater, was given the deed for the house and the land.

9. In a strange legal twist, Whitewater, not the owner—Hillary Rodham Clinton—regularly paid the principal and most of the interest payments on the personal loan she had taken out for the land and house.

10. In 1982, Lot 13 and the modular home were sold to Hillman Logan for approximately $27,000. There is no record of what happened to the down payment money of $3,000. It's quite possible that the Clintons pocketed the money, which is what McDougal once hinted at. The remainder of the sales price was to be made in payments over a period of years.

11. Since it was an "installment" contract, not an outright purchase, Hillary kept the deed to the land and the house.

12. Logan made several payments, then stopped making them and went bankrupt, after which he died.

13. Hillary bought back the land and house from the bankruptcy court for $8,000.

14. Meanwhile, Governor Clinton personally, without collateral, borrowed $20,000 from the Security Bank of Paragould, which was owned by Marlin Jackson, who became his banking commissioner not long after. Clinton used the proceeds to pay off the remaining balance of Hillary's loan from the Bank of Kingston. (Whitewater helped out by adding a $7,322.42 payment, at a time when its balance was less than $100.

The check was covered by a $7,500 deposit in the Whitewater account from Madison Marketing, a Madison Guaranty subsidiary run by McDougal's wife, Susan.)

15. Hillary resold the land and house to a couple for $28,000. She then paid off the remaining loan of $13,000, on which she had never made any prior payments. The Clintons kept the balance of the money and reported a capital gain of $1,640 on their income tax.

16. All this time, the Whitewater Development Co., Inc.—not Hillary Clinton—carried Lot 13 on their books as an asset.

17. Then there's the mystery of who paid the real estate taxes on Lot 13. If Hillary was the owner, and entitled to the profits, she should have paid the taxes.

I checked with the tax collector of Marion County, Arkansas, situated in the county seat of Yellville, and learned that mostly she did not. The records show that in 1981, the first year of her ownership, the $5.60 in taxes was paid by Chris Wade, the real estate agent. In 1982 and 1983, there was no notation of who paid the $143.65 (the model house was now on the lot). In 1984 it was paid by the Whitewater Development Corporation. In 1985 and 1986, the taxes were paid by Hillman Logan, the man who bought it on an installment purchase plan, even though the land was still in her name. In 1987, it was paid by "Ozark Escrow," an account related to the agent, Chris Wade. After that it was paid by the family that finally bought the house from Hillary.

(Marlin Jackson, the former banking commissioner, has reportedly recently claimed that the loan violated state rules anyway. Hillary's model house and her own residence—by then the governor's mansion—were outside the Bank of Kingston's lending area.)

Further Complications

The entire scenario has tax as well as legal implications.

Congressman Jim Leach, a Republican on the House Banking Committee, goes further in challenging the Clintons on the Lot 13 deal. Describing the sale price of $28,000 and a payment of $8,000, he says the Clintons made much more than the $1,640 they declared as a capital gain to the IRS.

"A taped conversation of Mr. McDougal in 1992 suggests Whitewater paid all of the mortgage, which would suggest that the Clintons netted approximately $20,000 on this single transaction," says the Congressman.

Then, in his statement to the U.S. House, Congressman Leach concluded: "The proceeds from the sale of Lot 13 are . . . substantially greater than the $1,640 reported in the Clintons' tax returns."

In fact, Congressman Leach believes that the Clintons *made money, not lost it, on Whitewater.* At least one critic says that Leach's accounting on Lot 13 was incorrect. We'll look at all of this later.

The Clintons do acknowledge one error—that they took deductions of $2,811 and $2,322—a total of $5,311— on their 1984 and 1985 income tax returns for interest pay-

ments on the personal loan taken out by Bill Clinton to
help retire Hillary's original loan for the model home. The
only problem is these interest payments were not made by
the Clintons, but again by the Whitewater corporation.
During the 1992 campaign, the Clintons filed amended IRS
returns, paying the back taxes plus interest.

"But," asks our federal source, "what about the Clintons' tax claims for supposed interest paid on the Whitewater loans for the years before 1984 and the years after
1985—interest possibly paid by Whitewater Development
but for which the Clintons took tax credit?"

Later, we'll look at the total tax problems of the Clintons, which may yet turn out to be enormous.

One Legal Opinion

Lot 13 is also an intriguing case for legal experts, who are
first perplexed, then somewhat shocked by Hillary's buying, borrowing money, and selling of the lot and model
house.

"If the facts are as presented, I too am perplexed," says
a prominent attorney, who like the Clintons, is a Yale Law
School graduate. He explains the case in semi legalese:

"The transaction fails to satisfy either one of two
possible legal theories. If she was acting as an agent of
the Whitewater corporation—which I understand she
claims—it looks like the Arkansas banking laws may
have been compromised. If the $30,000 loan to the corpo-
ration would have been improper, then the loan to
Hillary as the corporation's agent was equally improper.
And indeed if she was the agent of the Whitewater corporation, then she couldn't keep the proceeds of the sale of

Lot 13—as if she were a beneficial owner. But it appears that she did keep the money because she paid a capital gains tax on it.

"If, on the other hand," he continues, "the transfer of the title of Lot 13 from the Whitewater corporation to Hillary was a true fee title transfer, it seems to have been done without consideration—meaning she didn't pay for it. In this case, it was probably an *ultra vires* act of the corporation, or outside the Whitewater corporation's legal authority. This is especially true when the corporation continues to pay the mortgage and the corporation and others pay most of the real estate taxes, as appears to be the case. Overall, it seems to be a very questionable transaction."

For those of us not sophisticated in the law, what he is saying is that either Hillary really owned the land or she didn't. Either way, several improper activities took place.

So much for ingenuity and the stretchability of business and political ethics, especially for such knowledgeable attorneys as Mrs. Clinton and the Governor.

But despite all the effort and legal finagling, the model house proved of little value. They did sell half the lots in the first two years, but then sold "zero" in 1982. In the years of 1983 and 1984, they sold only two more lots, each for $10,000 to $12,000.

Meanwhile, the new Governor of Arkansas, thirty-two-year-old Bill Clinton, wasn't doing much better in his role at the statehouse. He had taken office in January 1979, for a two-year term. One of his first moves was an obvious conflict-of-interest, part of the political-money equation that plagues much of American life.

Even though McDougal was his business partner in Whitewater, Governor Clinton rewarded his old friend by naming him to his kitchen cabinet as a paid economic adviser. McDougal held the job until 1980 when he left to start his pyrotechnic career as a banker.

(Not long after Clinton took over the state capitol, a new two-mile road was built from the closest highway to the Whitewater property.)

A Burst of Energy

The Clintons came into the statehouse in a wave of academic exuberance, determined to remake Arkansas in their own image in the shortest possible time. But they found more resistance to their enthusiasm than expected.

"In his first term as governor, Bill Clinton surrounded himself with a group of flaming liberals," says Joe Woodward, a lawyer from Magnolia who came in second to Clinton in the 1978 gubernatorial primary, and is still supportive of the President.

"That group included not only Jim McDougal, but people like Steve Smith, a liberal intellectual who was his executive secretary, and had been a professor of political science at the University of Arkansas."

John Robert Starr, editor and columnist at the *Arkansas Democrat-Gazette* was then a regular, sometimes angry, critic of the new Governor. "Clinton divided the power of the governor's office among three young, bearded impractical visionaries," he blasted. Others pointed to the use of antibusiness jargon such as "corporate criminals" used by a top aide to describe some local business interests.

Joe Woodward tries to explain what happened.

"During his first term as governor, Clinton alienated a lot of people," Woodward says. "With the help of the environmentalists, he took on the timber industry, and he was generally too liberal in his viewpoints as far as the business community was concerned. There was also the Hillary question. She went around using her maiden name, Hillary Rodham, which made a lot of people angry."

The "Hillary Question" was quite important in the socially conservative state of Arkansas. She maintained the Wellesley hippie style even though she was now the Governor's wife. Her reputation was that of a strong feminist who advocated the equal rights amendment, which needed just two more states to ratify to become part of the Constitution. That too was unpopular in Arkansas.

"Then," adds Woodward, "there were the Cubans and the car tag tax."

The 1980 Campaign
"Cubans and Car Tags" was the motto of the 1980 gubernatorial campaign against Clinton, run by the Republican candidate, Frank White, a former S&L executive who had never been in politics.

White, a tall, portly gentleman with a familiar Arkansas drawl and the easy manner of the region, occupies the ground floor office of the First Commercial Bank Building in Little Rock, where he is senior vice president in charge of retail business development. A graduate of the U.S. Naval Academy, he is noted for his sometimes exuberant down-home charm.

"Hillary was a big-time feminist, and Bill was arrogant and power-crazy—thought he was smarter than anyone else," White commented when interviewed in Little Rock. "That doesn't go over in these parts. Not long after he got in, he put in a huge increase in the car license tax, the car tags, and a lot of people couldn't afford it. This is a poor state. We were forty-ninth in income when Clinton came in, and we're still that after fourteen years of him in office."

"What about the Cubans?" I asked. "What did that have to do with the Governor of Arkansas?"

White explained that a flood of Cubans had come into the army base, Camp Chafee, near Fort Smith, Arkansas. It was a relocation site for the boat people who had left Cuba, many of whom were former convicts let out of jail by Castro.

"First, the Vietnamese refugees came there. They were no problem and many of them have successfully settled in the southwestern part of the state. But we got about 30,000 Cubans and they were rowdy," relates White. "Carter didn't supply enough federal marshals and Clinton believed the lies Carter told him about the number of Cubans. Instead of cutting back, Carter said he was putting in 10,000 more and Clinton did and said nothing. One day the Cubans rioted and headed for the nearby town of Barling. They were stopped by state troopers and the local people, but Clinton never lived it down."

Unexpected Defeat
The election of November 1980, at the end of Bill Clinton's first term as Governor, was a shock. He lost to Frank

White by a 52 to 48 percent vote, which was extraordinary in the heavily Democratic state. White was only the second Republican governor in Arkansas history.

"There was virtually no Republican party in Arkansas then," says White, who entered the Governor's Mansion in January 1981. "The party primary usually drew about 8,000 in the whole state, with no Republican primary vote at all in six counties. I won because people were tired of Bill and Hillary and disappointed in their liberal programs."

Another reason was given by local columnist John Brummett, who pointed out that the young Governor had "acted too big for his britches." Clinton seemed to agree. After losing the election, Clinton himself commented that the public had seen him as being "too young, too ambitious, arrogant and insensitive."

Clinton took the defeat as if it were the end of the world.

"He went around like a sick puppy," recalls Joe Woodward. (Some observers remember that in a supermarket, he'd tell surprised shoppers that he had been the Governor of the state.) "But he's resilient. He doesn't take defeat as being final. You just can't kill him. He's like the Energizer battery. He just keeps on going and going."

Clinton did just that. To make a living, he took a job with the law firm of Wright, Lindsey and Jennings, where his present senior aide in the White House, Bruce Lindsey— one of the few Arkansas survivors—was a partner.

Once out of the Governor's Mansion, the Clintons needed a place in which to live. Flush with Hillary's $100,000 cattle futures coup, they decided to buy a relatively expensive house. It was, according to a Little Rock source, a "nouveau Victorian" reproduction of reasonable size. The house was in the Hillcrest section of Little Rock, which is below the Heights, the posh area where the Stephenses and other wealthy families lived. The price was high for the place and time—between $100,000 and $120,000—and the down payment of $60,000 came from the commodities winnings.

Now settled, Clinton traveled around the state making speeches at civic clubs. He bought a thirty second television commercial to confess to the people that he had made mistakes and had learned from them. He joined the Baptist church choir, and was seen on television every Sunday morning standing close to the preacher, singing hymns.

Remaking His Image

Those two years between his defeat in November 1980, and the next election for governor, November 1982, Bill Clinton remade himself, say both his friends and critics.

"He spent the next two years making up for his mistakes," remembers Joe Woodward. "He befriended those he had alienated, and actually apologized publicly for errors he had made. He pulled back on the corn in his speeches, and talked much less liberal. He got rid of the flaming liberals in his inner circle, and brought in seasoned Democratic party operators like Maurice Smith, who was the head of the Bank of Cherry Valley and had been around a long time, and Bill Clark, who had been head of the Arkansas Highway Commission. Clinton spent the time mending fences with business and everyone else he had offended. He knew it was the only way to get reelected."

After the defeat, Hillary Rodham also underwent a transformation, perhaps one even more radical than Bill's. She went on the stump with a new look and a new approach. The feminist image was downplayed and the traditional wife role played up. Her first change was a simple one. She stopped calling herself Hillary Rodham—a thorn in much of the public's side—and became "Mrs. Hillary Clinton," just like other Arkansas women of her day.

The Transformation

Equally important, she went through a physical transformation not unlike the ones portrayed in Hollywood films, where dowdy secretary Miss Jones takes off her glasses, loosens her hair, and voilà!

"In his second race against me," says former Governor White, "Hillary went through an amazing Hollywood makeover. It was done by her friend, Linda Bloodworth-Thomason, wife of the television producer. It changed her looks completely. She can thank me for that."

The makeover was nearly total. Hillary's oversize granny glasses gave way to contact lenses. Her hair, a kind of mousy brown, was lightened to a near-blond. Her hippy clothes, to which she stuck to so fervently because of their ties to her adolescent radical days, were discarded. She was now dressed by fashion consultants. It was a new woman for a new campaign.

That done, the Clintons decided they had to turn around their local nemesis, John Robert Starr, managing editor of the *Arkansas Democrat-Gazette*, who had daily needled Clinton and his programs, with exposés of waste and inefficiency.

(Rumors of Clinton's dalliances with women were being circulated, but were ignored by the press, including Starr.)

Hillary was assigned the job of bringing Starr around. Although she's never been noted for her charm, Hillary dredged it up and turned it on full force for this one target. Sometimes joined by the ex-Governor, Hillary often took Starr to lunch. She flattered him, talked to him about their education program (his wife was a teacher), consulted him constantly on his opinion, and sought his advice on any number of issues.

The top campaign workers, including Hillary, made sure that nothing important was said until it was checked with Starr. Ex officio, he almost became part of the Clinton circle. As Starr recently said to this author, despairingly: "I was conned."

It worked. Starr made a complete turnaround and supported Clinton for reelection in the 1980 campaign. There are several in Little Rock today who feel that the intellectual seduction of John Robert Starr by Hillary made all the difference in Clinton's reelection.

It all went as planned. In November 1982, Bill Clinton, now reconstituted as a pragmatic Democrat, defeated Republican incumbent Frank White by 55 percent to 45 percent and regained the Governor's Mansion, which he didn't relinquish until he ran for President in November 1992.

Meanwhile, the other half of the Whitewater coin, Jim McDougal, was just as busy, building an S&L empire, the star of which was Madison Guaranty Savings and Loan of Little Rock, the vehicle behind the Whitewater tale. Madi-

son was born from the small, ailing Woodruff Savings and
Loan of Augusta, Arkansas, just across the White River
from his hometown of Bradford, population less than nine
hundred.

After McDougal bought Woodruff and changed its
name, the new Madison Guaranty— of which he owned
some 63 percent, and his wife, Susan McDougal, owned
13 percent—had only a few million dollars in assets. But
McDougal thought big, and acted the same way. He started
offering jumbo CDs for just under $100,000 (the govern-
ment guaranteed the money up to $100,000) at a higher
interest rate than his competitors and sponsored some
flamboyant advertising.

He moved his operation from Augusta to a large aban-
doned factory in the historic Quapaw district of downtown
Little Rock, turning it into a maroon Art Deco temple at
enormous cost.

A Burgeoning S&L
His promotions paid off. Soon the depositors flocked in
and the bank's assets rose from $6 million to $123 million
in four years. James McDougal became "Diamond Jim,"
driving a dark green Jaguar (his wife had a twin one), and
for a while, a blue Bentley which the bank had repos-
sessed.

In a policy mistake, the Reagan administration had virtually deregulated the S&Ls, which were now allowed to
lend money for speculative ventures, especially real estate,
which was flying high in the early and mid-1980s.

McDougal's Madison Guaranty was expert at capitalizing on Washington's laxity. The bank started to lend

money for numerous real estate developments, including some prompted by McDougal and his wife. One called Gold Mine Springs was publicized by Susan McDougal, who had an excellent figure who went on television dressed in hot pants and riding a white horse around the property.

The loans were spread across the state, including several to members of the "political family," well-placed Democrats that included Jim Guy Tucker, former congressman and the present governor of Arkansas, and Senator William Fulbright.

One government spokesman estimated that the bank had lent $17 million to directors, officers, and executives of the S&L and its subsidiaries. Madison Guaranty, says Congressman Jim Leach of the House Banking Committee, was run "like a private piggy bank."

In the general picture, it was only one of 1,100 S&Ls that eventually went under, costing the taxpayers $200 billion dollars.

But this one was special, in so many ways, as we shall see. It was tied, through Whitewater and the "political family" to the personal lives and political fortunes of Governor Bill Clinton and his very active wife, Hillary Rodham Clinton.

Chapter Six

Hillary the Money Machine

Conflict Raised to an Art

Hillary Rodham was as busy as her husband, and their Whitewater partner, Jim McDougal. Almost like clockwork, as soon as Bill was inaugurated Governor, she was elevated to "partner" at Rose. This was no little reward, for the group was one of the three major players in the legal business of Little Rock.

Rose had a distinguished roster of clients: such local giants as Tyson Foods; Wal-Mart; Stephens, Inc., the nation's largest investment firm outside of Wall Street; ARKLA, the natural gas utility (whose former head, Thomas F. "Mack" McLarty, became President Clinton's chief of staff); TCBY; the *Arkansas Gazette*; the Worthen Bank, the state's largest, whose major stockholder was the Stephens organization. They even handled public agencies, from the Public Service Commission to the Little Rock Airport Commission, where Hillary had been house attorney. When firms outside the state, including General Motors and Prudential, had legal work in Arkansas, they hired Rose.

Hillary was not just another partner. She was the Governor's wife, and the glue of a quartet of lawyers who stuck together through thick and thick. The tightly knit group included Webster L. Hubbell, Vincent W. Foster, Jr., William Kennedy III, and herself—the "Famous Four," as they came to be known, joined inexorably in loyalty.

Hubbell was a politically active Democrat who had served on the Little Rock City Council, and as mayor of the city for two years. A very tall, beefy but soft-spoken man, he had been the star offensive tackle of the University of Arkansas Razorbacks that won the 1969 Sugar Bowl. The closest of the three to Arkansas politicians and Bill Clinton, Hubbell was Bill's golfing buddy and was even named chief justice of the Arkansas Supreme Court for a short while. As the firm's administrative partner, he decided whether there were conflicts of interest.

Vincent W. Foster, Jr., the mild-mannered member, was closest to Hillary. A graduate of the University of Arkansas Law School, he scored the highest in the state bar examination and was considered both the scholar and "soul" of the foursome. Foster was the firm's major litigator.

William H. Kennedy III was the head of the firm's executive committee.

(Eventually all four moved to Washington together with President Clinton. Hubbell officially became the number three man in the Justice Department, but was actually the power above Janet Reno, reporting privately back to Clinton. Foster became Deputy White House Counsel under Bernard Nussbaum, Hillary's friend, and functioned as the Clintons' personal lawyer, handling their tangled Whitewater affairs. Kennedy was a senior White House aide in charge of administration. Today Foster is dead, Hubbell is gone, and Kennedy has been demoted. Only Hillary is still in power.)

The Famous Rose
The Rose Law Firm, now housed in a renovated YMCA building in downtown Little Rock, is said to trace its roots back to 1820, before Arkansas became a state, and is therefore the oldest legal organization west of the Mississippi. It takes its name from Judge U. M. Rose, one of the founders of the American Bar Association, who joined the firm after the Civil War.

It has always been successful, but in the mid-1970s, C. Joseph Giroir, a former Securities and Exchange Commission attorney, took over and in a space of ten years quadrupled its volume, adding the corporate elite of Arkansas to its client roster, and expanding its staff to fifty-three attorneys, thirty of whom were partners.

Hillary's name proved invaluable to the firm. Rose partner William Kennedy called her the "Rainmaker," the one who attracts important clients. Not that Hillary had to go out and seed the clouds. Her name on the stationery—and a whispered hint that she was the Governor's wife—was good enough.

Hillary rapidly became a money machine, not only for the firm, but for herself. Hillary started out small, drawing only $23,000 as an "associate"—actually an employee—when she began in 1977. But by the time she left, she was making $203,000 a year in partnership earnings, sharing in all company proceeds except for *direct* business with the state of Arkansas.

Name Power

Corporations were also thrilled to have her name on their stationery. Before she was finished in 1992, she was taking in $64,000 a year just for serving on the board of such Arkansas-based giants as Wal-Mart and TCBY.

"Nobody thinks that anybody thinks she got all that money just for her skills," says Max Brantley, reigning, and sometimes biting, oracle at the *Arkansas Times*. (Even though he's a dedicated Clintonite.)

This was a far cry from the young anticorporate radical at Wellesley. Youthful hyperbole can often be overlooked as part of the maturing process, but Hillary is consistent. As a recently retired corporate honcho, she spoke at the 1993 University of Michigan commencement, offering the same unbending message. Hillary warned the graduates not to imitate the 1980s—the era that had been so good to her. That decade, she charged again, was a damned one of "too much individual gain" and an "ethos of selfishness and greed." So much for personal insight, or self-hypnotism, or whatever.

At Rose, Hillary was part of a team of litigators who earned their fees in court and in preparing cases. But despite her designation as a "litigator," Hillary was much too busy for that scut work. Observers say that in her fifteen years at Rose, she turned up in court only five times. She was more a power player, a draw for clients, a brief writer, a pinch hitter, a legal strategist, and an influencer with the statehouse and state agencies.

High Hourly Wage

She drew full-time pay but she was a part-time, probably from one-half to only a one-third time, lawyer. While
on Rose's healthy payroll, she was running the Governor's Mansion, raising a young daughter, helping Bill
Clinton run the state, directing his six campaigns for
election, and doing public work for children and in education. Hillary carried the education reform ball in
Arkansas, just as she now directs the health issue
in Washington.

Even her good friend William Kennedy admits that she
wasn't a regular *working* partner. "We're very proud of
Hillary," he told the *American Lawyer*, "and if she ever
quit having two lives and concentrated on the law practice,
she'd have been a superb lawyer." (Notice the use of the
past conditional.)

Why then, we might ask, did Hillary Clinton earn as
much as other working Rose partners when she wasn't doing as much, or even nearly as much, work?

The answer, of course, is that old equation: POLITI-
CAL CELEBRITY PAYS. Hillary was capitalizing on her
name, big-time, earning enormous private welfare in exchange for the use of her public persona. But at least then
it wasn't taxpayer money.

"My view," a former Rose lawyer (not Kennedy) was
quoted in *American Lawyer* as commenting, "is that she
does not contribute much as a lawyer. But she is Bill Clinton's wife and they feel good about that."

Good enough, we might ask, to pay her an enormous
six figure salary for part-time work?

But despite attempts to make the situation look normal, Hillary's work at Rose was bedeviled by daily conflict. On a scale of 1 to 10, it hit 12. Hillary was a director of TCBY, the yogurt giant whose headquarters is the tallest building in Little Rock. She received $12,500 a year as a board member at the same time she was getting her partnership share of the $275,000 in legal fees that Rose annually billed TCBY.

As both corporate director and partner in the firm that did their legal work, she was approving payments to herself. Is that appropriate, or ethical? Or do those in the political limelight so mesmerize themselves that they believe that all those favors, attention, and money are thrust at them because of their talents instead of their political influence?

Obsessed with Money

With Bill silently approving, over the years Hillary became more and more obsessed with money. McDougal called her "grasping" when it came to financial matters. Together with Foster and Hubbell, she put $15,000 into an investment pool called Midlife Investors. Little Rock money manager Roy Drew who opened the account, recalls that despite her superharried schedule as Arkansas's First Lady, a Rose attorney, and a mother— she called "all the time" to find out how her investments were doing.

Later on, she joined a fashionable Little Rock investment pool called Value Partners with a larger amount.

Hillary's compulsive nature zeroed in on money as laser-like as it did on politics. There's no doubt she had the Midas touch and used it to transmute opportunity—which flowed from her husband's prominence—into gold. Some of her financial coups are still little known.

An Unknown Deal

She has been very secretive about her moneymaking schemes, and has sworn her friends-in-investment to secrecy. The cattle futures bonanza was only uncovered in 1994. But there's at least one more relatively unknown Hillary deal. That involves cellular phones, and the profit margin here was almost as great as her commodities coup.

An old Little Rock friend, David Watkins (recently fired from the White House for his affinity for golf and helicopters), was putting together a syndicate to secure a cellular phone license for the Little Rock area from the Federal Communications Commission.

Originally, the licenses were going to be awarded by selection, which was based on many intangible factors. The name of the Governor's wife would look very good on such an application, Watkins was confident. He invited Hillary into the cellular phone group and she agreed to invest $2,000.

But the government switched signals and decided to award the license by lottery instead. Hillary's application didn't win, but Watkins turned around and bought the cellular phone rights from the lottery winners in their area. He then resold it to a cellular giant.

The result? Hillary's little $2,000 investment brought her in $47,630, a twenty-four-fold gain that rivaled her cattle coup.

In the mid-1980s, Hillary was very active financially, dabbling in a whole range of money instruments to make the family fortune. She bought oil-drilling partnerships that generated tax deductions, which she took, along with deductions for playing the market with losing stock index futures.

Hillary even turned her public service work into money for Rose. A group of local charities, with financial aid from the state, created the Southern Development Corporation, which would make loans to the poor—a well-intentioned scheme. Hillary was put on the board, and the legal business was directed to Rose. Over the years, Hillary's firm took in between $100,000 and $150,000 in fees, according to the director. Not bad, considering the money was coming from charity.

Smelling the Rose
Rose itself was another fertile field for ever-greater income, Hillary decided. Though she was earning a full partnership share for part-time work, she wanted more money. To accomplish that, she planned a palace revolt with her friends—Kennedy, Foster, and Hubbell—against the managing partner, C. Joseph Giroir, the man who had built the modern organization.

As litigators who prepared and tried cases in court, they earned less than corporate people like Giroir who dealt in multi-million-dollar buyouts, mergers, and other security deals. Their income was often double that of the litigators. Hillary started a battle to change the firm's compensation formula in order to increase the share for litigators such as herself— even though she had tried very few cases in court.

And *especially* for herself, she developed a new legal fillip. The Rose sharing formula, she insisted, should include extra money for such items as "public service," or as one Rose lawyer put it, "enhancing the firm's reputation"— Hillary's forte. It seems startling in retrospect that rather than be hesitant about being paid for her political name, she demanded *extra* compensation for it.

It worked. Her income and that of her friends went up, with Hillary getting a little something extra as a reward for her prominence, courtesy of Bill Clinton. Giroir agreed that up to twenty percent of a partner's income would come from such intangibles, custom-made for a Governor's wife.

Eventually, Giroir left the Rose firm, some believe pushed out by Hillary and her friends.

He had been involved in several business deals and lawsuits at the time. When interviewed in his spacious office overlooking all of Little Rock, Giroir denied that he had been "forced out" of Rose. It had been voluntary, he said. He had other pressing business obligations to take care of, but he did not dispute that the battle between litigators and corporate lawyers was an age-old one that Hillary had championed at Rose.

Money, Money, Money
Money, curiously, was a driving force of the Clintons during those years. I say curious because they were very well off for a young couple in their midthirties. In the early to the mid-1980s, the Governor's $35,000 salary and Hillary's substantial partnership profits combined reached, then passed, the $100,000 a year mark. That did not include the bonanza from the cellular phone deal, the profits from their stock pool, and the cattle futures windfall that had been invested in a home. That money was also banked

when the house was sold after Bill had been reelected governor in 1982.

There were solid perks that went with Bill's job: free room and board for themselves and their daughter at the Governor's Mansion plus a chauffered car and a generous entertainment allowance. It was an extraordinarily good income and lifestyle, especially for Arkansas in its time.

Despite that, the Clintons hid their wealth and cried poverty. One of their more curious attempts to get more money out of the political-legal system was described by their Whitewater partner, Jim McDougal, in an interview with the *Los Angeles Times*. The way he related it, McDougal often chatted with Governor Clinton when he jogged past his Madison Guaranty office. One morning, the Governor came by and dropped into McDougal's expensive new leather chair, sitting and talking for a while. McDougal was annoyed, fearful that Clinton's sweated body would stain the leather.

"Jim," Clinton finally said, "we're finding it hard to make ends meet. Can you help out?"

McDougal recalled that day. "I asked him how much he would need," the banker recalled, "and Clinton said 'about $2,000 a month.' "

McDougal immediately had his people call the Rose Law Firm and put them— ostensibly meaning Hillary— on a $2,000-a-month retainer. "I hired Hillary," McDougal later said, "because Bill came in whimpering that they needed help."

One of McDougal's aides remembers that Clinton jogged by and picked up the check personally every month. The Clintons admit that the retainer existed, but the White House denies that it was sought or picked up. The retainer eventually cost McDougal almost $24,000.

Here, we should ask three important questions:

1. Why, in God's name, we might wonder, would this public-spirited couple, with a sizable nest egg in the bank, a solid double paycheck, free room and board and more, plead poverty to get still more money they obviously didn't need?

2. Why would they risk their reputations by having Hillary and the Rose Law Firm become involved with the shaky Madison Guaranty Savings and Loan for $2,000 a month, creating a possible conflict-of-interest between their 50 percent stake in Whitewater and the state government?

3. Why would they be in Whitewater, and more important, stay in Whitewater, a real estate promotion with little prospects and enormous conflicts, to begin with?

The answer to all three seems puzzling but it was there all the time, just waiting in the wings. It comes as a surprise to some who thought the couple were obviously dedicated to politics but surely were not wealthy. Or so they thought. But what has come out is that the Clintons were not only compulsive about changing the world, they were equally obsessive about accumulating a fortune from a standing start. All of the risks, including Whitewater, were part of that overriding need to become rich.

A Sizable Fortune

They, and especially Hillary, succeeded. The secret was revealed in the spring of 1994 in the White House's official disclosure statement of the First Couple's net worth. It shows that, mainly in the decade of the 1980s— ostensibly one of "greed,"—they built and stashed away a fortune. They now have a net worth estimated as high as $1.6 million, and almost all of it liquid. Not bad for a couple still in their midforties, one of whom never made more than $35,000 a year.

It seems that the business of politics can be quite lucrative. But only if one understands just the right admixture of public service and personal profit. As the Clintons, especially Hillary, surely did.

Though it was lucrative, in retrospect it's still surprising that Hillary ever took the job at Rose in the first place. And more surprising, that she stayed there throughout her husband's five terms as Governor of Arkansas. The conflict of interest implicit in her role was so obvious that a first-year law student would have judged her unique role unethical from the get-go.

The vulnerable points were all over the legal map.

1. Several of Rose's clients—Tyson Foods, Stephens, Inc., the Worthen Bank, and others—were regulated by the state. The regulating was done by individuals appointed by her husband, often with Hillary's advice and counsel, even consent. The conflict was self-evident.

2. The Rose Law Firm was often hired by the state and quasi-public agencies to represent them. Although Hillary waived her income in such cases, her presence as a Rose lawyer had to influence state decisions.

3. Hillary and Bill were half owners in Whitewater, but, as we shall see, she represented the S&L owned by her partner before state authorities named by her husband.

4. As an active policy maker in Governor Clinton's administrations, she often helped select state supreme court justices to fill out terms. Some believe that she personally interviewed the judicial candidates herself—justices before whom her law firm would soon be pleading cases.

More Than Theory

That last conflict sounds like a one-in-a-thousand possibility, even a legal fantasy. But as it turned out, it wasn't just theory. It actually came up in a lawsuit naming Hillary as having unfairly tipped the scales of justice through her influence with her husband.

According to the *New York Times*, the Rose firm, working for Alcoa, appealed a $1.2 million judgment awarded an injured worker for alleged company negligence. The case came before the Arkansas Supreme Court, and specifically before one of the judges appointed by Governor Clinton to fill out a term.

That "special justice" (as he's called) wrote the majority decision in favor of Rose and Alcoa, vacating the money judgment awarded the badly injured worker. The plaintiff's attorney, Ted Boswell, a prominent Little Rock lawyer, yelled that Hillary might have prejudiced the case in a classic conflict of interest.

Because she was both a Rose attorney and wife of Governor Clinton, he intimated, she might have helped select the special justice who ruled against his client. He also surprised the court by claiming that the Governor's wife had been directly involved in the case as well, on Alcoa's side.

Rose denied that Hillary had anything to do with it. But Boswell presented his view in a statement to the court. He even produced an affidavit from another attorney who swore that Mrs. Clinton had performed legal services for Rose in that case. Hillary had sought advice from him on the selection of the jurors for the trial, the lawyer revealed.

Then he added the embarrassing clincher, which was quoted in the *New York Times*:

"It is generally believed among the bench and the bar that Hillary Rodham Clinton has played some part in the selection of special justices in the past."

Boswell lost, but the message survives.

(When contacted, Boswell's office said that the attorney declined to talk about the subject.)

Ongoing Conflicts

Hillary's ongoing conflicts of interest—which didn't seem to bother either her or Bill— can be seen over and over. One of Rose's clients, Tyson Foods, the nation's largest poultry producer, was perhaps Bill Clinton's largest and most reliable campaign contributor. So, naturally, Tyson was important, pocketbookwise, to both Hillary and Bill.

Tyson's environmental activity was regulated by the state, especially the problem of getting rid of tons of chicken feces. That was, and is, a deadly threat to Arkansas rivers and the drinking water supply. No one in the state doubts that Tyson always got a generous deal from Governor Clinton. Tyson was excused $9 million in taxes as part of the state's development program. But more important, Tyson seemed the beneficiary of lax environmental rules shaped by Governor Clinton.

The strange connection between money and power ended up sending tons of extra chicken feces into Arkansas rivers and ground water, forcing at least one town to close down its polluted drinking water system.

In 1977, the state pollution regulators reissued the license for a Tyson plant in the town of Green Forest. But the order was never enforced, and in May 1983, the waste seeped into the drinking water. Governor Clinton had to declare the town a disaster area.

Tyson has been a faithful friend, both as a contributor to Clinton's campaigns for Governor and Rose partnership fees for Hillary. The firm even managed a few trips for the Clintons on the Tyson jet.

No More "St. Hillary"

Does this all prove anything? Yes, especially when it comes to political spouses. In the American tradition, wives (and husbands) of public officials have silent power in our democracy. No one can stop the spouses of members of Congress, a governor, or the president, from lobbying at dinner, or even in bed. But the nature of Hillary's role at the Rose Law Firm was unprecedented and tailor-made for both conflict and later "exposure."

The trouble called Whitewater was inevitable. It's merely the end result of bad theory, one in which both Hillary and Bill Clinton were overconfident, even cocky (or as the Greeks say, filled with hubris), and therefore insensitive to ethical concerns that would be obvious to our first-year law student.

By playing too many roles and seeking to make money on many of them, Hillary the Invincible became Hillary the Vulnerable because she was immersed in a day-to-day conflict of interest. She was a major stockholder in Whitewater, and a lawyer whose clients, including Madison Guaranty, had concerns that regularly came before public officials who were named, often with her advice, by her husband.

That wasn't all. She also served as the Governor's chief policy aide. Not only didn't Bill—who's in awe of his wife's mind and legal skills—object. He encouraged her, and still does. "Read my lips. Buy one, get one free!"

Ernest Dumas of the *Arkansas Times* believes Clinton has a "mystical faith" in Hillary's political acumen, a sign of naïveté that's troubling in such a powerful political leader.

In the old days, Hillary's conflict would simply be called nepotism and cut out quickly. But today, there's a powerful attempt to make nepotism more palatable. It's being disguised as a "political partnership." Despite that fashionable excuse, nepotism is doomed (we hope) to eventual failure in a democracy, especially in the glare of Washington's kleig lights.

Unfortunately, some people have confused Hillary's role in all this as part of the "new profile" of women, as in the feminist movement. But the reality, of course, is exactly the opposite. Despite her obvious competence,

Hillary's rise in public life was not orchestrated by the voters. It was done years ago by the minister who married them, surely an outmoded route to female success.

Part of it *(there seems to be no end!)* came to a head in 1984 and 1985, when both Hillary and Governor Clinton threw their weight, directly and indirectly, into a campaign to help keep their partner, Jim McDougal's Madison Guaranty Savings and Loan, afloat. And Whitewater with it.

This, perhaps more than any other of Hillary's expansive Arkansas adventures as a well-paid attorney for the Rose firm and wife of the Governor, was—as we shall see—the *denouement* of a misjudged, misrun, inappropriate, even dangerous, chapter of the Whitewater fiasco.

Chapter Seven

How to Keep Alive
A Bleeding S&L

Did the Clintons Cost Us
Multi-Millions?

By 1985, it was obvious to anyone within financial smelling distance of the Madison Guaranty Savings and Loan in Little Rock that it should be closed shut, tight.

Everyone, it seems, except Whitewater partners McDougal, Bill and Hillary Clinton, and those beholden to them, politically and economically.

That adventure in money politics— delaying the inevitable demise of Madison— ended up costing taxpayers millions of dollars each month, all part of the final loss of the S&L. Most recently, a spokesman at the Resolution Trust Company in Washington, when interviewed, estimated that loss at an unhealthy $68 million—$21 million more than previously.

The White House washes its hands of the whole affair, denying any involvement by the Clintons in Madison Guaranty, and thus Whitewater. But it's best for the public to understand the full scenario, then make their own decision.

It began in 1984, when it appeared to federal investigators that Madison Guaranty was getting shaky, suffering from too many risky loans, especially for flamboyant real estate deals.

Madison Guaranty was a state-chartered savings and loan and thus regulated by the Arkansas Securities Department. (Only regular banks were handled by the Banking Department.) But since its depositors were insured up to $100,000 each by the FDIC, the federal government had as much—or more—to say about its operation.

The oversight group, the Federal Home Loan Bank Board (FHLBB) out of Dallas, became concerned about Madison's health, especially when they keyed into problem loans and potential conflicts. Especially loans to insiders. One that concerned examiners was a $45,000 loan to a top officer of the S&L.

A Red Flag
The Dallas FHLBB office scheduled a "Special Limited Examination," as they called it, and put up the federal red flag. The "viability of the institution is jeopardized," the feds said after the examination. They found "unsafe and unsound lending practices," including a host of insider loans. Madison had losses in shaky real estate projects, had paid too much for land, and their reserves were dangerously low.

After a meeting in Dallas on June 21, 1984, the then-chief of the Arkansas Securities Department, Lee Thalheimer, reportedly called the situation "very serious."

One of its investments, for example, was for a resort on Campobello Island in Canada, near Maine. The island was made famous as the summer resort of Franklin Delano Roosevelt, who contracted polio there. McDougal and his partners spent almost $4 million for the resort, which was so isolated that it was three and a half hours by car from the nearest airport. The investment went sour.

But out of the bank board's examination came only a slap on the wrist—if with a threat of future action. Madison was issued a "Supervisory Agreement," which was a reprimand with a promise to do better.

But there was an implied threat in the mild rebuke: the bank had to raise more reserves and watch its lending habits if it didn't want to be closed down, as had been happening with so many Arkansas S&Ls. From 1975, when Arkansas had fifteen state-chartered S&Ls, the number has dwindled to three.

Bill Clinton (and ostensibly Hillary) should not have been surprised. He had an early warning in 1983 from the banking chief, Marlin D. Jackson, an old friend and political aide, who informed the governor that McDougal's outfit was issuing a host of bad loans.

But both warnings were unheeded by the Governor. The S&L was permitted to stay open, and the losses—finally to the taxpayers—continued.

Turn to Rose
The Madison Guaranty went into a protective stance. It authorized a study by an accounting firm, Frost and Company, which strangely showed the bank as being solvent.

Then it turned to its legal guns, the Rose Firm, which had been paid Hillary's $2,000 a month retainer by McDougal for just such an emergency.

Almost immediately after his inauguration in January 1985, Governor Clinton replaced his Securities Department chief, Lee Thalheimer—who had been appointed by the Republican governor Frank White—with a friend, Beverly Bassett. Ms. Bassett came from a law firm that had worked for Madison Guaranty. She was also the sister of Clinton's campaign chief in Washington County.

The Rose Law Firm outlined a strategy to keep Madison going, and even to expand it. It was a unique plan to raise capital by selling preferred stock in the failing operation. Not only that, but Rose petitioned the Arkansas Securities Department to permit Madison to start a stock brokerage subsidiary.

An assistant of Hillary's worked on the case, and wrote Ms. Bassett at least two letters on behalf of Madison Guaranty. One was quite optimistic—for no reason—and noted that "the applicant anticipates that no deficiency will exist in the near future."

The next month, the Rose lawyer was even more upbeat. The second letter to the Arkansas Securities Department said that Madison "anticipates improvement of its financial conditions and services provided to its customers." (Later, the attorney said he was just passing on what Madison had told him.) The letter to Ms. Bassett was signed "Rose Law Firm."

Check It With Hillary

But the woman who the White House later swore was not involved had her name plainly printed on the letter. The

Rose letter stated that if the Securities Department wanted more information they should get back to Hillary Rodham Clinton or her assistant.

Let's put this in simple perspective, so far:

1. Madison Guaranty was considered shaky by the federal government, which had warned it to change its ways if it wanted to stay open.
2. Clinton's own banking chief had warned that Madison was making bad loans. Clinton did nothing.
3. Madison needed more capital to keep going. It also had to get the Arkansas Securities Department to be cooperative.
4. The Rose Law Firm was already on retainer from McDougal through a $2,000-a-month fee arranged by Governor Clinton for his wife, Hillary.
5. Right after his inauguration in January 1985 for a third term, Bill Clinton replaced the head of the Securities Department.
6. The new appointment, Beverly Bassett, had been an attorney at a firm that worked for McDougal, setting up a potential conflict of interest.
7. Then, an attorney at Rose who worked with Hillary, sent in a plan to Ms. Bassett (now Mrs. Beverly Bassett Schaffer), asking for permission to raise capital through preferred stock, and to open a brokerage operation.
8. Hillary Clinton, who supposedly wasn't involved, had her name plainly advertised on Rose's submis-

sion— only the first clue to her real role, which was
probably managing the whole operation.

What happened as a result? Ms. Bassett quickly approved the plan, despite its basic impracticality, as
we shall see. It was a simple, conflicted deal. The plan
had been agreed to by an official just appointed by
the Governor, and pled for by the law firm of which the
Governor's wife was a partner. And on behalf of a man
who was the business colleague of both of them in
Whitewater. Amazing!

Not everyone was happy with the result. The head of
the professional staff handling financial oversight, Charles
Handley, originally disagreed with the decision, but when
he was overruled, he joined the team.

What about Lee Thalheimer, the previous head of the
Securities Department? What did he think of the lenient
attitude the state was taking toward Madison?

"I really don't know what I would have done," Thalheimer, an attorney who now represents the present governor, Jim Guy Tucker, said when interviewed. "I wasn't
there at the time that Madison asked the Securities Department for permission to sell more stock. But I suppose I
could be criticized as well. I'm the one who approved the
Campobello investment."

Zone of Fear
Ms. Bassett has several times denied that she gave Hillary
and Rose any special treatment, but what would we expect
her to say? She should not have been put into the position of having to respond to both her boss, the Governor,

and his wife—who were partners of the owner of Madison Guaranty.

The great fiction of the whole operation was that Hillary was not involved. Naturally, that would be a great embarrassment—pleading for a client who was also her business partner in Whitewater before a state agency head appointed by her husband, probably with her aid.

To escape such criticism, the Clintons, their friends, then later the White House, developed a whole hands-off theory. Not only wasn't Hillary involved in the preferred stock deal, they said, but she had *nothing* at all to do with Madison's failing operation and its loss to taxpayers. Strictly remote.

Nonsense. It turned out that it was more a ploy than a theory, a charming political fairy tale. That exposure was accomplished by a series of memos uncovered by the Resolution Trust Corporation, which took over what remained of the Madison Guaranty's assets when it was finally closed.

The first memo showed Hillary's strong intervention on behalf of Madison Guaranty with her own boss. Rose had billed Madison a significant amount and McDougal had refused to pay. Giroir, then managing partner of Rose, decided he wanted to throw the Madison account out. It was too much trouble and provided too little legal income. However, Hillary quickly mediated between the two men. On October 13, 1983, Giroir sent McDougal a new, smaller, bill along with a notation: "Pursuant to your discussions with Hillary Rodham Clinton."

In April of 1994, Mrs. Clinton tried to distance herself from the Madison project by saying that when Rose appealed to state authorities, she was only "the billing lawyer," as if that was nothing. An associate, she says, did the real work. Supposedly she had no contact with the state agency head named by her husband.

Again, nonsense. The reality is that the letter from the Arkansas Securities Department granting approval for the speculative refinancing was addressed not to the Rose Law Firm, but simply: "Dear Hillary."

Meeting With Hillary

Perhaps the most incriminating memo, tying Hillary directly in, was written by McDougal himself on July 11, 1985. It was addressed to John Latham, then the chairman of his Madison Guaranty. In it, McDougal talks about the influence he expects Hillary Clinton to exercise on his behalf:

"I need to know everything you have pending before the Securities Commission (of Arkansas)," wrote McDougal, "as I intend to get with Hillary Clinton within the next few days."

Another fiction is that people like Hillary and McDougal had no input into who was chosen as state regulator.

McDougal has bragged that he recommended Beverly Bassett in the first place to Clinton—that it was "to his advantage." That's been denied by the Clintons. However, a prior memo showed that in matters of choosing oversight people, McDougal had considerable power with the Governor.

On February 7, 1985, McDougal sent the following memo, addressed to "Governor Bill Clinton." It reads in part:

"Kathy called yesterday to ask for my recommendations for two people to fill the vacancies on the State Savings and Loan Board. For the industry position for the 2nd

Congressional District, I recommend John Latham, who is chairman of the board of Madison Guaranty and Loan" he wrote, then added that "he is a major contributor to your campaign." The other was for another S&L man McDougal wanted. Both his recommendations were taken.

Failed Plan

But even if McDougal and Hillary had paved the way for the unprecedented preferred stock plan for Madison, it never got off the ground. It's probable that Madison's weak condition would have shown up in the disclosure document ("Red Herring") and no one would have bought the stock. Meanwhile, the state government, with the help of Hillary, had agreed to a plan to save Madison, at least for the time being.

What did Bill Clinton, the man ultimately responsible for the S&L's safety, know about all this? Probably *everything*.

A top professional in the Arkansas Securities Department, Charles Handley, now the assistant commissioner, points out that the red flag on Madison was up, if anybody wanted to look at it.

"We were worried about Madison Guaranty's financial condition as far back as 1983, when the S&L already had a weak net worth," Handley pointed out when interviewed. "The federal government had done an examination that year and I agreed with it. I also concurred with the 1984 examination, which showed that Madison had a net worth of only 1 percent of total assets. The benchmark was 3 percent, which wasn't very high itself."

Handley expressed his opinion, but no one listened. No one in authority, neither the Governor, Hillary, or the regulators did anything to close, or inhibit the operations of Madison. They permitted the S&L to stay open—even tried to find ways to keep it open—putting the Clintons deeper into the morass of money politics, while Madison Guaranty devoured millions more of the taxpayers' money.

McDougal was temporarily stymied, but he didn't give up. A more formal Home Loan Bank Board examination was scheduled for 1986, less than a year later. When the preferred stock plan failed, McDougal needed additional capital from someone. The person he sought out was a tall, somewhat heavy man his age. His name was Judge David Hale, the "judge" being a title granted him by Bill Clinton.

Hale was a member of what McDougal called "the political family." A former head of the Young Democrats of Arkansas, Hale had been named by Clinton as a judge of a new municipal court in Little Rock, which became the busiest in the state. In addition to his official duties, which paid $59,000 a year, Hale had gone into business—with the U.S. Government. His company, Capital-Management Services, Inc., was the state's only SBIC (Small Business Investment Company), a firm dedicated to lending money to *minorities and the disadvantaged.*

But Hale didn't quite see it that way. The government didn't check on his activities, and instead of granting loans to minorities and the poor, as Congress had planned, most of the loans went to Caucasians with college educations making at least $40,000 a year.

The state was sprinkled with millions lent out by Hale, and McDougal saw in the federal moneylender a possibility for survival. (The loans were easier made than others because they were guaranteed and subsidized by the Small

Business Administration, one of the most wasteful agencies of the U.S. government.)

"McDougal told me he wanted to clean up some problem loans with our friends in the 'political family,' " Hale said. He was speaking of loans made to leading politicians by McDougal, which were making the books look bad for the upcoming FHLBB examination.

Chance Meeting

McDougal pitched Hale for a loan, then some time passed. Hale says the second time it came up was just before Christmas when he was waiting for a ride while standing on the steps of the Capitol building, which sits at the end of Capitol Street, the main drag of Little Rock.

Governor Clinton spotted him and came racing up, Hale says. "Are you going to help Jim and me out?" the Governor asked, according to Hale. The judge responded: "We're working on it." (Later, Hale confessed that he knew he really had no choice. He had to do it.)

The next meeting was in February. Hale told the *Los Angeles Times* that it was held in the sales office of the Castle Grande real estate development in the suburbs of Little Rock. McDougal and Clinton were already there when he arrived, Hale says.

(Both Clinton and McDougal have denied that the meeting ever took place.)

The idea of the project, which took up 1,100 acres, was to provide low-cost housing and commercial development for people who wanted to leave the city. The idea was sound, but the outcome was a disaster. A later federal report on the development read nothing like the brochure.

"The land is swampy and cannot be developed without considerable cost," said the federal bank examiners. "There is no evidence that there is a viable market for the land."

According to Hale, the three men tried to figure a way to get Hale to lend Madison $150,000. Governor Clinton allegedly offered to put up Whitewater as collateral, but Hale informed him that the Small Business Administration frowned on raw land as security.

Cherchez La Femme

Then someone had an idea. Since the SBIC was designed for minorities and/or the "disadvantaged," Susan McDougal, a woman, would qualify for the loan.

Hale agreed with the idea. McDougal convinced him to increase the loan to $300,000 and a check for that amount, No. 458 from Capital-Management—really federal funds appropriated without an appropriation from Congress—was handed to Susan McDougal. All the money was defaulted.

Meanwhile, Whitewater was going through dying pains. By 1985, more than half the lots were still unsold. They were finally sold to the rental agent, Chris Wade, in a swap for a Piper Seminole airplane ostensibly worth $35,000 and for a $35,000 pickup of the unpaid mortgage. Later, the plane was reportedly sold to Seth Ward, Hubbell's father-in-law, for a large loss.

But Whitewater was not dead, at least not in McDougal's mind. In a twist that surpasses fiction, McDougal decided not to close Whitewater, but to *enlarge* it. In fact, he planned to virtually start over again with a new piece of land. He received help from two sources—indirectly from

Clinton and directly from Hale. Of the loan of $300,000 to Susan McDougal, $110,000 reportedly found its way into the Whitewater account, Hale says.

Clinton had helped stimulate the idea of enlarging Whitewater by giving a massive $22 million tax break to the International Paper (IP) company—the owners of a choice piece of land. It was accomplished through a special piece of legislation he had pushed in the state legislature.

Whitewater II

The ground was set for Whitewater redux. Whitewater II? Yes, at least for a while.

The land development was known as Lorrance Heights, and it was a project of the Whitewater Development Corporation, still owned equally by the Clintons and the McDougals—who apparently hadn't had enough of failure. The land, located about ten miles south of Little Rock, was originally owned by International Paper. It was a raw softwood forest that was uneconomical to cut for paper.

"The sale to Whitewater was made on October 10, 1986," Carl Gagliardi, IP's director of external affairs, and a former Reagan-Bush official, said when interviewed. "The sale was for $550,950 for 810 acres—$80,000 down and $30,000 in a sixty-day note. We took the mortgage, which was for $440,000 over a six-year term. Whitewater was going to develop and sell plots of land for vacation and regular homes." (Shades of the 1978 hopes!)

The $80,000 plus $30,000 down payment nicely matches the $110,000 of the loan to Susan McDougal that Hale said found its way into the Whitewater account.

Talk was that the deal was a quid pro quo with White-water because of the giant tax break Clinton had pushed through the legislature (Act 529) for International Paper. But IP denies that.

"Actually," the company spokesman laughed, "White-water paid well over the market price. I don't think the land was worth $700 an acre."

Then in a strange twist, in December 1986, McDougal transferred Lorrance Heights to a new entity, the Great Southern Land Company. This may or may not have been done without the signatures of the Clintons, who sud-denly lost their ownership in the second land deal. But they must have had some knowledge of what was going on. On their tax returns for that year, the Clintons de-ducted $10,131 for interest paid to Great Southern.

What finally happened to this second Whitewater land scheme?

"Well, in September 1988, McDougal stopped paying the mortgage," says Gagliardi, the IP spokesman. "We fore-closed and got a $514,000 judgment. Then we turned around and sold the property to another developer. Over-all, we made money."

The Examiners Return

While Great Southern was aborning and a-dying, Madison Guaranty had to face the regulatory music. In June 1986, examiners from the Home Loan Bank Board made their feared revisit to the faltering S&L. One report said that when they saw two Jaguars parked outside in the em-ployee spaces, they said, "Let's close the place down."

Less apocryphal is the damning negative report the examiners delivered. Madison had multiple problems, they said, including "conflicts of interest, high risk land developments, poor asset quality . . . inadequate income and net worth, low liquidity, securities speculation, excessive compensation (to officers), and poor records and controls." (Otherwise, it was fine.)

The portfolio of loans outstanding was larger in dollars than the value of the security behind it. The profits of the bank had been inflated, the examiners said. Just the losses of three pieces of its real estate projects, if figured accurately, would place the S&L into insolvency, the examiners lamented.

McDougal was almost immediately removed from office by the bank board and a staff member—actually the former government examiner—was put in charge.

And what of Governor Clinton and Hillary? Together they had worked to forestall Madiso.ᴛs end, but events overtook them.

The ledger was not complete. As we shall see, Madison and Whitewater, two allied debacles, were to come back to haunt the Clintons at least once, and perhaps twice, more.

Chapter Eight

Political Souls
for Sale
Bill Clinton's Campaign
Contributions

Bill Clinton never met a campaign contribution he didn't love.

In that he's no different from thousands of other American politicians who live and die on the cash people give them, or at least they think they do. We see the flood of money for influence in a simple statistic. In the 1992 presidential year, $1 _billion_ was raised and spent just by candidates for federal office. Add another $300 million for state and local elections and you have some idea of the sickness that permeates American democracy.

Bill is no different from the others, except that maybe he's better at it than some of his colleagues. And—now with Whitewater and a few other scrapes—he may be demonstrating a tendency to too closely mix his politics and money.

People give to candidates for any number of reasons.

There's sympathy with their ideology, personal friendship, and businesses especially sometimes fear that if they don't give to a winner, they'll be punished, or at least they'll be granting their competitors unfair advantage with the city, state or Washington.

People don't necessarily give because they want a candidate to win. Often it's because they're afraid he will win and they'll be left out of the spoils.

Overall, then, campaign fund-raising in America should be seen in three lights. One is love. The second is blackmail. And the third, the really powerful motivation, is to buy influence, and as much of that as possible.

One former senator from Minnesota gave out a book of blue stamps to those who gave him $1,000. By placing a stamp on their letter to him, it received immediate attention. That's real good access.

In other cases, like the reprimand given to former Senator Alan Cranston for lobbying the federal regulatory agencies on behalf of Bob Keating, the failed S&L king who went to jail, it was buying influence with large campaign contributions.

A True Exception

And totally on the other side of the coin, as in the case of former Senator William Proxmire of Wisconsin—who would not take one nickel from anybody—it bought absolutely nothing. In fact, in his last two senatorial races he spent only $150, for stamps to return unwanted contributions.

But Proxmire, the creator of the Golden Fleece Award for government waste, was an exception. Most politicians are not only ready, willing, and available, but they often solicit the money themselves. Givers like it that way. They look the politician in the eye as the check passes hands, expecting at least access, and maybe more, sometime down the line.

It's really an obscene system, but it's the American Way. And Bill Clinton was an enthusiastic, even eager, part of it. Only now he's in some trouble over it—trouble that will be investigated by the Independent Counsel and adjudicated by the American public about the quid pro quo involved with some of his political cronies.

Bill Clinton, the innocent of the 1974 campaign for U.S. Congress, didn't fully understand the system at the time. He reportedly raised only $44,000, mainly from his union friends, and aides say he spurned money that he feared was tainted, generally from business interests.

But as time went on, that naive Clinton disappeared from the Arkansas political landscape. He was replaced by one of the great money raisers in the state, or any state's, history. In 1982, for example, Clinton raised $1.6 million in his quest to regain the statehouse from Governor Frank White. That doesn't sound like a lot of money when compared to campaign chests today, as, for example, the $11 million each raised by Democrat Barbara Boxer of California and Republican Al D'Amato of New York in their quest for a Senate seat.

But $1.6 million in that small state of 2.5 million people, was a fortune there, and for its time. If we compare that spending with California on a per capita basis, for example, it would represent $20 million. If it were adjusted for the larger state's higher standard of living, it would come closer to $30 million. And today, compared with 1982, it would be more than double that amount.

If we look at Clinton's 1990 campaign for governor, where he raised $2 million, that's equivalent to $25 million or more in California. Now that's a man who has learned, and well.

A Search of the Records

In the hope of exploring the campaign funds of some Clinton races in detail, I contacted the office of the Secretary of State of Arkansas and asked for the list of contributors going back to 1974.

"I'm sorry I can't help, except for Bill Clinton's last race for governor in 1990. That's the only records we have," a spokesman in the statehouse answered.

"What happened to the others?" I asked incredulously.

"We have destroyed them," he answered.

"On purpose?"

"Well, yes. The Arkansas law then only required that we keep them for four years, so they have been destroyed. The law now requires us to hold them for eight years, but all we have is the last gubernatorial election, the one in 1990," he said, then added that those will be destroyed as well when the time comes.

"Don't you have any backup—microfilm or microfiche, or computer discs?" I asked, now more incredulous.

"No, nothing."

Apparently, the state either has something to hide, or it believes that the less time researchers have to review the cash flow from citizens and corporations to politicians, the better. And the less embarrassment in the future. History apparently has no friends at the statehouse.

But he did give me a tip. "Try the Pulaski County Court. They may have kept some records on their own."

I did, and found that although the county—which covers Little Rock—didn't have the older ones, they have kept records from 1984 on. For a nominal fee of $35, I bought the 1984 package, a 127-page printout of monies coming into the Clinton gubernatorial campaign coffers.

It was this campaign and some of its contributions that are getting Bill Clinton in trouble and drawing the attention of Congress and the Independent Counsel.

The Contributors
In that 1984 race, Clinton ran against three people in the Democratic primary, and then against the Republican, a Jonesboro contractor named Woody Freeman. The records show the usual type of contributors. First there are anonymous people from all over the state, contributing anywhere from $50 to $1,500, which was the maximum then allowed.

Then there are banks, insurance companies, utilities, business corporations from Reynolds Metal to the Union Pacific Railroad to Coca-Cola and Pepsi Cola to Weyerhaueser, to the Worthen Bank, the state's largest, and even Wendy's. Then there are the unions, including the United Auto Workers, the United Paperworkers, and the ILGWU, among others.

Most interesting are two other categories. One of them is out-of-staters who had some special interest in Bill Clinton, the evolving star of the Democratic party, who in 1984 was already the subject of conjecture about a future candidacy for President or Vice President. (Many of the rumors were started by Clinton himself.)

Bill Clinton attracted contributions from Pamela Harriman, later rewarded as ambassador to France; Bernard Nussbaum of New York, a friend of Hillary, who became the President's counsel; the securities firm of Donaldson, Lufkin and Jenrette, also in New York, who were apparently placing a political "call" on the future; George Ball, former State Department official and Democratic warhorse; PaineWebber; and John Gutfreund, then head of Salomon Brothers—an unusual collection of eastern glitterati contributing on behalf of someone who most easterners considered a "hick" governor back in 1984.

Added to that were contributions from what McDougal has accurately called "the political family," the friends who stuck together in power, and in the search for power. Those contributors included Webb Hubbell; $3,000 from three members of the Lasater family (later to play a vital, negative role in Clinton's career); over $1,000 from his own assistant, Betsey Wright; $1,000 from his former law firm, from which Bruce Lindsey emigrated with Clinton to Washington; $1,100 from Vincent Foster, who took his life in Washington; and Patsy Thomasson, who is now his administrative chief.

There was $1,000 from John Latham, the chairman of McDougal's Madison Guaranty; $1,000, and then a strange additional $10, from Marlin D. Jackson, the director of the Arkansas Banking Department; $1,000 from C. Joseph Giroir, who was then Hillary's boss at the Rose Law Firm; $1,000 from Diane and James Blair—he the genius who parlayed Hillary's $1,000 to $100,000 and earned a sleepover at the White House; $1,000 from Harry and Linda

Thomason, the Hollywood couple with Arkansas roots who did the physical makeover of Hillary Clinton; and $1,500 from W. Maurice Smith, who described himself as being on the "governor's staff/banker," and who was to play a vital role in the charade that follows.

His Own Contribution

But surely the most interesting, and largest, contribution to Clinton's 1984 campaign for governor was listed on page one, top of the report, showing that the payment was made on October 29, 1984, one week before the election.

The contributor was listed as Bill Clinton, living at 1800 Center, Little Rock. His occupation was noted as "governor." Bill Clinton had contributed $50,000—cash— to his own campaign, starting a chain reaction that has not stopped. It was to provide a perfect case history in the exchange of favors, favoritism, cronyism, twisting of banking rules, political debts paid, and worse.

A week before the election the polls showed Clinton way ahead of Freeman, a relatively weak Republican candidate. But Bill's typical preelection anxiety took over. He told his aides he wanted a flood of thirty-second television commercials to be run all over the state that last week.

When his surprised staff asked where the money was coming from, he said, "Me."

Where in the world would Clinton get $50,000 in cash, and so quickly? He was not about to get credit from the television stations. His salary was only $35,000, and the family money was mostly in Hillary's name. Surely, she was not about to deplete her carefully nurtured, growing nest egg for her husband's campaign vanity. But the answer was close at hand.

The Friendly Banker

One of his top aides was W. Maurice Smith, who also happened to be an owner of the Bank of Cherry Valley, a small federally insured institution. Clinton asked him for the loan but had no collateral to offer. His Whitewater stock was virtually worthless, and there was still a partial mortgage on the land anyway. But Smith was a friendly banker, and the loan was made to Bill and Hillary Clinton without any collateral whatsoever.

The television commercials, surely unneeded, were run with the $50,000. Clinton beat Freeman with a handy 64 percent, the same margin that the polls had predicted.

Once the flush of victory had worn off, Clinton had to find a way to repay the loan. His first move displayed enormous gratitude towards his banker friend. Not long after the inauguration for Clinton's third term, W. Maurice Smith was named director of the Highway and Transportation Department of Arkansas, a powerful position which is virtually independent of the governor and the legislature, with considerable power to decide where and how roads will be built.

The next step was to get $50,000 cash to repay the rather unconventional loan. Clinton turned to his friend, Jim McDougal. The Madison Guaranty was then in trouble, but few besides the Governor, Hillary, state banking and securities people, and a few close friends, knew it. McDougal had been King of the S&L Walk in Arkansas for some

time, and the world assumed he was as solvent as his flamboyant personal lifestyle and his bank's promotions.

He was the only one Clinton could turn to to raise a
sum that large.

"Jim, can you help me knock out my campaign deficit?"
Clinton asked.

The Madison Gala

The answer was a gala affair on April 4, 1985 in the lobby
of the bank. Scores of officers and employees of the bank
attended. According to a former Madison bank official, Mc-
Dougal said, "Bill's in trouble and we're going to have to
get together and help him out."

They did, and shortly afterwards, McDougal presented
Clinton with checks totaling $30,000. The money was then
given to the Bank of Cherry Valley to cut way back on Clinton's indebtedness.

(As an important connection in time, the "Dear
Hillary" letter from the Arkansas Securities Department
granting McDougal the right to sell more stock in his failing S&L and open a brokerage subsidiary, came just
three weeks after the McDougal-arranged campaign
deficit party.)

Who paid the money to Clinton? Was all of it contributors' money, or was some of it Madison Guaranty's own
funds, which wouldn't be cricket, or even legal. Was part of
the $30,000 a not so subtle way of diverting money from
what was becoming a failed S&L—and therefore eventually taxpayer debt—into Bill Clinton's campaign fund? Or
since it was a personal loan, did it, indirectly or directly, go
into the Governor's own pocket?

Those queries are part of the new Independent Counsel's job. But an investigation by the RTC in the interim shows that Clinton may have been the recipient of monies he shouldn't have had. It all revolves around the possibility that Madison Guaranty, not contributors, put up part of the funds. In fact, RTC investigators have turned up four bank checks drawn on Madison. Three were cashier checks and one was drawn from McDougal's personal account. Each was for $3,000, for a total of $12,000, as contributions to the Clinton payoff fund. Could it have been Madison's own money masquerading as individual campaign contributions?

One of the supposed contributors was Ken Peacock, whose name appears on a $3,000 cashier's check made out to the Clinton campaign fund. But he has denied making any contribution to Clinton.

I spoke with Mr. Peacock, a pleasant young man who was then a law student at the University of Arkansas and is now a trucking broker. I asked if it was true that he did not make the contribution.

"It's very much true," he responded. "I made no contribution to Clinton whatsoever."

"What about your father, Charles Peacock?" I asked.

(Peacock senior had loans outstanding with Madison and had been on the board of the S&L at one time.)

"I don't know anything about that, but my father and grandfather, like myself, are Republicans," Ken Peacock says. "I've met the Clintons and McDougal too, but I'd never contribute to a Clinton campaign."

"I suppose you've been contacted by the FBI or the Independent Counsel's people?" I asked rhetorically.

"No, no one from the government has approached me," he answered.

I commented, to myself, that it was one hell of an investigation by Mr. Fiske if he never called Ken Peacock, a vital "phantom" contributor in the plan to pay off Mr. Clinton's personal debt. Peacock should be a key witness in the mystery of whether Madison funds were diverted to Clinton. Other possible "phantom" contributors, according to the RTC, include Senator Fulbright himself, an old friend of Clinton and McDougal; Susan McDougal; and a now-deceased employee of Charles Peacock.

Senator Fulbright's lawyer stated that his client never made, or authorized, such a donation.

Had Fulbright been subpoenaed by Mr. Fiske? we might also ask. Obviously he should have been.

The Missing List

Of course, the investigation would be much easier *if* a list of those who attended the bank lobby affair, and how much they actually contributed, were available. Those names do not appear on the official list of 1984 contributors I received from the Pulaski County office.

But where is *the other list*, which covers the post-election contributions? It should have been reported to the Secretary of State by Clinton's committee, and/or his chief of staff, Ms. Betsey Wright. (Incidentally, she is now a highly paid lobbyist for the Wexler group in Washington, working her old friends in the White House with unprecedented access and success.)

The whereabouts of the April 1985 contributions report are unknown, one of the great mysteries of the Whitewater affair. In fact, reasonably suspicious people might think someone is not fully forthcoming. When questioned about it, Betsey Wright told the press that she recalls filing it with the Secretary of State but "can't find those reports" today.

The next step in checking out the April mystery was the County Clerk's office again. But neither do they have the list. Their last report on the 1984 campaign was published in December, five months before the Madison party.

After that, I rechecked with the Secretary of State's office, which has destroyed all records prior to 1990. They appeared to be helpful—at first.

"We have no record of that 1985 fund-raiser at all," says Phil Hoots, a decade-long member of the Secretary of State's office. "We used to do some microfilming here, but we discontinued that around 1986. When I was first approached about the list of the 1985 contributions, I decided to check the microfilm. But when I went down to where they were stored, which was near an old boiler room, I quickly saw that the film was injured. When we opened the drawers, the acetate stench was horrible."

"So what happened to the microfilm?" I asked expectantly.

"We turned it over to the Arkansas History Commission here at the capital," Hoots responded.

The trail was getting warmer, I thought. I called the History Commission and spoke with Dr. John Ferguson, the director, and repeated the story in detail.

"No. We have no microfilm of campaign contributions here," he stated forthrightly. He went on to say that the

Secretary of State's office tells everybody that they turned over the records to the History Commission, but that it's not true.

Full circle, and the records are gone.

Personal Payoff?

The RTC and the Independent Counsel are now ostensibly trying to learn if some Madison money did end up in the Governor's campaign fund. Congressman Leach, of the House Banking Committee, for one, thinks so. "Some of these funds (Madison's) were used to pay off personal and campaign liabilities of the Governor," he says.

The truth of that ten-year-old mystery has still not been pinned down. We may have to wait for the new Independent Counsel, Kenneth W. Starr, who hopefully is conducting an honest, thorough, investigation. We shall soon see.

The brouhaha over the $50,000 unsecured loan taken out personally by Governor Clinton is far from over. But it may be superseded by a revelation of other loans he took out from 1983 to 1988 that have even more severe ramifications—politically, morally, legally, and tax-wise.

It seems that the $50,000 loan from the small Bank of Cherry Valley (small, but with a big heart) was just the tip of the green iceberg. According to the Associated Press, which broke the story, the final amount was $400,000, in the form of twelve loans, taken out from 1983 to 1988, and all signed for personally by Clinton. No security or collateral was asked for, or given. Yet the bank depositors' money was made freely available to Bill—acting not as Governor, but as plain William Jefferson Clinton, private citizen.

The fairy godfather was again W. Maurice Smith, top aide, campaign finance chairman, and highway commissioner under Clinton. By coincidence, Smith was also one of the owners of a bank which opened its vaults to create that giant slush fund for the Governor.

According to Smith, this time reported in *The Washington Post*, which followed up the AP story by speaking with the banker, $300,000 of the borrowed money was used by Clinton for his own political campaigning. The rest of it (or perhaps more) was used by Clinton to buy television commercials, hire consultants, send out direct mail, etc., so that he could lobby the legislature to pass his initiatives—whether on education or otherwise. He didn't do this as a public official, but as a private citizen using his own borrowed cash.

What a unique wrinkle for someone in public life! As far as I know, it's never been done before. (In the Nixon "Checkers" era, some $18,000 was raised, extra-campaign, for a private expense fund for the vice presidential candidate, and he almost got bounced from the ticket as a result.)

But here we're talking about $400,000. How did private citizen Clinton expect to pay it back on his measly $35,000 salary?

He didn't. Clinton again went to the well, to the people who had supported his campaigns over the years. The contributions went into special funds with such fanciful names as "America 2000." They were not campaign donations, as we shall see, or registered non-profit corporations. If Maurice Smith, an old Clinton buddy, is correct, they were just vehicles for Bill Clinton—a way to collect money to pay back his personal loans used for political purposes.

Bizarre.

Frank Hickingbotham, major owner of TCBY, who had put Hillary on his board, contributed $25,000. Tyson Foods contributed $15,000. The Union Bank (which had given the Clintons the $20,000 for the down payment on Whitewater) donated $11,500. Arkansas Power and Light chipped in to this unique potpourri. Even Wal-Mart contributed $1,000 to help pay back Clinton's indebtednesses.

The gimmick of the slush fund was that it circumvented the state's $1,500 limit on contributions, since reduced to $1,000. Common Cause of Arkansas calls it an "end run" around the election laws.

These special "funds" raise all sorts of questions. We have to look at the $400,000 borrowed by Clinton and paid back by others in two parts. The first part of the $400,000 are those loans that were used for electioneering. If, as Smith says, $300,000 was for election campaigns, was the money reported to officials as required?

Most of the donations were too large to begin with. The contributions of $1,500 or less could be reported, but since they were used to pay back money Clinton borrowed personally, they would have to be reported as part of money he contributed to his own campaign on which there is no limit.

If not, they would—the Secretary of State's office informs me—be breaking the election laws of Arkansas.

Governor Clinton did report the famous $50,000 in 1984, money he declared on his election return, then was partially paid back by the famous Madison S&L fund-raiser in 1985.

But did he contribute $300,000 to his gubernatorial campaigns for 1986 or 1990 (there was no election in 1988) to make these donations legal as campaign funds?

I checked with the Pulaski County Clerk's Office.

"Did Governor Clinton contribute any money to his campaigns in 1986 and 1990?" I asked.

They searched their records and responded: "No, we believe the only contribution by Governor Clinton to his campaign was in 1984, and that was $50,000."

To double check, I ordered all 748 pages of contributions to the Clinton campaigns for 1986 and 1990. ($178 for the two reports.)

I scoured every page—a total of over 5,000 contributors. There were no contributions by Clinton himself, just $180,000 in three loans from the Perry County Bank. The loans were made to Clinton personally, who then lent the money to the campaign. Apparently, this is not part of the $400,000 Mr. Smith says he loaned Clinton over seven years in a dozen loans, three-fourths of which went to election campaigning. (Are we now up to $600,000 in personal loans?)

In any case, none of that *slush fund*, for want of a better term, was contributed by Clinton to his campaign, raising grave questions about the legality of those funds.

"The money given by contributors to pay back borrowed money a candidate has spent in a campaign is not a violation of Arkansas election laws—*if* the candidate contributes that amount to his own campaign," says an attorney in the Arkansas Secretary of State's office. "But if he collects it and doesn't contribute to his own campaign, and report it to us, then he's breaking the law."

That doesn't take too much thinking to understand its implications.

What about the larger contributions above the legal limit, such as the $15,000 from Tyson Foods?

Betsey Wright, former chief-of-staff to Governor Clinton who kept the records of these enormous, unprecedented funds had turned them over to Special Counsel Fiske, and they are now in the hands of Independent Counsel Starr. Wright says there was nothing wrong with collecting these monies even though they were not for regular campaigns. Press Secretary Dee Dee Myers says "it certainly was legal. It was permissible under Arkansas law."

Our attorney in the Secretary of State's office doesn't know what they're talking about.

"At the time we had no lobbying law. It just went into effect in 1990," he says. "And the contributions over $1,500 were not legal for election campaigns."

Scott Trotter of the Arkansas Common Cause sees them as an influence buying on a grand scale. He says: "Wealthy special interests were offered another opportunity through unlimited contributions to influence Governor Clinton and the administration."

"We gave that money to the Governor in order to promote education," stated Archie Schaffer, the public relations director of Tyson Foods and husband of Beverly Bassett Schaffer, former chief of the Arkansas Security Department that dealt with Hillary Clinton in 1985.

"But your corporation's money went to pay off Bill Clinton's personal loans," I interjected.

"None of the people who were solicited knew there was a personal loan involved," Schaffer replied.

I asked his help to find out in what category Tyson Foods had placed the expenditure. Was it deducted as a business expense? Was it a consulting fee? An election campaign expense? Or what?

Schaffer bristled. "You can find that out from some other source," he barked. "It's none of your business."

Of course, it is the business of stockholders who should look askance at money given to personal slush funds of politicians that circumvent the election law. Was it a personal gift? That, of course, is not permitted in a public corporation like Tyson.

On the other hand, maybe Tyson's $15,000 was well spent—for Tyson. They have a history of contributing to Clinton, and of having influence at the statehouse, and maybe now at the White House.

Just recently, President Clinton showed that Tyson chickens are as close to his heart as to his pocketbook.

In the July 25, 1994 issue of *Time*, the magazine shows Tyson's power with the administration, specifically with Mike Espy, head of the Department of Agriculture. Espy had reportedly accepted plane rides and football tickets from Tyson, which he then had to pay back with his own money when it was revealed.

Tyson was having trouble getting its chicken parts into the flourishing Puerto Rican market. In fact, thousands of their parts were being held on the docks because the importer's name wasn't printed on each package—a Commonwealth rule that lets them spot the source if the parts become spoiled.

"It (the chicken parts) was going to rot," said Guillermo Garcia, Tyson's executive importer on the island. He called Tyson headquarters in Arkansas and was promised help. "We expected a good result because of Tyson's support of Clinton," Garcia said.

But Garcia was told it wouldn't look good to seek Espy's help directly. Instead, Garcia said, the National Broiler Council "would be used as a kind of shield."

Eleven days after Clinton was inaugurated, on February 1, 1993, the regulation was suspended by Agriculture at Espy's request. Tyson chickens were allowed into Puerto Rico —sans the name of the importer.

To get back to the slush funds that Tyson supported, it's clear their donation couldn't be a *legal* campaign contribution. The substantial ones were too large. Neither were they for charity, because Mr. Clinton, though perhaps charitable, is not himself a legal charity. Neither were they for a governmental activity.

Then what in God's name was the small fortune circuitously paid into the Clinton bank account?

Probably personal income for the Governor, which may well be subject to tax.

The question here is whether the money he spent lobbying the legislature, or in unreported campaign contributions, was legally deductible from the $400,000 taken in—less the $50,000 reported in his 1984 campaign. The Federal Tax Code, as reported in the *Federal Tax Coordinator 2d* says that "a deductible expense must be an ordinary and necessary expense of carrying on that trade or business."

Bill Clinton was governor at the time. Was his private, extravagant spending of his own money—which was neither an official act nor an election expenditure—an "ordinary" or "necessary" expense? Was it a business at all, and therefore entitled to a deduction in the first place?

The argument that Clinton defenders seem to be developing is that the money was spent for "good works," and therefore should not be taxable, which is a rather ridiculous response. Even a public-spirited citizen who spent a million dollars sponsoring ads for peace in the world who had not set up a nonprofit organization couldn't take it as a "business deduction," and neither should Clinton.

In any case, the Governor never filed the money as income, or even claimed it as a deduction. It's still sitting out there in fiscal limbo.

Money is the Achilles Heel of the Clintons, especially because they try to present such an unmaterialistic, idealistic face to the nation. In Hillary's case, she seems to have an obsessive need to use every neuron of her considerable intelligence to make, save, and invest as much money as possible, mainly by cashing in—sometimes embarrassingly— on her political celebrity.

In Bill's case, it's quite different. But money still presents a powerful vulnerability for him. Clinton has an adolescent view of money, and his attitude toward it borders on contempt. To him, money is just sheaves of printed green paper which he uses with wanton disregard to borrow and collect, then to get elected and re-elected.

For him, it has no meaning outside of power. And there he uses it with less than candor. But in that arena, he has made himself a master of the cash-politics-influence equation that so dominates, and defiles, our democracy.

Campaign money may have been very important to Clinton in the 1984 election, when he took out his $50,000 loan, but he was also then undergoing a powerful personal battle.

Clinton's tussle involved his half brother, Roger Clinton, and it exploded right in the middle of that campaign. To his credit, Bill Clinton met it head on, a trait that seldom surfaces in the Whitewater affair.

The incident was also tied to Clinton's compulsion for more and more campaign contributions, and for the beneficial attention given by him to those who made them.

Roger Clinton, who is Bill's junior by ten years, had run into considerable trouble. The younger Clinton had developed a cocaine habit, and in the heat of the 1984 campaign was arrested. What to do? The governor could have intervened to help him, but instead he gave the go-ahead to a sting operation by the Arkansas State Police, one that snared Roger when he sold cocaine to an undercover agent.

Double Trouble

Roger was in trouble on two fronts: with the Arkansas police, and with drug dealers who had extended him $8,000 in credit. That tab was picked up by a good friend of both Clintons, and a heavy contributor to the Clinton campaigns—Dan Lasater, a local millionaire. Lasater had hired Roger as his limo driver, then lent him $8,000 to pay off his drug debt, and even sent him to his thoroughbred racing stable in Florida to work for a while.

Roger was finally sentenced to two years in jail for drug use and peddling. The Governor showed up in court during his brother's trial, and made a public statement explaining that drugs were nefarious and could strike any family. His was a prime example. (Roger served one year of a two-year sentence in a federal prison in Texas.)

Roger's benefactor, Dan Lasater, held a special, and eventually troubling, place in the life of the Clintons. A securities and bond broker, he had been a major contributor to the Clinton campaigns and had also held successful fund-raising affairs for Bill. They had become very friendly, and the Clintons sometimes rode cross-state in his expensive jet.

Most important, Lasater had assumed a vital part in the state's bond operation, which had previously been controlled by Stephens, Inc.—who people said "owned" Arkansas. Stephens had backed the Republican Frank White twice, and were still not sure about their young Governor. Just as he was not sure about them.

As a former Lasater partner told the FBI about Bill Clinton's favorite new bond broker: "Because Lasater & Co. backed the right individual in Governor Clinton, Lasater & Co., received the contract."

Clinton wanted to help stake an alternative to Stephens, especially since he had started an economic development program based on state-backed bonds. And Lasater & Co., Inc. was the company of his choice. Before the relationship to Lasater was severed—by a crime—the broker had handled $664 million in Arkansas bond sales contracts, all approved by Clinton. Lasater earned $1.6 million in fees on two dozen different state bonds.

State Power

The program, started in 1985 and called the Arkansas Development Finance Authority (ADFA), would put the

state's credit behind low-interest often tax-free bonds being issued for private businesses. In a strange system, the
governor, not the legislature, had veto power over who received the loans, and could grant the bond brokerage business, in effect, to anyone he wanted through his appointed
board of directors. It was one of the strongest money-
power tools granted to any politician. And Clinton regularly used it.

The *Los Angeles Times*, which had anonymous talks
with federal investigators, quotes one of them as saying
that it was "common knowledge" among investment
bankers in Arkansas that companies headed by political
supporters of Mr. Clinton received favored treatment.

One former official of the ADFA reportedly sent a letter to the FBI in which he stated that Clinton appointees
engaged in "power brokering." He said that many ADFA
bond sales were intended as "political favors or repayments for campaign support."

So what's new?

Local Critic

One energetic, well-known local critic of Clinton and
ADFA is Roy Drew, a Little Rock money manager, who
used to work for Stephens, Merrill Lynch, and E. F. Hutton,
and who was the one who opened Hillary Clinton's Midlife
Investors account. He believes that the ADFA gave Clinton
the power "essentially to create money." Since the governor appoints the board and has the right to approve or dis-
approve every bond issue, and has no regulatory or
legislative oversight, Drew believes that the arrangement is
a "prescription for abuse."

I interviewed Mr. Drew on this and other issues at lunch in the Hilton in North Little Rock. (He didn't want to meet in my hotel, the Capitol, in order to avoid the typical crowd who know him.)

"My criticism of the Clintons and the ADFA pretty much cost me my livelihood," said the tall, spare Arkansan who speaks, like most Little Rockers, with a soft drawl, somewhat quieter than their Texas neighbors. He related how his financial customers had left him in droves after he came out against what he considered ADFA and other Clinton abuses.

"For example, the legislature passed a rule that 10 percent of the pension funds of state employees should be used for direct investments in companies, not just in listed stocks or bonds," he says. "Many times those investments were politically motivated to begin with. The auditor of the state asked me to look into one as a third party, and I came back saying that the deal was a 'flimflam.' The newspapers picked that up, and within a week my three best financial accounts, which were bringing me in $6,000 a month, left. Somebody was putting on the heat."

He adds that he doesn't think that the state-sponsored ADFA should be involved in ordinary businesses by "backing sorority houses, motels, and car dealerships."

Drew has remade his career by becoming a money manager, and is now independent of political pressure, which can be intense in Little Rock. By the way, he points out that there never have been third-party reviews of ADFA bond issues. The board, appointed by the governor, oversees itself, a not uncommon phenomenon in American politics. In fact, ADFA is now the third-party review for direct investments of the state employee retirement fund. Thus full circle.

The Lasater Case

It was a controversial bond issue question that got Dan Lasater, Clinton's favorite bond broker, into trouble. Simultaneously, it cast doubt on the Governor's seeming inability to separate himself cleanly from major contributors and political friends. It appears that he suffers from "political loyalty," a detrimental, somewhat antique, concept in modern government.

Clinton had been lobbying for a police improvement project, a $30 million bond issue for a new radio system. It was to replace the World War II–vintage one that had cost the life of a state trooper under attack who couldn't reach his colleagues by radio.

The Governor pushed hard for the project and for Dan Lasater to handle the bond issue, which would bring the dealer $700,000 in commissions. But during the investigation of Lasater by state police, the securities dealer confessed that he used cocaine.

Despite that incrimination, the Governor approved the bond dealer's participation. Six months later, Lasater was arrested and pled guilty to charges of "social distribution" of cocaine.

The young millionaire, whose fortune was made when his Ponderosa chain of restaurants went public in 1971, confessed to police that although he had never sold the narcotic, that he had given it to friends on a mass basis. He kept a regular supply on his person, and snorted it in the office. At parties in his home, he gave away vials of cocaine as souvenirs, and kept ashtrays full of cocaine dispersed around the house. On his jet plane, it was freely available to all passengers. In total, he guessed that he had used it 180 times.

While the investigation was going on, Lasater continued to sell ADFA bonds and take his commissions from the state. Finally, in December 1986, he was sentenced to thirty months in prison. He served only six months in jail, followed by four months in a halfway house and two months under "house arrest."

While he was away, Lasater turned over effective control of his company to Ms. Patsy Thomasson, who was then Clinton's chief of the Arkansas Highway Commission.

Return to Little Rock

In November 1990, Lasater was pardoned by Governor Clinton. He returned to live in Little Rock, where he became chairman of the Phoenix Group, a company which, among other things, bought assets from the RTC at rock-bottom prices. (An ironic twist.)

Ms. Thomasson, who was not involved in the cocaine charges, stayed with Lasater upon his return. Then after the 1992 election, President Clinton put her in charge of administration in the White House. She is still there today, despite her involvement in what is known as "Travelgate." Ms. Thomasson was one of three staffers who entered Vince Foster's office soon after his suicide.

In a strange— or perhaps not so strange— development during the Lasater investigation, federal investigators found a June 1984 agreement between Susan McDougal and the Lasater firm. It stipulated that McDougal would buy and sell securities in conjunction with Lasater & Co. That probably was behind Madison's application to the Arkansas Securities Department requesting permission to open a stock brokerage subsidiary for the public.

Congressman Leach, who has been frustrated in getting Congress to hold full hearings on Whitewater, has said this about the partnership: "Madison and its institution-affiliated parties had significant dealings with Lasater & Co., a now-defunct Arkansas securities firm. It has been reported that Lasater & Co. was connected with significant abuses in the municipal securities market."

The Lasater connection— one of excessive friendship and favors given by a governor for equally large campaign contributions—is being investigated by the Independent Counsel. And just recently, Senator Pete Domenici of New Mexico has announced that the Counsel is investigating a giant resort in his state, Angel Fire, which had been owned by Lasater and is now in bankruptcy.

The 1985 cash gala at Madison Guaranty, which may have diverted taxpayer money into a political campaign, is today a main target of the federal investigation. It will try to unravel a complex, somewhat hidden skein Bill Clinton wove in his continual drive to raise money for his political campaigns.

Clinton's problem is instructive for us all. He has yet to settle it with the nation, and we have yet to face its implications for our entire political system, which is mired, in all fifty states and most of our 86,000 governmental units, in the same ugly equation of quid pro quo—influence for money.

Until that is faced and solved, there will be many more Whitewaters to plague us.

Chapter Nine

Hillary in
A China Shop

Conflicts, Legal and Moral

"The first thing we do, let's kill all the lawyers."

This bold statement comes from the master philosopher, William Shakespeare, and specifically from Act IV of his play *Henry VI, Part II*. It was written in the sixteenth century, but it smacks very much of today.

In the case of Whitewater-Madison Guaranty, that skepticism about lawyers might stick to Hillary Rodham and a few of her colleagues, who sometimes earned their fare by casting a blind eye when it came to conflicts of interest. In 1985, as we've seen, Hillary helped represent Madison before the state Securities Department, which in Arkansas is in charge of regulating S&Ls.

One major plank in her plea to Securities chief Beverly Bassett was an audit from accountants Frost & Company, which claimed that Madison was solvent. At the time, of course, it was hopelessly insolvent, losing millions of dollars of taxpayer money a month through imprudent investing and loans, often to members of the Arkansas "political family."

It's safe to say that by helping extend the life of Madison Guaranty, Hillary and Bill cost the federal government—meaning me and you—at least $30 million. Her efforts, and the lack of oversight by the regulators appointed by her husband the Governor, kept the leaky financial ship afloat.

But once Madison Guaranty had been shut down by Washington, not by Arkansas, which had the closest control of the state-chartered S&L, Hillary gained a chance to switch her considerable legal talents to the other side, again for a fee. By this time, the FSLIC, the savings and loan insurer, had gone bankrupt and the work was shifted to the Federal Deposit Insurance Company (FDIC). The FDIC decided to sue to recover some of the $68 million in taxpayer funds lost in the Madison debacle.

Sue who? McDougal, his wife, and his closest colleagues were now broke.

The decision was to sue the accounting firm, Frost & Company, which had produced the Madison audit, which the government now claimed was "defective." That, of course, was the same audit that Hillary had used to convince the Arkansas state government that Madison really was *solvent*.

Rose Redux

Who should handle this lawsuit? Naturally *not* the legal firm that had contributed to the trouble in the first place? But in a strange twist, the government decided that was just the thing to do. Rose was given the assignment and Webb Hubbell was put in charge. Inevitably Hillary Rodham put in her expensive two cents.

The government claim against Madison's accounting firm was for $20 million—$10 million in damages, and $10 million for punitive damages. Guess what the result was for taxpayers?

Hubbell, Hillary, et al., settled with Frost & Company for a mere $1 million, only 5 percent of the claimed amount, and even less than the firm was insured for. Their fee? $400,000. That left $600,000 for Uncle Sam, a piddling 3 percent of the claim and less than 1 percent of the loss. Hillary had managed to help waste the taxpayers' money. Not once, but twice, in the very same case.

If Hillary had a conflict with her first attempts as a lawyer in serving several masters, including Madison, Rose, Arkansas and her husband the Governor, then in this case the conflict was multiplied many times over.

It seems it's unethical when representing the government to sue a former client, or someone closely involved, without revealing that fact to Uncle Sam. It was *absolutely* incumbent on Hillary and Rose to inform the FDIC that they had represented Madison Guaranty before state regulators back in 1985. Not to do so was a breach of ethics, perhaps even worse.

Did they inform the government? Apparently not. Webb Hubbell did tell the FDIC that Seth Ward, who was involved in both loans and litigation with Madison, was his father-in-law. But federal authorities say that they were never told by Hubbell or Hillary, who *really* knew, of the prior Madison case, either in writing or verbally.

Did the business just happen to fall into Rose's legal lap? No. Actually, it was solicited in a letter to the FDIC from the late Vince Foster, written just a few days before the government took over Madison on March 2, 1989. To cover the firm's proverbial rear, he put their former representation of Madison in the *present* tense, saying Rose *does not* represent any S&Ls at the time. He failed to mention their prior work for Madison.

They got the business, with miserable results for the people and excellent results for Rose and Hillary.

This wasn't Hillary's first conflict as an attorney in cases involving both the federal government and old friends and political supporters of Bill and Hill. Remember Dan Lasater?

Lasater & Co., his investment firm, had been involved with the First American Savings and Loan in Oak Brook, Illinois, a Chicago suburb. Like Madison, it had gone belly-up. The government claimed that Lasater's firm was partially responsible because of unauthorized trades using the thrift's funds.

The S&L hired the Rose firm and started its own lawsuit against the Lasater interests. Then, in 1987, when the S&L failed, the FDIC took it over and kept Rose on as their attorneys. And this time, one of the two lawyers chosen to sue Lasater's company was Mrs. Hillary Rodham Clinton. Hillary, of course, was the sister-in-law of Roger Clinton whose drug debts had been paid off by loans from Lasater. She was also the friend, political ally, and social buddy, recipient of entertainment, jet plane rides, and cash contributions to her husband's campaign, from the man who owned the company being sued.

Too cozy, you ask? So what's new?

Hillary to the Rescue

Vincent Foster, later a suicide victim, was the lead attorney and Hillary signed on as the number two. The amount of the lawsuit was $3.3 million. What was the outcome for her friend, Mr. Lasater, who was then in jail? Would the government break him? Hardly. Hillary and Foster settled the case for a piddling $200,000, much of which was eaten up by their legal fees.

The White House, in commenting on the Lasater-S&L case, resorted to its usual defenses when it comes to Whitewater, et al. They obfuscated, and worse. They said Hillary had little to do with the case, when in reality, she actually had signed four official documents.

(In a second FDIC lawsuit against Lasater, this time involving the failed Home Federal Savings and Loan of Centralia, Illinois, Rose settled a $4.6 million suit for $250,000 on Vince Foster's advice.)

Was it ethical, or sensible, for Hillary to represent her powerful political ally and Bill Clinton's bond broker, who had been convicted of distributing cocaine? Hardly.

And was it fair to the taxpayers, whose money the government was trying to recover? Worse yet. Her work helped yield a healthy legal fee for Rose, which strengthened her own pocketbook, which as we have seen, has a strong pull on her psyche. And virtually nothing was left for the taxpayer.

Did Hillary purposely help her friend, Dan Lasater, at

the expense of taxpayers? We'll never know, but we do know that she should never have put herself—and by inference her husband, the Governor—in that position in the first place.

It's all quite bizarre. It's even shocking to our first-year law student, who would have known better than to come within a mile of the case.

More Fees For Hillary

Despite these two nonvictories, the Rose Law Firm has been hired to represent the RTC—successor to the FDIC in this type of case—twenty-two times. It has earned $1.27 million in fees, part of which went into Hillary's ample pockets. It also has $600,000 more in new business lined up with the RTC.

(Incidentally, in 1988, Rose and its insurers paid a fine of $3 million to the FDIC regulators for guess what—a conflict of interest—in connection with the failure of First South Savings and Loan, the largest loss to that date in the entire S&L debacle. But it didn't seem to hurt Rose's government business which, according to sources, contributes 40 percent of their entire gross. And therefore a large part of Hillary's pre–White House take-home pay.)

We need to fill in some gaps before and between those federal lawsuits in 1987 and 1989. In 1986, as we've seen, McDougal was removed from his stewardship of Madison. But the S&L was kept open for three full years, accumulating still more losses. Finally, in 1989, the RTC closed Madison Guaranty, and took over its assets, and put the former bank examiner in as CEO. The main office that McDougal had so loved was sold off to the Central

Bank and Trust, and its other branches were sold to local banks.

"We were stuck with some of the real estate properties like Campobello up in Canada, which we now have up for sale," an RTC spokesman in Washington explained when interviewed.

"How big a loss was Madison?" I asked. "Newspaper reports say anything from $47 million to $60 million."

"No, it's more than that. It changes, but right now it's $68 million," the RTC spokesman responded.

That, of course, does not include the overhead of the RTC, which should be added to Madison's piece of the crumbling pie.

McDougal's Travails

McDougal himself fell on hard times. For a period in 1987, he went through a mental trauma that has been described as everything from a temporary blood shortage to his brain to a manic-depressive incident. He was treated by a psychiatrist, even hospitalized for a short period. His wife, Susan, divorced him, and he found himself alone, deserted by his "political family," especially by his old buddy and partner in Whitewater, Governor Bill Clinton.

His best friend turned out to be the taxpayer. He went on Social Security as a disabled beneficiary.

In 1989, McDougal was indicted on eight counts of fraud and tried in federal court in Little Rock, along with some of his associates. His lawyer pleaded that it was a case of financial mismanagement, contributed to by Mc-Dougal's mental state, and that nothing illegal was involved. One of McDougal's associates was convicted on some charges and spent a short period in jail. But James McDougal, represented by leading criminal defense attorney Sam Heuer, was exonerated on all charges and walked out of the Little Rock courtroom a free man.

During this period of McDougal's troubles, Whitewater became a problem. Who was going to handle the business while he was sick? Installment payments were coming in from land buyers, and there was no one to mind the store— except for Hillary, the active partner of the Clinton half of the Whitewater partnership.

Contrary to the White House pap that she was a "passive" investor in Whitewater, Hillary now hopped in with the same involvement she showed in the Lot 13 deal. She actually had the monthly payment checks from Whitewater land buyers sent to her during 1989 and 1990. In fact, she sought power of attorney to completely run Whitewater. That happened when Chris Wade, the rental agent, called her at the Governor's Mansion in 1988 to tell her that he couldn't reach Jim McDougal and had some documents that needed signing.

Hillary wrote McDougal a letter asking for the power of attorney, adding that she hoped it could all be cleared up by the end of the year. But McDougal suddenly showed up and the power of attorney never went into force.

Bill Focuses In

Governor Clinton said nothing publicly, but it would be naive to assume that he didn't know what was going on. He may not care for money *per se*, but his eyes have always stopped glazing over when the conversation turned to campaign contributions. Then, Bill Clinton's peripatetic manner suddenly slowed and he focused in on the matter at hand.

In fact, that same year, Clinton moved aggressively to stop a voter Initiative that could have cramped his style, present and future. Aware that there was too much backscratching in the state, a voter Initiative (Arkansas is one of the twenty-three states where voters can place proposals on the November ballot through petition) demanded that the state put a law into effect that would require disclosure of potential conflicts by public officials.

Since conflict of interest had been the meat and potatoes of the Clintons, Bill and Hillary both moved to restrict what the voters had demanded. Clinton appointed Webb Hubbell to draft the regulation. But the First Family, including Hillary, participated behind the scene. The final result dramatically altered the wishes of the voters. The new conflict-of-interest law required state legislators to hew the line, but *specifically excluded the governor and appointed officials*. So much for democracy in Arkansas.

Just before that, Whitewater, a prime example of conflict of interest, came forcefully to mind in the Clinton camp as Bill seriously considered running for President in 1988. But two shadows clouded the dream at that time. One was that stories of his sexual pecadilloes were starting to leak out. The other was Whitewater, with its complex machinations recorded in thousands of documents. But the Clintons didn't have the papers. They were in the hands of the McDougals.

Hillary personally called Susan McDougal, the Whitewater corporate secretary, and asked her to bring all the

Whitewater papers, including the general ledger, to the Governor's Mansion. Susan arranged that, and five boxes full were delivered to the Clintons' office. Susan McDougal later stated that she had arranged the delivery of "every last piece of paper" to Hillary. (When things got hot at the White House, the Clintons said they had "only some" of the Whitewater papers.)

Presidential Ambitions

In any case, the way now seemed clear for Clinton to compete for the Democratic presidential nomination in 1988, for there were no stellar candidates. But at the last minute, he and Hillary changed their minds. As history records, the nominee, Mike Dukakis, was soundly defeated by George Bush.

At the time Hillary Clinton had a strong political nose. In 1988, she decided that the time was not ripe. They would wait until 1992, which turned out to be a propitious piece of intuition.

Today, Hillary's sixth sense has been injured by the hubris that's emerged with her unprecedented new power, and by the defensiveness she has picked up in the White House trenches— one reminiscent of the atmosphere of the Nixon years.

Her current political failings seem to come from her frustrations, especially her propensity to be a "control freak," as modern parlance terms it. With her brains and her golden girl history of being in charge of whatever she wanted, she is confused by not being able to manipulate events as she used to.

Playing on the larger, more sophisticated national

stage is considerably more difficult, and riskier than it was in the carefully nurtured and controlled Arkansas zone of privacy, an almost conspiratorial climate of the "political family," and an accommodating press. In a way, the sharp Wellesley and Yale woman has become a vulnerable *amateur*, suffering much of the same fate that sent her Rose Law Firm buddies back to Arkansas.

Lackluster Speech

At the 1988 Democratic convention, Clinton was treated respectfully as a leading governor, even if he wasn't a candidate. In fact, he was honored with the job of nominating Governor Dukakis as the presidential candidate. For any other politician, Clinton's lackluster performance, one of the worst in modern political history, would have been the dirge of death. He spoke, actually droned, for a full twenty minutes, reading a dull speech while impatient delegates paid attention to everything else.

Clinton received major applause only one time, when he said he was concluding. Funeral orations were written in the press over the next weeks about his political death. But as friends in Arkansas, and now the nation, know, he's not only the Energizer battery, but much like the opera star who has been stabbed six times, and refuses to die before the aria is completed.

In 1990, Clinton had to decide whether or not to run for a fifth term as governor of Arkansas, his only road to the White House. He had served ten years, already a record.

"A number of people were saying that Bill was not going to run for a fifth term in 1990," Tom C. McRae IV, scion

of an old Arkansas family, and former director of Winthrop
Rockefeller's foundation, said when interviewed. "He
seemed to be burned out. So I decided to run for governor
as a Democrat, and in the fall of 1989, I signed up for the
Democratic primary."

The talk of Clinton's burnout was not just political.
Things had deteriorated in the Clinton marriage, no doubt
stimulated by his infidelities. The brilliant political team
seemed on the verge of breaking up. In fact, there was talk
about Hillary taking his place and making the run for the
statehouse herself. (She wouldn't have to move if elected,
even if they got divorced.)

"No one knew up until the last minute, whether he
was going to run or not," recalls McRae. "I don't think he
had made up his mind even that very morning. It seems to
me that he had written his speech so that it could go either
way. But he did finally announce."

McRae seemed to be making headway, which annoyed
the Clinton camp. Rather than answer him personally, and
thus give him credence, it was decided that Hillary would
do the hatchet work. One morning, McRae was holding a
press conference, which is generally considered the one
time a candidate has total freedom of expression. Heckling
is generally limited to the press.

Hillary Suddenly Appears
But not long after the conference began, in walked Hillary,
saying she had just been passing by. In the space of ten
minutes she let loose a barrage of charges against McRae,
taking over his conference and leaving the press and
McRae with open mouths.

"I had never seen anything like this. I didn't know what to say," McRae recalled about the upsetting incident. "I suppose I was limited by my gentlemanly instinct not to fight with her. After all, she was not the candidate."

McRae stayed in the race, and to everyone's astonishment, got 39 percent of the vote to the Governor's 53 percent. The general election was against the Republican candidate, Sheffield Nelson.

Mr. Nelson did not win the 1990 race, but his intrusion into the Whitewater picture—as an enemy of Clinton—was to later make a big difference.

Whitewater did not emerge as an important issue in the election.

"The local papers ran a few stories on Whitewater, but they were routine," explains Max Brantley of the *Arkansas Times*. "People already knew that the Clintons and the McDougals were in partnership. A few people thought of the quid pro quo idea, but since the stories had nothing new, they were largely ignored. The man who was feeding information to the press was Sheffield Nelson. Later, he helped break the story open more, but not at that time. Then it made very little impression."

At this point, it might be wise to connect Sheffield Nelson and the powerful Stephens, Inc., interests in Arkansas, which became very valuable to Hillary and Bill.

Called the people who "own Arkansas," Jackson T. (Mr. Jack) Stephens and his brother, Winston (Mr. Witt) Stephens, have accumulated an estimated $1.7 billion in their investment business and various subsidiaries, including the largest interest in the Worthen Bank, the state's biggest. The glass Stephens tower dominates the Little

Rock skyline along with the TCBY building, and President
Clinton keeps his Little Rock White House there, and it's
listed as "Bill Clinton's Arkansas Office."

Initially, the Stephenses were rabid enemies of the
Clintons. They saw them as radical usurpers who might
threaten business interests in the state. In the 1978, 1980,
and 1982 races, especially, they supported the Republican
candidates, including Frank White in his two bids, one successful, for the statehouse.

But little by little, the Stephenses had begun to view
Clinton as unbeatable, and started, slowly, to shift their allegiance away from his competitors. Clinton had helped
build up Dan Lasater as an alternate bond dealer for his
Arkansas ADFA, but Lasater had been convicted and
gone to jail. Clinton had no choice but to deal with the
Stephenses, and he even helped them gain a large bond
issue along with a sizable commission before the 1990
election.

King of the Hill

For their part, the Stephenses had to come to terms with
reality, which was that Bill Clinton was the king of the political walk. The Stephenses' first step was to try to get
Sheffield Nelson, the strongest Republican, out of the
1990 race. They backed former Congressman Tommy
Robinson, but despite their support, Robinson lost the primary to Nelson.

Nelson had once been a fair-haired Stephens boy, and
had even been chief executive of their gas company,
ARKLA. But the Stephenses and Nelson had management
disputes, and he left, persona non Stephens. Now, in the

1990 election, having failed to block Nelson's nomination, they threw all their weight behind their onetime nemesis, Bill Clinton—who for years they had accused of increasing taxes, swelling the bureaucracy and continuing a deadening one-party control of the state.

But, as financial man Roy Drew, critic of ADFA operations, says of that marriage, "The Stephenses don't particularly like Clinton, but they wanted to hedge both sides."

The strange bedfellows of Democrat Clinton and Republican Stephens worked closely together in the 1990 gubernatorial election. Before every election, as in 1984, when he borrowed $50,000 in unneeded money, Clinton gets slightly hysterical. This happened again in 1990. Just four days before the election, Clinton called Warren Stephens, the heir and his contemporary and new friend, in a panic. The opposition Republicans were running a series of ads calling Clinton a "tax-and-spend liberal," Bill told Warren. Could Mr. Stephens raise $10,000 overnight for a last minute rebuttal?

The answer was yes. Based on the guarantees of four other $10,000 fund-raisers, Clinton borrowed $50,000 and threw the money into a countercampaign.

Wins a Fifth Term

With or without the ads, Clinton handily won the 1990 race for Governor of Arkansas. Bill Clinton won election to his fifth term with a margin of 61 percent to 39 percent.

Now all Arkansas was abuzz with talk that Bill was running for President. During those two years, he and Hillary had apparently come to a modus operandi of sorts in their marriage, and the goal of the White House was a uniting force. The girlfriends could be outflanked if the couple stuck together. The efforts of Nelson to embarrass them on Whitewater had fallen on deaf ears. That, they were sure, was a nonissue, and would stay that way.

In May 1991, just five months after his inauguration as Governor for the fifth time, Bill, with Hillary alongside, announced that he would be a Democratic candidate for President of the United States— exactly what he had pledged to the editor of the Little Rock paper he would not do.

But destiny was calling. The road to New Hampshire lay straight ahead, and Whitewater—they thought—lay behind them.

Chapter Ten

The Cover-up Begins
Yes, There Are American Heroes

The place was New Hampshire and the fateful period was February 1992. In the chill of winter, the quadrennial presidential primary was about to get under way, with Bill and Hillary Clinton worried about the upcoming vote. Polls showed former Senator Tsongas of Massachusetts with a solid lead, with Clinton holding a tenuous second or third.

Suddenly, there was a political explosion. The two time bombs in their past—Bill's promiscuity and Whitewater—had been relatively quiet, for which the Clintons were thankful. Then, near the eve of the primary, Gennifer Flowers, blonde extraordinaire, announced that she had had a twelve-year sexual affair with presidential candidate Bill Clinton, with phone tapes to at least give her claim some credence.

Media frenzy took over, and when the levers were finally pulled in New Hampshire on February 18, 1992, the Clintons were happy with a second-place finish.

But New Hampshire was only the preliminary. The real contest would come on Super Tuesday, March 10, a collection of eight primaries, mainly in southern states, that seemingly were arranged for candidates like Clinton. That primary day—in states with twenty-five times more electoral votes than New Hampshire—was viewed as a make-or-break situation for Clinton. If he couldn't win his party's vote in his native South, the old Confederacy, pundits said, he couldn't win anywhere.

What was missing was money. The Clinton campaign believed that Gennifer, as attractive as she was, wouldn't sway many votes against him, especially with Hillary at Bill's side, staring up adoringly. But money was another story. It was hopelessly short, and contributions had started to dry up in the aftermath of the bedroom accusation.

Needed Cash

What was needed was enough money, quickly, to run an avalanche of television commercials in the Super Tuesday primary to counter Gennifer and remind voters that a native son, a fellow Southerner, was seeking the presidency. (A technique, incidentally, that helped elect Jimmy Carter. The rest of the country, it seems, is immune to such corny regional pride.)

How much money? At least $3.5 million, Clinton's people believed, sufficient to keep things going until they could raise enough on their own to secure the matching federal funds.

Who? Where?

Who indeed but two of the richest men in the world, who happened to live in Arkansas? Where indeed but Little Rock, where gubernatorial favors had been strewn around for ten years? Who but Jack and Witt (actually Jackson and Winston) Stephens and their son Warren, of Stephens, Inc., fellow Arkansans who had heavily supported Governor Clinton's reelection bid in 1990.

Just as important to Clinton was the Worthen Bank, also headquartered in Little Rock, which had $2 billion in assets. That was the institution which came to his rescue. They bailed Clinton out after his failed New Hampshire primary by giving his broke campaign a giant $3.5 million line of credit. The Worthen's CEO is Curt Bradbury, a contemporary of Clinton who apparently felt almost a kinship for the Governor.

"I would like to be in a position to think I could call the President of the United States and give him my views—on the Federal Reserve, for example," Bradbury told the *Arkansas Times*.

What's the connection between the Stephenses and Bradbury, if any? Firstly, Bradbury is a former Stephens executive and onetime boy brokerage genius. But more significant is that skeptics believe that the Stephenses indirectly have considerable power in the Worthen bank.

It's all part of a decade-long federal debate over the connection between the two giants. The Glass-Steagall banking law does not permit an investment firm to own 50 percent of a bank, a sensible separation of functions. But skeptics say that the Stephenses, who have owned between 20 and 38 percent of the bank at various times, pull too much weight with Worthen. If that's true, the $3.5 million for Clinton, these skeptics say, indirectly came from the Stephenses, who handle at least half the bond business in Arkansas, much of it in collaboration with the Governor.

A Matter of Percentages

Investigations have been undertaken by the federal government on the Stephens-Worthen connection. There have been suspicions, especially by the Federal Reserve, but since 50 percent is the magic number, they have never ruled against Stephens or Worthen. It seems that friends, associates, employees, relatives, etc., of the Stephens family just don't count in counting percentages of Worthen ownership.

But in Arkansas they laugh at the idea. If you walk into the lobby of the Worthen Bank building in downtown Little Rock, one of the first things that hits you is a computer terminal that allows you to open an account at the Stephens brokerage office. (There are no terminals, by the way, for Merrill Lynch or E. F. Hutton.)

Sure, Worthen and Stephens are separate, Arkansans say. Then they give you one big knowing wink. In any case, having the Worthen bank back Clinton with millions surely won't hurt Stephens when the question of who owns what comes up again in a subsequent Federal Reserve inquiry.

The Clinton campaign pulled down $2 million of the line of credit and flooded the states in the giant primary with television commercials and other advertising. On Super Tuesday, March 10, 1992, Bill Clinton was the big winner, with the vast majority of delegates' votes. From then on, it was easy. Money came pouring in, and with that and matching federal funds, Clinton paid off the loan to

Worthen. By the late spring, barring another public relations disaster, the nomination was as good as his.

What could possibly injure Clinton's name now that he
had survived Gennifer and the largest primary of the campaign? The hidden nemesis was, of course, Whitewater,
waiting in the wings all this time.

On March 8, 1992, two days before Super Tuesday, the
good, gray *New York Times* ran a flamboyant—for it—
front page story. It was headlined CLINTONS JOINED S. & L. OP-
ERATOR IN AN OZARK REAL-ESTATE VENTURE and featured an
inside eight-column story that offered the details of the
Whitewater investment, with the clear implication that it
was a sweetheart deal for presidential aspirant Bill Clinton
and his wife. There was little risk of real financial loss, plus
the specter of a strong conflict of interest involving the
Madison Guaranty Savings and Loan, owned by their business partner in Whitewater.

"It raised a flurry of interest in the media for the next
few days," Jeff Gerth, author of the story, explained when
interviewed. "But after that it seemed to fade away. I don't
think many people really understood its significance."

A New Gimmick
But that didn't include the Clintons, who quickly went into
damage-control mode. They invented what is really a new
public relations device, as unprecedented as Bill's $400,000
in unsecured loans from his favorite bank.

Why not have a trusted friend make like an arbiter,
and have him report his appraisal of the situation to the
media—just as if it were an objective third-party audit?
The friend was James Lyons, a Denver attorney who had

met Clinton in Little Rock and had given him legal and
campaign advice over the years.

Lyons hired what he called a "forensic accounting"
firm to delve into Whitewater and provide the public with
the details. They examined check stubs, ledgers, etc., and
came up with a number that seemed to refute the *Times*
piece. The Clintons, he said, had actually *lost* a great deal
of money—$68,900 specifically—in Whitewater as against
about $92,200 for the McDougals.

Where was the so-called free ride? Lyons asked. In
fact, what could possibly be wrong when they had lost
money? Lyons's only caveat was that "in many instances,
documentation as to various transactions was incomplete
or unavailable."

The Lyons report, as we now know, was heavily
flawed. The loss figure was hopelessly false. The Clintons
never paid a penny of the $203,000 mortgage and did get a
free ride, and there were many other failings. But at the
time the report was a stroke of sheer genius. You wouldn't
think that the media—which knew that Lyons was an old
Clinton buddy—would fall for it. But they did.

Media Failure
The ingenious ploy worked because the national media
amateurishly failed to do their job and took the self-serving
report as gospel. The result was that no one followed up on
the *Times* story. Whitewater virtually disappeared as a
campaign issue during the 1992 presidential campaign, an
indictment of the press.

The only candidate to forcefully bring up Whitewater was Jerry Brown, former governor of California,

who futilely fought Clinton almost to the end in the primaries.

When he challenged Clinton about Whitewater in a debate and mentioned Hillary as a major participant, the front-runner became furious. "You ought to be ashamed of yourself," Clinton responded with indignation about an attack on his wife, then added a fillip for himself: "Every time I have ever run for office, because I have been a change agent . . . the people who have run against me attack me personally."

What about the incumbent President, George Bush? Between the *Times* exposé in March 1992 and the election in November, he said nothing about Whitewater, which seemed to fit in with the tenor of his whole inept campaign.

What was behind that? In a moment, we'll speculate on this strange political behavior.

But Whitewater was not as dead as it appeared in the media during the 1992 campaign. Behind the scenes a game of power, intrigue, and politics was being played out in the Resolution Trust Corporation, in a Justice Department still controlled by the Republicans, and in the U.S. attorney's office in Little Rock. It was a game that managed to keep suspicions bottled up until after election day, then into the new Clinton administration and beyond, when the cover-up truly began.

The story goes as follows:

In July 1991, long before anyone had heard of Whitewater outside of Arkansas, criminal investigator L. Jean Lewis, working out of the Tulsa regional office of the Resolution Trust Corporation, was assigned to Madison Guaranty. The S&L was slated for a follow-up, a sort of cleanup exam, in the fall of 1992. But there was no urgency. Besides, Jim McDougal, its owner, had already been tried for fraud and acquitted just the year before.

RTC Responsibility

The RTC had taken over from the FDIC, and was responsible for the full spectrum of activity: closing down S&Ls, investigating their books, trying to collect what they could from those involved, recommending the criminal prosecution of others to the Justice Department, and selling off the remaining assets. As a routine operation, they collected whatever documents they could from the closed S&Ls.

In the summer of 1991, civil investigator Wyatt Adams traveled to Little Rock. In an old warehouse down by the river he found an enormous number of Madison records—from officer correspondence to land documents to investment folders—strewn haphazardly around and not inventoried. The scene told the story: No one seemed to care.

Nothing much happened until March 1992, when the *Times* story broke. The media may not have been stimulated by the Whitewater article, but a Washington RTC official was. Senior Investigator Jon Walker read the Gerth piece and contacted the Kansas City office, which covers Little Rock. He asked them to look into any possible link between Whitewater and Madison's failure.

They were to look for any collusion that could result in a "criminal referral," which would then be given to the Justice Department to examine and possibly prosecute. But on the other hand, there could be more smoke than fire.

At first, L. Jean Lewis spent two weeks looking at some Madison documents in the Tulsa office. She found no mention of Whitewater. It looked like a dead end.

Then it was discovered that a former employee of Madison allegedly had fabricated two years of minutes for a Madison subsidiary, the Madison Financial Corporation. Even though the FBI decided to take no action, the records were shipped to Tulsa. After examination, the RTC people were encouraged to continue the probe.

Back to the Warehouse

Adams and Lewis were sent from Tulsa to the riverfront warehouse in Little Rock to try to make sense out of the mess. They started by rearranging the haphazardly strewn boxes of records to make room for a table and two chairs so that they could begin working.

They began the hard, boring work of white-collar crime spotting, going through everything, searching for Whitewater documents. They located the White-water checking accounts for 1984, 1985, and 1986, then hit their first pay dirt, something that could connect Whitewater with Madison's failure. On a ledger sheet marked "Reserve for Development—Maple Creek Farms," a Madison-financed operation, was a notation of a $30,000 item for an engineering survey, charged to Whitewater.

The team continued to search. They found Whitewater checks payable to the Bank of Cherry Valley and numerous checks payable to such real estate entities as Pembroke Manor, Rolling Manor, and Madison Marketing and others with the notation of "loan." Up through the end of April they followed up twelve Madison-related accounts, including Whitewater.

By the end of July 1992, the Tulsa office was closed and criminal investigator Jean Lewis was transferred to Kansas City, which took over the Madison-Whitewater case. During that summer, she continued to assiduously comb the records. She was startled by what she found. Lewis decided that a crime, or several, may have been committed.

The result was a "criminal referral," a twenty-one-page document labeled COOO4 that alleged that a giant $1.5 million check-kiting scheme had been developed at Madison involving the S&L itself and several related entities— including Whitewater. What's more, she believed that at least $70,000, and perhaps as much as $100,000 or even more, was funneled from Madison to Whitewater, which was half-owned by the Clintons, by paying checks even though there were insufficient funds. The diversion of Madison Guaranty taxpayer-insured deposits to Whitewater was, of course, the finding the White House would love to hate.

Lewis now turned to the Justice Department to learn if it was going to follow up on her suspicions.

The Hot Document
"COOO4" soon became the hottest federal document in Washington. Not because of its description of S&L fallibilities— dozens had already been prosecuted—but because the names of presidential candidate William Jefferson Clinton and his wife, Hillary Rodham Clinton, appeared in its pages. Not as participants in the "criminal referral" but as "possible beneficiaries" of, or "possible witnesses" to, the alleged crimes.

Jim McDougal, acquitted in 1990 on eight fraud counts in regard to Madison, and his ex-wife, Susan McDougal, have denied any wrongdoing in Madison and all related enterprises, including Whitewater.

On September 2, 1992, the referral was submitted to the Department of Justice, beginning a saga for Jean Lewis in which she emerges as the true hero of the Whitewater story, persistent, resistant to overwhelming bureaucratic pressure from above, determined to learn the truth.

(Yes, there still are heroes in the convoluted, corrupt mess known as American politics.)

Ms. Lewis is a forty-year-old who grew up in Houston, Texas, the daughter of a retired U.S. Army major general. She is not an attorney or an accountant but a political science grad from Sam Houston College, earning $54,000 a year in her RTC job. "Jean loves digging out facts and details," says a Dallas executive who worked with her at an S&L before she joined the government.

Back then in Kansas City, her work was appreciated and the RTC office turned her criminal referral on Madison-Whitewater over to Chuck Banks, the Republican-appointed U.S. Attorney in Little Rock. The presidential campaign was heating up. In fact, by that time Clinton was edging ahead of Bush in the polls.

What Happened to CO0O4?

There is no definite word on what happened to the report in Little Rock. Mr. Banks will not talk until the Independent Counsel approaches him— or Congress subpoenas him as a witness.

"I can't say anything about it until then," he told me

personally. But reports indicate that no action was taken by Justice during the 1992 Bush-Clinton battle, either because Banks did not take it seriously, or because Washington decided not to touch it with the proverbial pole and made Banks the patsy by holding him to inaction.

In any case, the criminal referral of Jean Lewis of the RTC involving Madison and Whitewater finally arrived in Washington and came to the attention of Attorney General William Barr and President Bush in early October 1992.

What to do?

The answer, surprisingly, was nothing, which was rather symptomatic of the entire Bush effort. The Republicans were intimidated by a report that might have been received with partisan glee, especially since Bush was behind in the polls by seven points. Apparently they were being held back by several considerations.

1. The entire S&L scandal, of which Madison and Whitewater were a part, was costing the nation an anticipated $200 billion, not just Madison's $68 million. And who had loosened the regulations on S&Ls to make the debacle possible in the first place? The Republican administrations of Reagan and Bush, that's who. The fear that an attack on Clinton's Whitewater could bounce back against Bush was real.

2. The Bush administration had been chastised for checking Bill Clinton's travel visas in the State Department, and a vendetta now might look McCarthyish.

3. Bush's son Neil had been involved in an S&L scan-

dal, the Silverado in Colorado, and the family was happy to hear the last of S&Ls.

4. Perhaps most important, it was late in the campaign. There was a fear of how the electorate would receive an October surprise. Aggressive last-minute attacks are highly unpredictable, even dangerous, if the information is not solid enough to make the charge stick. Best to leave it alone, President Bush and his advisers decided.

(In some ways, it's similar to the Democratic party's dilemma over Watergate in the months before the 1972 presidential election between McGovern and Nixon. The *Washington Post*'s Bernstein-Woodward investigation had not yet taken place, and the Democrats didn't have enough ammunition to press forward on what the White House had called a "third-rate burglary." So Watergate, like Whitewater, became a nonissue in the presidential campaign.)

After the Victory

Clinton, of course, won the 1992 election and quickly moved to clean up the loose ends of Whitewater, which was still operating. In December of that year, Vince Foster, who was at the Rose office in Little Rock, decided that it was best to get the First Family out of the picture. He negotiated a sale of the Clintons' 50 percent interest in Whitewater to Jim McDougal for $1,000, only to learn that no corporate taxes had been filed for the last three years. Foster was given the responsibility of handling it.

Incidentally, the Clintons have never filed a capital

gains tax for the $1,000, or $500, gain on the Whitewater
sale. Nor have they ever taken any of their purported losses
on Whitewater on their IRS returns.

The supposed losses can be subtracted against capital
gains. And if there are none of those, they could take $3,000
each year against their regular income—which they haven't
done. But perhaps they don't want to confuse Internal Revenue. Or their Whitewater tax matters are hopelessly tangled anyway, as we shall see.

But though Whitewater was in a state of suspended
political animation after the election, it was far from dead.
In fact, it was searching for a resurrection.

Now that the Republican Justice Department was a
lame duck until Clinton's inauguration on January 20, 1993,
Whitewater languished during those three months. Soon
after, Jean Lewis picked up the crusade, pestering the
Little Rock FBI office with calls. What had happened to her
COOO4 on Madison? she asked. Finally, the FBI special
agent in charge sent a letter to the RTC acknowledging
that both the FBI and the local U.S. attorney had received
the referral.

This took her up through May 1993 and into the fifth
month of the new administration. Republican Chuck Banks
was no longer the U.S. attorney. There was an interim acting U.S. attorney in Little Rock, but he was about to be replaced by Paula J. Casey, a former law student of Bill
Clinton's at the University of Arkansas back in the 1970s.

Finally, desperate about the stalling, Lewis sent a letter to the Little Rock U.S. Attorney's Office, asking for the
status of the criminal referral, which surely had burned a
hole in someone's desk. Lewis did get a response. The re-

ferral, she was told, had been sent to the Department of
Justice in Washington, Lewis should contact them.

Numerous phone calls to Janet Reno's department
produced the same result—nothing.

On May 19, 1993, for example, a second call was made
by Lewis to the Office of Legal Counsel at Justice. She
asked the secretary if she had determined the status of the
Madison referral.

"No," came the response. "We have no record of that
referral, it is not in the computer system, it has not been
given to an attorney."

Try, Try Again

Ms. Lewis tried another Justice Department section, the "Executive Office for the U.S. Attorneys." There she spoke with
someone who remembered the referral. "Oh," she blurted
out, "the one involving the President and his wife." The government employee then explained that "any time a referral
comes in that would make the department look bad, or has
political ramifications, it goes to the attorney general."

A week later Lewis received a phone call from Justice.
The referral had been given to a special counsel, but he was
now in private practice. They would continue to try to find it.

By early June 1993, the Kansas City office of the RTC
was also annoyed by the stonewalling, and decided to
take some action on their own. Three more investigators
were added to the one-person Jean Lewis task force. Two
of them, including Lewis, went back to the Whitewater
fountainhead—the dank old Little Rock warehouse.

They did more scavenging of pertinent papers, and
then all four spread out into several Arkansas counties,

studying land records related to property sales, loans, and
mortgages involving Madison and its many entities, including Whitewater. The investigation looked more promising
than ever. They had found new evidence that made the
"criminal referrals" even stronger.

At the same time the investigation was progressing,
Justice called again, with news. The referral had finally
been found. It had been in the Fraud Section, but the person assigned to the case "didn't want to deal with it" (ostensibly with the proverbial pole) and had returned it to
the executive office of the U.S. Attorneys.

Lewis told the spokesperson that the RTC now had new
evidence that made the case stronger, and "whatever the decision [by Justice] is," Lewis said, "I need something in writing."

Her Eighth Call
Another fortnight passed. Justice called again. They had
sent the entire package to Associate Deputy Attorney General Doug Frazier but had gotten it all back. Frazier had
been appointed U.S. Attorney in Florida. This was, Lewis
noted, her eighth conversation with Justice.

That same day, Justice called again. They had spoken
with Frazier, who said that he had met with the director of
the executive office for U.S. Attorneys. They had decided
that referral C0O004 should go back to the newly appointed U.S. attorney Paula Casey in Little Rock. Ms. Casey
had recused herself from the case because she had once
been Bill Clinton's law student. Frazier said that that "was
no basis" for such a recusal and, like it or not, she was getting the case back.

Meanwhile, the RTC and Ms. Lewis were active in

their new investigation of Madison-Whitewater, which they
had begun in June 1993. The culling of records and the
preparation of the new report took four months. On October 8, 1993, Lewis and the others submitted a new document—this time with nine new "criminal referrals," for
Justice to handle, for a total of ten.

The new investigation had turned up leads, including
the suspicion that money had flowed from Madison funds
into both Whitewater and Governor Clinton's 1984 campaign fund to help pay back his $50,000 personal loan. And,
the referrals reportedly repeated the charge that Whitewater had gained upwards of $100,000 that had been diverted
from Madison accounts.

(With or without their knowledge, the Clintons—
according to the criminal referral—had been enriched
by the taxpayers, making their supposed "losses" on
Whitewater even more ephemeral.)

Soon after, the new criminal referrals were sent to the
FBI in Little Rock and to Paula J. Casey, U.S. Attorney for
the eastern district of Arkansas. Casey no longer claimed
the right of recusal just because she knew the President
personally.

Finally, A Response
Just weeks after Jean Lewis submitted the new referrals,
she got a response. On October 27, 1993, almost one year
into the Clinton administration, the mammoth U.S. government finally acted on the case. Not to the new criminal referrals—that would have been too much to ask. The
response from U.S. Attorney Casey was about *the original
referral, going back to September 1992.*

The answer was simple and of course expected. Clinton-appointee Casey said in a letter to Jean Lewis that the criminal referral had been turned down. Why? "Insufficient information."

"There is," Casey said, "insufficient information in the referral to sustain many of the allegations made by the investigators or to warrant the initiation of a criminal investigation."

The result was simple and predictable. L. Jean Lewis was kicked off the case. The new evidence, some-one must have feared, would force action on the Madison and Whitewater case. Lashing out at Ms. Lewis, the messenger, was natural—but may be finally destructive for the administration.

On November 10, 1993, the RTC, yielding to some-one's pressure, removed Jean Lewis as lead criminal investigator on the Madison-Whitewater inquiry. The pressure from above was particularly onerous because just that year the RTC had awarded Lewis $1,000 for her excellent work on Madison and had recommended her for a second award in the form of bonus pay and time off.

"The Powers That Be," she memoed her bosses when she was removed, "have decided that I'm better off out of the line of fire. . . ."

Mike Forshey, a Dallas attorney who now represents Lewis, was quoted as saying that her supervisor in Kansas City, Richard Iorio, was "ordered" to remove Ms. Lewis and was never given a reason. As the cliché goes, we don't need a neurosurgeon to explain that one.

The decision to dismiss Ms. Lewis may have seemed smart to the people at the White House, or to some officials in the FDIC, the RTC, or Justice. But whoever made the decision, it was the stupidest move of the operation.

Those handling the stonewalling and obfuscation, whoever they are, had forgotten their high school civics lessons.

There are three independent branches of the U.S. government, according to the Constitution—the executive, the judiciary, and the legislative.

The Clintons might be in control of the executive and perhaps much of the judiciary through the Justice Department, its entry point to the courts. But they seem to have forgotten about the third branch, the legislative—the U.S. Congress.

Jean Lewis remembered her schoolbook civics. She had been stymied at Justice and then dismissed from the Madison Guaranty investigation by the Resolution Trust Corporation, part of the executive branch. She then decided to go where she would be welcome—to the U.S. Congress, specifically the House of Representatives.

She didn't bring her case to Congress immediately. Her suspicion that she was a patsy in a larger plot occurred to her two months after her removal. On January 6, 1994, Lewis wrote an E-mail memo to her supervisor.

"It's beginning to sound like somebody, or multiple somebodies, are trying to carefully control the outcome of any investigation surrounding the RTC referrals," she wrote, "and that the beginnings of a cover-up may have already started months ago."

Lewis became even warier when she heard that an at-

torney from the investigative department of the RTC—
someone who had helped hire Hillary's law firm to sue
Madison's accountants—wanted to speak with her.

The attorney, April Breslaw, came to Kansas City
from Washington. It wasn't long into the conversation
before Lewis realized that Ms. Breslaw was talking like
she was there on behalf of the "Powers That Be," as
Lewis called the Washington brass.

The meeting took place in the Kansas City RTC office
on February 2, 1994, from 3:50 P.M. to 4:35 P.M.

Judging from Ms. Lewis's detailed memo on the discussion, it was a less-than-subtle attempt to convince the
federal investigator to report what someone wanted her to
report.

"The people at the top" keep getting asked about
Whitewater, Breslaw explained to Lewis. Therefore, the
"head people" at her agency would like to be able to say
that Whitewater *did not cause a loss of money to Madison*, which is the key to the case. Breslaw made it clear
that there were certain answers Washington would be
"happier" about, because it would "get them off the
hook."

Debating the Referral

Breslaw continued her pitch. She said she figured that
Whitewater really wasn't culpable because so many
checks had gone in and out of the account. For example,
Breslaw pointed out, the work papers on Maple Creek
Farms didn't seem to have any apparent tie to Whitewater, even though the money ($30,000) was slated to come
out of Whitewater's account. "I concurred that it didn't

have any legitimately defined tie," Lewis noted, "which is precisely why it was included in the referral."

Breslaw persisted. She asked Lewis how she could get a clear-cut answer as to whether Madison had lost money as a result of Whitewater, making the Clinton investment a loser for the American taxpayer.

Lewis answered: "As far as I am concerned, there is a clear-cut loss from Whitewater." She pointed out that just her six-month window on the transactions showed a loss of some $70,000 to Madison Guaranty Savings and Loan as a result of diversion of funds to Whitewater—and therefore an eventual loss to the taxpayers. But if the "window" were extended to the entire span of their two-year study, "the losses to Madison from the Whitewater account alone would easily exceed $100,000."

(We're talking about taxpayer monies from the insolvent Madison that went to maintain Whitewater, half-owned by the Clintons.)

Not Politically Correct

Lewis was not cowed by the senior official. "I further pointed out," she later related in notes of her meeting, *"that I would produce the answers that were available, but that I would not facilitate providing the 'people at the top' with the 'politically correct answers just to get them off the hook.'"*

April Breslaw "categorically denied" Lewis's account of the meeting. Which version is more accurate—that of Lewis or that of Breslaw, the investigator or the emissary from Washington?

"Ms. Lewis was smart enough to secretly tape the

conversation, which is quite legal," explains an aide to
Congressman Leach. "The tape exists, and Ms. Lewis's re-
counting is accurate."

(On August 17, 1994, the full transcript of the Lewis-
Breslaw meeting was obtained by *The Wall Street Journal*.
The nine page, single-spaced document confirms everything that Lewis said—that senior agency officials "would
like to be able to say that Whitewater didn't cause a loss"
to Madison and Jean Lewis's belief that it actually did. But
it does add several comments by Breslaw that she didn't
want to appear to be pressuring Lewis, or that the people
above her necessarily wanted a certain conclusion. In reality, the new transcript detracts little or nothing from
Lewis's detailed tape recorded reporting of the meeting.)

Laura Jean Lewis has the tape hidden in a safe place
and guards it zealously. It is the proof of her integrity, her
most prized possession. The dialogue with the RTC attorney from Washington had convinced the general's daughter that the administration fiasco should not be permitted
to continue without exposure.

She could have gone to the press and television but
decided that contact with the right member of Congress
might in the long run be more effective.

The right congressman was Jim Leach of Iowa, ranking Republican on the House Banking Committee, which
has jurisdiction over S&Ls and her own agency, the Resolution Trust Corporation, as well.

(She didn't call Henry Gonzalez, the chairman of the
Banking Committee. Gonzalez, a friend of the President,
was in no mood to promote any cause that could hurt the
administration. Unfortunately, that's the nature of politics

today—heated adversarial stances by both Democrats and Republicans in which partisan interests almost always outweigh patriotic, decent ones—if any of the latter are still alive in the Washington arena.)

Jean Lewis was wary, cognizant of the power of her information. She refused to speak to any of Congressman Leach's aides, insisting in telling her story only to him. She got through, and within days, sometime in mid-February 1994, Leach secretly flew to Kansas City. He met with Ms. Lewis, who played the audiotape for him and gave him a collection of her E-mail memos to her bosses. Leach has since confirmed the accuracy of Ms. Lewis's version of the shocking Breslaw meeting.

Was the Clinton administration— either from on high or by officials in various agencies—trying to stifle the truth about Whitewater?

Obviously.

Jean Lewis, once an anonymous federal bureaucrat, was on her way toward being elevated as St. Jean (not St. Hillary). The actions of the "Powers That Be" had stimulated a revival of a Whitewater inquiry that had been dying for lack of news, and good reporting, in the press.

The fourth-rate real estate deal in the rural northwestern corner of Arkansas was now truly headed for political immortality.

Chapter Eleven

Cover-up II

Panic in the White House

Whitewater is not just the story of government gone astray—an age-old tale of destructive arrogance that comes with power.

It is also a human story, one in which people win and lose and some suffer. The political cronies of Bill and Hillary who came with them to Washington have been among both the spoilers and the victims.

First among the victims was the Clintons' best friend, Vincent W. Foster, Jr. No one was closer to the First Family than Hillary's former law partner, who was the "soul" of Rose and supra-confidante of the Clintons.

Named deputy counsel to the President, Foster nominally reported to his boss, White House counsel Bernard Nussbaum. But Foster was actually above the chain of command and spoke directly and regularly to Bill and

Hillary, just as did Reno's nominal aide, former Rose partner Webb Hubbell, at Justice.

As part of his responsibility, Foster handled the Whitewater affairs for the Clintons. His "job" also included handling their personal tax returns and financial disclosure forms. In a way, his confidential work for the President and Hillary was quite illegal. Foster was being paid by the U.S. Treasury to do the President's official chores, not to handle Whitewater and other personal affairs.

Be that as it may, Foster was totally trusted by the Clintons as the guardian of all their family secrets, and rightly so.

Day of Decision

As everyone now knows, July 20, 1993, was a fateful day for Foster. He had been depressed for weeks but was hiding the severity of it from his colleagues, including the Clintons, who had no inkling of his mental state. Foster had been thinking of seeing a psychiatrist. He had even unsuccessfully sought to reach one but hadn't yet decided to become a patient, possibly for fear of revealing Clinton secrets. But he had taken some slow-working antidepressant pills prescribed by his family doctor a few days before.

He left the office about 1 P.M. and said he would return. He never did.

At 5:45 P.M., his body, with a .38-caliber shot through the mouth and exiting from his skull, was found in the small Fort Marcy National Park in Virginia, on the other side of the Potomac. The gun was a Colt Army Special revolver.

Mr. Fiske was empowered to determine if his death

was indeed a suicide, but the forensic details of the investigation were so casually handled that an entire conspiracy
industry that rivals the "man on the knoll" of the Kennedy
years has begun to flourish.

The Fiske report, which was issued on June 30, 1994,
described a series of strange factors discovered by the effi-
cient FBI, but in most instances it offers no explanations
or follow-up. The FBI found:

1. Blond and light brown hairs on Foster's undershirt,
   pants, socks, and shoes.
2. Semen stains on his undershorts, which might indicate a very recent sexual contact.
3. Even though he was found in a park, there was no
   dirt on his shoes, only traces of mica.
4. Carpet fibers of various colors were found on his
   suit, shirt, and underclothes, as well as pink wool
   fibers of an "unknown source."
5. An exhaustive search of the area was made, but
   the bullet was never found.
6. There were no skull fragments from the pistol
   shot.
7. There were no fingerprints on the antique gun.
8. Despite its investigations, the FBI was unable to
   learn where Foster had been between 1 P.M. and
   5:45 P.M. that day. One piece of missing evidence
   was the pager Foster carried on him when he was
   outside the office. It seems that the Park Police had
   removed the pager—with possibly its memory of
   phone calls made to him—and returned it to the
   White House.

These and other discrepancies have fed the conspiracy theory that Foster was not a suicide victim but was murdered somewhere else and brought to the park site. (One of the most popular, and imaginative theories is that Foster and other women or men in the White House maintained a secret apartment in suburban Virginia and that's where the death actually took place.)

In fact, several congressmen, including Dan Burton of Indiana, have raised questions regarding the forensic inconsistencies. Whether or not the suicide verdict is true or false, the unusual findings should have been followed up more thoroughly.

The logical questions to be asked, whether or not one believes Congressman Burton's radical theory, are:

1. The report says the position of the head was "inconsistent" with the position of the blood stains. Why?
2. Why didn't Fiske follow up and try to learn the source of the blond hairs which were on Foster's underclothes?
3. Why were there semen stains on his undershorts?
4. What was the source of the carpet fibers on his underclothes, of which Fiske's report says has an unknown "possible significance"?
5. Why, despite a search by sixteen FBI lab men, was no bullet found?
6. The exit hole in the skull was an enormous 1¼" x 1" in size, yet—despite the hand-sifting of soil to a depth of 18 inches—no brain and bone fragments were found. Why?
7. Why were there no fingerprints on the gun?

Despite these failures of investigation, the chances are still quite strong that it was a suicide, just as Fiske said. But the frustration among some Americans about the paucity of candor on Whitewater and Fiske's lack of follow-up of FBI forensic evidence has nourished extreme theories. One of them strings together recent tragedies tangentially connected to Whitewater into a conspiracy that even involves murder.

Conspiracy of Violence?
The latest "victim" in this conspiracy theory is Stanley Huggins, a forty-six-year-old lawyer who died in June 1994 of viral pneumonia. He was one of the examiners who investigated Madison Guaranty in 1987 and produced a 300-page report on the S&L's.

The list of the newly deceased, besides Foster and Huggins, also includes the ex-wife of the Arkansas state trooper named as a codefendant in the Paula Jones suit, who died of gunshot wounds in a purported suicide; the boyfriend of that woman, also an Arkansas police officer, who died separately of a supposedly self-inflicted gunshot wound; an RTC investigator who had inquired about Madison and who leapt to his death; and the death by gunshot (not suicide) of the private security chief for Clinton's Little Rock campaign headquarters, who had investigated Clinton in the 1980s.

In addition, an attorney and next-apartment neighbor of Gennifer Flowers was beaten so badly that his spleen had to be removed. And three attempts were made on the life of Dennis Patrick, in whose name tens of millions of dollars in bonds were traded by the Lasater organization.

FBI agents assigned to the Whitewater case were seeking to interrogate him.

(The British publication *The Economist* has published stories on this, but I'll leave that to others more conspiratorially inclined. Whitewater itself has enough elements of political chicanery to keep anyone busy.)

Failure of Security

To return to Foster's suicide, it's painfully apparent that there was no security at his White House office that night, either through oversight or on purpose. Three people are believed to have entered the room in the evening sometime after 10 P.M., with full access to the sensitive papers of the President, Hillary, and Whitewater.

One of those who breached what should have been an isolated area was Bernard Nussbaum, the President's counsel and Foster's boss.

The other two were allegedly Patsy Thomasson, once Dan Lasater's right hand who ran his company while he was in jail, and is now in charge of White House administration. Ms. Thomasson declined to comment on press speculation that she tried to open Foster's safe that night. The other participant in the nocturnal confab was Margaret Williams, Hillary's chief of staff. (Did you know that spouses have taxpayer-paid chiefs of staff, with a salary in the range of $100,000 or more?)

The trio, according to Nussbaum, stayed there only ten minutes and did not destroy anything or take any papers, but the Park Police believe they were in there longer. When they left, Foster's office was unlocked. The next morning, Foster's secretary came in and cleaned up, and it wasn't until mid-morning that the Secret Service officially sealed the room.

Not until the second day after Foster's suicide was there an official investigation of the office. On July 22, thirteen people, including representatives of the FBI, the Justice Department, and the National Park Police, jammed into the small room to watch the strangest procedure.

Nussbaum so dominated the scene one would think that he, not the federal agents, was in charge. Nussbaum insisted that his own White House attorneys be present when staff witnesses were interrogated, a sure way of keeping people from talking frankly.

The feisty lawyer also reportedly screened every piece of paper before letting the police see them. Nussbaum wouldn't let the police examine certain papers at all and wouldn't relinquish others. He carefully separated the papers out and gave the "official" papers to the FBI. Foster's personal papers were sent to his attorney, and according to the White House, certain papers involving the Clintons were supposedly handed over to David Kendall, the First Family's personal lawyer.

(I say "supposedly" because the White House has changed their story about the papers three times, and not until a year later did the truth come out.)

One investigator reportedly said that he saw Nussbaum open Foster's briefcase, look in quickly, then close it. But Nussbaum has denied that.

The White House said the papers had been sent to the appropriate places, but conveniently omitted mentioning that those supposedly given by Nussbaum to Kendall included Whitewater files.

In December 1993, the White House finally admitted they had Whitewater papers, and that they were being turned over to the Department of Justice. In April, 1994, Hillary Clinton was asked at a White House news conference if Margaret Williams, her chief of staff, was one of those who had removed documents from Foster's office. She said she "didn't think so," that it was Mr. Nussbaum who had done so.

The truth finally came out on August 2, 1994, when the White House confessed that it had given a misleading account all this time. Dee Dee Myers, the press secretary, when questioned, admitted that Mr. Nussbaum had not given the papers to David Kendall as they had first said.

What, then, happened to the Whitewater papers?

Nussbaum had given them to Margaret Williams, who quickly called Hillary Clinton in Little Rock, who told her to put them in the safe in the family quarters on the third floor of the White House, where they sat for five days before being given over to Mr. Kendall.

The White House explanation was tragically underwhelming, one of many such instances involving Whitewater.

"I think in hindsight we should have been more clear about exactly what the chain of custody on those documents was, and I think that was a mistake," the White House press secretary confessed.

Unknown File

The FBI agents and police who searched the office had no knowledge that Foster had even kept a Whitewater file. It was not mentioned on an inventory of items that Nussbaum had given them. Nor was there any mention of a Foster diary in which the Arkansan had made observations, including some about the 1992 campaigns and the cost of overruns in decorating the White House, and surely many other items. The diary had also been scooped up and sent to James Hamilton, the Foster family lawyer.

Apparently awed by the White House environment, the National Park Police, who were in charge, permitted this peculiar behavior. But months later they issued an official report which described Nussbaum's activities, and which some observers believe showed that he had "impeded" their investigation.

Mr. Fiske went to Federal Court and received authority to keep the Park Police report secret. *The Wall Street Journal* has sued the Justice Department for its release, thus far without results.

A search was made for any possible suicide note. Then, abracadabra, a White House aide suddenly discovered it six days after the suicide, torn up into twenty-seven pieces. It had been in the folds of Foster's briefcase all the time and was reconstituted, except for a corner that probably contained a signature— or some now-missing mysterious notation. Foster's note lamented that he was not meant for "the spotlight of public life in Washington," a city he hated.

Again, someone held up the evidence for thirty additional hours until the President and others could see it before it was turned over to the police.

Criminal Referral

Within a few months the anxiety over Foster's suicide subsided. The hope at the White House was that Whitewater would go away. But it did not. It was only to be replaced by a new Whitewater alert, what the Clintons feared the most.

The first "criminal referral" on Madison and Whitewater seemed to have been quashed, but now news arrived that the persistent investigator L. Jean Lewis had prepared a second group of nine criminal referrals related to Madison-Whitewater. Contents of one of them hit the Washington brass in the political breadbasket.

The first word of this came secretly to the White House on September 29, 1993, from Jean E. Hanson, General Counsel of the Treasury Department, which oversees the RTC. Former Senior Vice President of the RTC, William Roelle, who received the information from the Kansas City office a few days before, then relayed it to Ms. Hanson at the request of Roger Altman, acting chief of the RTC. Roelle reportedly told Ms. Hansen not to share her information on the criminal referrals with *anyone*.

In a meeting at the White House, Ms. Hanson alerted Bernard Nussbaum that within a few days a criminal referral involving Madison Guaranty would be sent to the Justice Department. Most important, the President and Mrs. Clinton would be named as "possible witnesses" to the alleged criminal acts. A previous referral may have named them as "possible beneficiaries" as well.

On September 30, 1993, Ms. Hanson wrote a memo to Roger C. Altman, acting chief of the RTC and deputy secretary of Treasury.

"I have spoken with the Secretary [Lloyd Bentsen of Treasury] and also with Bernie Nussbaum and Cliff Sloan. I have asked Bill Roelle to keep me informed. Is there anything else you think we should be doing?"

That was quite enough. Nussbaum, the President's counsel, was a direct pipeline to the President and Mrs. Clinton, who quickly learned the details of the referral. (At a press conference in March 1994, Mr. Clinton—who had avoided the subject—acknowledged that he had been told about the criminal referral by senior aide Bruce Lindsey in early October, before it had been sent to Justice.)

RTC investigations are supposed to be privileged and nonpublic but word of the twenty-one page referral mentioning the Clintons spread rapidly, like a Japanese tsunami wave.

The referral reportedly suggested that certain monies from Madison had been used to pay off Governor Clinton's $50,000 personal campaign debt in 1984 and that at least $70,000 had flowed secretly from Madison into Whitewater.

Anxious White House

The executive branch went into a frenzy of anxiety and action. By October 8, 1993, when the referral was sent to Justice, top officials at the White House and Treasury were scurrying about and secretly conferring.

On October 14 a strategy meeting was held in Bernard Nussbaum's office in the White House. Attending were key players from both the President's staff and the Department of the Treasury. From the White House there was Nussbaum; Bruce Lindsey; Mark D. Gearan, White House director of communications; and Clifford Sloan and Neil Eggleston, White House attorneys. From Treasury were Ms. Hanson; Joshua L. Steiner, Lloyd Bentsen's chief of staff; and Jack DeVore, the Treasury press secretary.

Whitewater, which had been pleasantly dormant, was coming back with an unpleasant vengeance.

The networking (Fiske had since recorded at least twenty contacts) was between Treasury and the White House. All were in conflict of interest because non-investigatory or non-law enforcement departments other than the RTC were now privy to, and could influence, a potential criminal investigation, a definite federal no-no.

It was during those weeks that someone in the government decided that the next step in the cover-up was to block the investigation by getting Jean Lewis off the case. That happened in early November, when her boss, L. Richard Iorio, in the Kansas City RTC office was "ordered" to do it without being given any reason, according to Jean Lewis's attorney. (It takes little imagination to understand why.)

The move may have temporarily relieved White House angst, but it only triggered more news coverage. On the first day of November 1993, newspapers got word of Jean Lewis's new criminal referrals. They printed the leaked stories, followed by word that Lewis had been rudely yanked off the Whitewater case by someone, possibly even by a frightened White House.

The fourth-rate real estate deal was now back strongly in public view. There was the added drama of "criminal referrals," the possible involvement of the First Couple, and the feeling that a high-level cover-up was definitely in the works.

Missing Files

Media and public interest started to build. Now speculation mounted that Foster's personal papers, including the

Whitewater file, had been taken out of his office the night of his death. In December 1993 —five months after the suicide—someone tipped the Justice Department about the missing files. The administration waffled in its response, commenting only that "all the files in Vince Foster's office were properly handled."

When pressed again, the White House relented. Yes, papers had been taken from Foster's office that did not appear on the inventory. They were now in the hands of the respective personal attorneys. Those related to Whitewater were in the possession of David Kendall, the First Family's lawyer.

And, said the White House, with confidence, *they would not be released.* Insisting on her zone of privacy, Hillary claimed they were the private property of the Clintons and nobody else's business.

Just as in every stage of Whitewater, Hillary's insistence on secrecy only triggered more public interest and antagonism, raising still more doubts about Whitewater. Through her take-no-prisoners legal attitude, Hillary was becoming an anti–public relations committee of one.

Within days of the announcement of the secret papers, a tug-of-war began to keep the Whitewater file from being released to the press. The Justice Department, reacted to the national uproar by appointing three career prosecutors— one of whom had originally been named by Bush—to look into Whitewater. A grand jury was convened at the federal district court in Washington.

(By this time, of course, the Whitewater papers might be missing even more than the metaphorical Nixon "eighteen minutes of tape.")

The press and several members of Congress called for release of the papers. Why wasn't the White House showing them? There must be something in them the Clintons didn't want the public to know. But the Clintons resisted the calls and came up with a winning scheme— one that has been keenly successful in outwitting the public, the press, and Congress.

Moved to Action

As soon as a freedom of information request was filed on December 23, 1993, for the Whitewater papers, the White House plan went into action. On Janet Reno's orders, the Justice Department announced that the grand jury would "subpoena" the files. That way, the Whitewater papers, including Foster's file and those returned by Susan McDougal, would be *sealed and placed in official custody*, whatever "official" really meant in this case.

The Justice Department of Janet Reno was, after all, the Justice Department of Bill Clinton, the real boss, along with Hillary. And most important, under that arrangement, anyone who released the papers to the press could be prosecuted!

So clever was the plan that the Clintons' attorney David Kendall reportedly asked Justice to broaden its demand for Whitewater papers so that virtually everything Bill and Hillary owned on the subject could be sequestered from the press's prying eyes.

It worked. The subpoena was served on Christmas Eve, and by January 10, 1994, all the papers were sealed and delivered to the grand jury. The time, says the White House, was used for "cataloging." The First Family now rested easier in the Family Quarters.

But it was a temporary lull, once again. The critics, aroused by the news, were calling for congressional hearings and for an independent investigator to look into all Whitewater-related matters, posthaste.

The calls fell on deaf White House and Democratic congressional ears. But there was a groundswell forming. Even such distinguished liberal sources as the *New York Times* pitched in. In an editorial called "Open Up on Madison Guaranty," the paper added its voice to the protest, along with a call for a special investigator.

Said the *Times*: "This is a man [Clinton] who rode into Washington on a pledge to end politics as usual and every time the White House dodges inquiries about the old days in Arkansas, reasonable people begin to wonder about a cover-up and Mr. Clinton's sincerity. The matter clearly needs ventilating."

The call was joined by some Democrats who were more secure than the White House. Senators Pat Moynihan of New York and Bill Bradley of New Jersey broke with their bunker-mentality colleagues by agreeing that a federal investigation was necessary. That seemed to do it. In early January 1994 the President announced his agreement. The Justice Department would name a "Special Counsel" for all matters Whitewater.

Not the Same Thing
Here it's important to understand the difference between a Special Counsel and an Independent Counsel. Up until 1992, there had been an Independent Counsel law, which *separated* the counsel from political influence and made him truly independent. He was chosen by a group of three

federal judges, who in turn were named by the Chief Justice of the Supreme Court, and was answerable only to the American people.

But that law had expired in 1992, and now the Special Counsel would have to be named by the President through his attorney general, Janet Reno. So basically the President would be investigating himself— except, of course, for the integrity of the man named.

Janet Reno understood that clearly. In fact, when she was stonewalling the request for a Special Counsel, she said that if she appointed the counsel under the present law, "no one would believe he was truly independent."

But the counsel was named anyway. The choice was Robert B. Fiske, Jr., a Wall Street lawyer and a registered Republican. After an appointment by Gerald Ford as U.S. attorney in New York, Fiske served for four years as a Carter administration attorney until Reagan was elected, when he left the job. Conservative Republicans considered him too liberal, and when he was nominated as Deputy U.S. Attorney by President Bush, Republicans in the Senate blocked his appointment.

A former law partner of Lawrence Walsh, Iran-Contra prosecutor, he had also been chief of the Bar Association screening committee when it blocked several Supreme Court nominations made by Reagan. But he did have a strong reputation for integrity.

Fiske was no stranger to some people at the White House. In fact, he and Bernard Nussbaum had worked together before and Nussbaum had previously recommended Fiske for a job with the Iran-Contra investigation staff.

Reno labeled Fiske an "Independent Counsel," and he adopted the name, although it is a misnomer. He should have been referred to only as a "Special Counsel." He worked for Janet Reno and President Clinton and could have been fired by them on a second's notice. He definitely was not "independent."

(On June 30, 1994, the truly Independent Counsel law was reenacted by Congress, and a new Independent Counsel was chosen in August.)

In the White House, before they caved in, the toughest holdout against a Special Counsel was Hillary Clinton, who, according to Roger Altman, was near-paranoid about such an appointment.

In his "scrapbook," as he called it, Roger Altman wrote about Hillary's reaction to the naming of the investigator. "On Whitewater," he wrote, "Maggie [Margaret Williams, Hillary's chief of staff] told me that HRC was 'paralyzed' by it. If we don't solve this 'within the next two days' you don't have to worry about her schedule on health care."

Altman also wrote that Mrs. Clinton did not want any Special Counsel "poking into twenty years of public life in Arkansas" and that the White House was trying to negotiate limits on the scope of his investigation.

Temporary Gain

Hillary warned everyone in the inner circle that in the short term it was the best balm—by temporarily pushing Whitewater news off the pages and heading off *full* congressional hearings, which the administration desperately feared. But Hillary prophesized that in the long run the Special Counsel was the worst possible remedy.

On January 20, 1994, Fiske took the oath and promised
to find and prosecute "any individuals or entities" who had
broken the law regarding Whitewater.

It's important here to understand that Fiske's assignment, as specified by Janet Reno, involved only law-
breaking. Or as his orders from Reno read, to prosecute
those who "have committed a violation of any federal
criminal or civil law relating in any way to President
William Jefferson Clinton's or Mrs. Hillary Rodham Clinton's relationships with (1) Madison Guaranty Savings
and Loan Association, (2) Whitewater Development Corporation, or (3) Capital-Management Services [Hale's
company]."

His orders from Justice also added: "or any obstruction of the due administration of justice, or any
material false testimony or statement in violation of
federal law."

Note carefully that Fiske was not empowered to root
out any deal making, impropriety, cover-up, conflict of interest, undue influence, immoral behavior, hanky-panky
or simply lying, or any other actions by the Clintons and
their administration appointees that would degrade the
democratic process, which is at the true root of the Whitewater fiasco.

February 2, 1994, just two weeks after Fiske's appointment, was an important date in the cover-up. On that day,
three meetings were held, all of which backfired.

In Washington, at exactly 8:00 A.M., there was a crisis
meeting on Whitewater on the Hill—in Speaker Foley's
office. Present were all the top House chairmen who
might become involved in the subject. Foley's aide read

them the riot act, and each pledged that they would not
hold hearings on Whitewater *under any circumstances*.
They would hold the line.

That same day, in Kansas City, RTC investigator Jean
Lewis, who was handling the Madison-Whitewater criminal referral, was being visited by the emissary from Washington, who told her that the "people at the top" would be
"happy" if her report showed that Whitewater did not
cause any loss of money to Madison Guaranty—and thus
to the taxpayers.

At the White House that same morning, acting RTC
chief Roger Altman held a meeting with top staffers on the
Madison-Whitewater affair, what is known in the trade as a
"heads up," Beltwayese for a "briefing."

Present were Bernie Nussbaum; Harold M. Ickes, the
deputy chief of staff; Mr. Neil Eggleston, one of the White
House attorneys; and Margaret Williams, Hillary's chief of
staff. Known as Hillary's alter ego, Williams was probably
the most important person in the room.

Liable for Losses

The first subject on the agenda was the statute of limitations on civil suits by the RTC against anyone liable for
losses from a failed S&L. In this case, the concern was the
failed Madison Guaranty and the Clintons. Since the First
Family had considerable wealth and might have benefited
from Madison's lost deposits, they could be subject to such
an action— if the RTC decided to move on it.

The key question was how long the President and Mrs.
Clinton might legally be in jeopardy on the *civil* side of
Whitewater. The cut-off date, Altman told the group, was

February 28th, 1994, just twenty-six days from then. If no action were taken by that time, and if the statute was not extended, the Clintons would be home free. That, of course, had nothing to do with the criminal referrals, on which they were listed as "possible witnesses," and reportedly "possible beneficiaries" as well.

As acting head of the RTC, Altman was in a position to determine the fate of his good friends. Suddenly, he had been thrust into the Whitewater game, a position he did not invite or enjoy. A millionaire Wall Street investment banker, Altman is a close friend and former classmate of Bill Clinton's from Georgetown back in the 1960s. His position in the RTC was key because he was politically trusted by both the President and Hillary.

He might—in a real crunch—be called upon to throw his weight on their side in case of a civil suit. But as a personal friend of theirs, was it ethical, he pondered, to remain in the fateful game at all?

Or should he "recuse" himself from the entire Whitewater matter?

(Recusal is another piece of Washington jargon designed to keep ordinary citizens at arm's length from the political discourse. In English, it just means to "excuse" yourself from a responsibility.)

Altman's Debate
What to do?

Virtually everyone, including Jean Hanson, advised him to get out, fast. There was only pain and no gain in staying.

On the other hand, if he did recuse himself and things

looked bad for the Clintons, he'd be leaving the decision *totally* in the hands of career RTC people. He had told the White House that he would leave the decision to the professionals anyway, but they wanted—needed—Altman as an insurance policy.

Without Altman, the White House was afraid that too much power would transfer to Ellen Kulka, the chief counsel of RTC who Bernie Nussbaum considered a "tough" lady. As it turns out, Nussbaum and Kulka had been opposing lawyers in an S&L case, and he considered her a formidable opponent.

Suddenly, on February 11, 1994, in a big surprise, the odds changed for the Clintons, both good and bad. The statute on the Madison case was extended by Congress through 1995, and the President signed it. They were no longer open to a quick lawsuit, nor would they have to sign a "tolling agreement," in which they voluntarily extend the time limit—the publicity fall-out of which would be unpleasant. They now had breathing room, but maybe too much. The RTC also had plenty of time to make up its mind.

During that February 2 meeting, Altman told the White House staff that he was recusing himself—that he was walking away from Madison-Whitewater altogether. They were shocked. The staff knew that the Clintons were of a far different mind on the subject. They talked and talked, and Altman finally agreed to sleep on it.

He surely spent a fitful night. The very next morning, February 3, 1994, he anxiously called Harold Ickes. (Margaret Williams remembers that he called her.) Altman wanted a quick meeting at the White House. Could he get some people together?

Loyal Soldier

Moments later, he was at 1600 Pennsylvania Avenue
telling them the good news. He had changed his mind and
was *not* going to recuse himself. Loyalty to Bill and Hillary
had won out over self-preservation. He would play good
soldier for the administration.

Altman was still in charge of the RTC (his term was
up March 30, 1994), but he was busy getting ready for a
regular Senate Banking Committee review of the agency
on February 24. He, Jean Hanson, and others went into a
lengthy rehearsal, drawing up "talking points," one of
which was a discussion of the recusal question—why he
had decided to stay on the Madison-Whitewater case despite his friendship with the Clintons.

But when the hearing took place, Altman struck out. He
was never asked a question on recusal and he didn't volun-
teer any information. When Senator Gramm asked if he, or
his staff, had any contact with the White House on the
Whitewater matter, he blithely answered: "Just one substantive contact," thinking only of the February 2 White House
meeting.

(That one line was to become the catastrophic point in
Altman's public life, which has now ceased to be.)

Sitting in the Senate hearing room was Neil Eggleston,
a White House counsel, who flipped when he heard Altman's answer. He ran out of the room and, with his cellular
phone, instantly called the White House, alerting them to
Altman's great error. Altman had not told the Senate the full
truth, a cardinal White House worry ever since the days of
Oliver North.

White House staffers quickly convened, and turned

the problem over to John Podesta, the executive secretary, who called Altman to straighten him out. Podesta reminded the Deputy Secretary of Treasury that he knew of
more than one meeting. In fact there were several contacts on Whitewater-Madison. He had also forgotten to
tell the senators that he had discussed the recusal issue
with the White House. Altman had a "legal duty" to correct his testimony with the committee, post haste,
Podesta said.

The next day the situation worsened. Altman received a phone call from Howell Raines, editorial page
editor of the *New York Times*, who informed him that
he was being slammed, strongly, the next day in an editorial on his February 24th Senate testimony. Right on
the phone, all the indecision, all the back and forth, vanished. There and then, Altman recused himself from all
things Whitewater.

A little at a time, he started to fill in the Senate Banking
Committee about his incomplete testimony—with a series of
letters, each miserly in their admissions, and slow in forthcoming. There was one on March 2, another on March 3, another on March 11, and the fourth on March 21.

He *thought* he was filling in the record, but it was all to
come back to haunt him, as we shall see.

Lawyerly Comment
While Altman was still in the shadows of the cover-up,
Bernie Nussbaum was taking the heat from some of the ear-
liest revelations. Word had leaked out about the removal of
the Foster–Whitewater papers from the office the night of
the suicide. When asked why he hadn't revealed that, Nuss-

baum reportedly answered with lawyerly confidence: "No one had asked for them."

(In the whole story of the Clintons' dodging and obfuscation, lawyerly manner and phraseology—learned well by the Clintons at Yale Law School—dominate the scene. At the time, no one outside the White House knew about the Whitewater papers being spirited away to a private White House safe.)

On March 3, one of the stalwarts of the administration, seventy-three-year-old Lloyd Bentsen, Texas millionaire and former senator from Texas, was ostensibly shocked by the news of the Treasury–White House cover-ups. He made a public statement.

"I did not attend any of these meetings, nor was I informed of any of these meetings."

If Jean Hanson's memo of September 30, 1994, is accurate, then Bentsen was not telling the truth. In addition to the memo, Ms. Hanson told congressional investigators that in early February she had briefed both Mr. Altman and Mr. Bentsen about the meetings.

Treasury chief counsel Jean Hanson is shaping up as a key to this part of the Whitewater story. Roger Altman, in his various statements, once claimed he was not aware of her meeting at the White House last fall. Actually, Ms. Hanson has told congressional investigators, it was Altman who *instructed* her to brief the White House!

Ms. Hansen has reportedly also told investigators that she urged Mr. Bentsen to go before Congress in March and admit that he knew White House officials had been briefed by Treasury on the Whitewater criminal referral. But he rejected the suggestion.

Bentsen's aides have denied the charge, and Mr. Bentsen has told Congress that he knew nothing about the briefings conducted by his two subordinates.

An ironic touch is that Mr. Bentsen is *chairman of the oversight committee of the RTC*, empowered to see that the agency's activities are ethical and lawful.

Obfuscation and stonewalling became the order of the day. At an earlier hearing in the House, Representative Toby Roth of Wisconsin asked one witness, Emil A. Ludwig, comptroller of the currency, the man who regulates banks, if he had any conversations about Whitewater. Roth was immediately ruled out of order, and he answered with the charge of "stonewalling."

Roth was right. The truth came out in the summer of 1994, prior to the Whitewater hearings. Mr. Ludwig revealed that on the New Year's weekend, President Clinton approached and asked him—an old friend from Yale Law and now the nation's top banking regulator—to provide legal advice on Whitewater and its ties to Madison Guaranty.

But after first inquiring about receiving Whitewater background from a White House counsel, the comptroller wisely begged off, saying that in his circumstances such advice would be "inappropriate."

The Rule Book

Ludwig apparently knows more about acting correctly in public office than does the President. A *New York Times* editorial, found Clinton's behavior with Ludwig "embarrassing" and "disturbing," then commented: "As a lawyer who has spent his life in politics, Mr. Clinton cannot claim ignorance of the commonsense rules that apply to conflict of interest at all levels of government. This is sloppy behavior and a dangerous example in an administration that wants to throw away the rule book."

Meanwhile as Whitewater gained center stage, the pressure was now building against presidential counsel Bernard Nussbaum for his part in the Treasury–White House talks and his role in Foster's Whitewater papers. And besides, somebody had to go. On March 5, after showing himself to be politically tone-deaf, Nussbaum resigned to return to his hardship job as a $1.5-million-a-year corporate lawyer in New York. His sin? He used his sharp lawyerly skills on behalf of his bosses, Bill and Hillary.

He was replaced by seventy-six-year-old Lloyd Cutler, a former Carter counsel noted for his old fox ways in maneuvering through the Beltway forest.

The day before the Nussbaum resignation something took place that was equally historic in the Whitewater story. In what looked like a touch of legal bravado, Fiske subpoenaed ten members of the White House and Treasury staffs, everyone from Bernard Nussbaum to George Stephanopoulos. The object—supposedly to flush out any cover-up. The legal concept was "obstruction of justice," Section 1505 of Title 18 of the U.S. Code.

Each of the "Gang of Ten," as they were quickly labeled, then hired lawyers and trekked into the federal district courthouse in Washington, followed by television cameras and newsmen, all making headlines—as if something were really happening. As we'll see, it was an exercise in legal futility.

White House Hardball

One of the ten, George Stephanopoulos, senior aide to Clinton and boy genius of the winning 1992 campaign, had just played typical Clinton White House hardball, which was one reason why he was subpoenaed.

He had learned that Jay B. Stephens, formerly the Republican-appointed U.S. attorney for the District of Columbia, who had been handling the Rostenkowski investigation before he was canned by Janet Reno (as were ninety-eight other Republican-appointed U.S. attorneys in an unprecedented one-day massacre), had just been hired by the RTC—an independent agency—to work on the civil fraud side of the Madison Guaranty investigation.

Young George, who has the office next to the President, went ballistic. Immediately he was on the phone to Josh Steiner, chief of staff of Treasury Secretary Bentsen, barking out his anger in unseemly tones, even with a touch of vulgarity. Stephanopoulos feared that the Republican could cause trouble somewhere down the line. Steiner took copious notes of the phone conversation.

Steiner wrote that Stephanopoulos wanted to "find a way to get rid of" Jay Stephens. Finally, Steiner "persuaded George that firing him would be incredibly stupid and improper."

Time magazine interviewed several White House people and put together the following enactment:

Stephanopoulos called Steiner and opened with a sophomoric caveat: "This conversation never happened," he said. After expressing his anger over the Stephens appointment, he asked, says *Time*: "How can we get rid of Stephens?"

Soon after, both Stephanopoulos and Deputy Chief-of-Staff Harold Ickes reportedly called Roger Altman, and then, says the report, "Altman was almost immediately asked to help think of a way to fire Stephens."

Altman reportedly said he wouldn't be a party to such a scheme and later commented about the incident: "These guys are nuts."

But again, as we shall see, none of these shenanigans seemed to make any negative impression on the "Independent Counsel."

Hearings To Be Held

Fortunately, all this was not lost on Congress. The House voted 408 to 15 to discuss holding hearings on Whitewater, with a pledge not to grant anyone immunity in order to avoid the now-famous Oliver North problem.

Once again, the White House, working hand in Machiavellian glove with the congressional leadership, outfoxed the critics. Fiske was their key weapon. Now that the President had appointed him, he had to be allowed to work without interference. Therefore, since there was no immunity being granted, Congress could call only those witnesses whom Fiske had finished interrogating.

The Special Counsel informed the congressional leadership that if they wanted the first hearings to be held in July, 1994 as scheduled, they should not include anything about the Arkansas phase of the investigation—which made the leadership quite happy. Only witnesses involved in the attempted cover-up of Foster's suicide would be entertained. Fiske even needed more time to handle the disappearance of the Foster papers.

He promised to deliver the first part of his report prior to the hearings in late July.

Meanwhile, Fiske had fallen into a ready-made criminal case. It had been sitting, just waiting for his arrival, in Little Rock. In fact, he had inherited it from the local prosecutor—a Clinton appointee and former law student of his—who had failed to move it ahead, possibly because it was too politically explosive.

The case had begun in the fall of 1993, when the new U.S. Attorney, Paula Casey, had to deal with someone who represented the gravest potential threat to the President, Hillary, and Whitewater.

His name was Judge David Hale, and in September 1993 he was being indicted for swindling money from the Small Business Administration (SBA), as we've seen. The vehicle was his supposed minority-oriented SBIC (Small Business Investment Company), which gave away almost $1 million of taxpayer money to the Arkansas "political family" and lost over $3 million in SBA funds.

Hale had privately told the prosecutor's office that he had done business with Clinton. Not only was the Governor aware of the $300,000 loan to Susan McDougal, Hale said, but on more than one occasion Clinton had personally pressured him to make the loan. In addition, Hale claimed, $110,000 of the $300,000 had found its way into the Whitewater bank account.

Presidential Denial
The President has flatly denied that he ever spoke to Hale about this and has accused Hale of talking a

"bunch of bull." McDougal has likewise denied that the supposed meeting of the three—Clinton, McDougal, and Hale—at the Casa Grande, or anywhere else, ever took place.

But a witness at the pretrial hearings, a Louisiana businessman named Gayland Westbrook, testified that as far back as 1989 Hale boasted to him that Governor Clinton was actively involved in Hale's company, Capital-Management Services.

Early on, Hale and his lawyer, Randy Coleman, offered to cooperate with the U.S. attorney in Little Rock in exchange for a lessened plea. Hale even suggested that he act as an undercover agent, "wiring" himself so that he could record conversations with his unsuspecting colleagues, even the President.

Paula Casey must have found that a little frightening. She turned him down flat. Hale's trial, which normally would have come up in the spring of 1994, would have granted Hale's attorney the right to call witnesses and cross-examine others. Anything could emerge at such a trial, what with ten years of money and power exchanges in Arkansas to be exposed.

Negotiations began between Hale's attorney, Randy Coleman, and Paula Casey. In fact, the correspondence between them was actually printed in the *Wall Street Journal*. It was a definite nonmeeting of minds, and no deal was made.

Hale was indicted on September 21, 1993, on several felony counts, but by November the Justice Department in Washington had taken over the sensitive case. Because of her personal friendship with President Clinton, Casey was out, having exempted herself or having been taken off it, or both. Justice sent in a special prosecutor, but within weeks he had turned the case over to the new "Independent Counsel," Robert Fiske, who had set up shop in Little Rock.

Guilty Plea

A deal was soon cut between Hale and Fiske. On March 21, 1994, Hale pleaded guilty to just two counts of fraud, and awaits a jail sentence estimated to be forty-six months. Fiske said he was pleased because in addition to the information made public by Hale, there was more secret information coming—what Fiske called "other allegations he made during the time he cooperated with us"—perhaps more material about Hale's charge that then-Governor Clinton had pressured him into making a large loan that benefited the Clinton family. An aide to Fiske said the prosecutor believed that Hale had extensive knowledge of the Whitewater deal.

(In Arkansas, a retired state supreme court justice, Jim Johnson, a longtime friend of the Hale family, told me that "that boy Dave knows the whereabouts of every dollar of the Whitewater deal.")

What do we know of Hale's case? First off, his was the biggest of the "piggy banks" for the fancy bubbas. Congressman John L. LaFalce, Democrat of New York, asked the General Accounting Office to check up on Hale's Capital-Management organization.

Every literate American knows that the federal government's distribution of our tax money—whether to the poor through welfare or in subsidies to business—is mired in stupidity, extravagance, and fraud. That's what the GAO, in its understated style, says about this Small Business Administration operation, calling the SBA's oversight of Hale's company "clearly inadequate." The GAO said the agency failed to recognize "red flags," a failure that cost the American taxpayer $3.4 million in wasted money.

The cash went everywhere, it seems, but mainly to friends of Hale. The $300,000 loan went to Susan McDougal, even though she and her husband had a net worth of $2.2 million at the time and Hale's loans were supposedly designed for the "disadvantaged."

He gave a loan of $150,000 to the present governor of Arkansas, Jim Guy Tucker, himself a wealthy man, and another to Tucker's wife, on the grounds that she was a woman, and therefore eligible under the Small Business Administration definition of an "economically or socially disadvantaged individual."

(It's shocking that the government would be so nonsensical as to lend out money on the *sole* basis that the recipient was a woman.)

Sometimes, the friendship between Hale and Madison went the other way. During the heyday of 1985–1986 Hale *received* $825,000 in loans from Madison, much of which was returned to Madison in other loans that helped both companies "clean up" their books, as Hale put it.

Hale's value to the Whitewater investigation will have to wait until the new Independent Counsel delivers his Arkansas report, probably in 1995. Or until hearings are held in Congress on the *full* Whitewater scandal.

Presidential Press Conference

About the same time as the Hale indictment, President Clinton decided to make one of his periodic televised press conferences—this one to quiet the mounting disaffection with the obfuscation on Whitewater.

He used the forum to make still another change in his version of the tale. Backed by the Lyons report, written during the 1992 campaign, Clinton had originally said that they had lost $68,900 on the ill-fated real estate venture.

A correction, please, the President now told the press. (The White House term for that is "It's inoperative.")

He had forgotten, but a $22,000 loss he had attributed to Whitewater belonged in another column. It had come to him after ten or more years as he was reading the galleys of his mother's autobiography. That money, he now realized, had not been spent on Whitewater but on a log cabin for mother Kelley. The Whitewater loss was now down to $46,636.

The press looked up at the President and dutifully took notes. Some even believed it.

The whole question of money lost (or made) by the Clintons would require an army of statisticians. The finances of the Clintons, at least when they involve Whitewater or their taxes, are a statistical nightmare. Numbers change routinely, and it all seems too complex for interpretation. The real loss, or gain, on Whitewater by the Clintons is still not accurately known, but we should at least try to divine it.

Probing The Money

Congressman Leach, ranking minority leader on the House Banking Committee, has his own view on this—which is that the Clintons *made*, rather than lost, money on White-water.

On March 24, 1994, Leach intended to question several witnesses at a previously arranged Whitewater minihearing. But when Chairman Henry Gonzalez heard the identity of the witnesses (Jean Lewis, for one), he canceled it. Instead, Leach made a long speech on the floor of the House and then issued a series of papers on Whitewater.

On the question of money, he made the following summary: The Clintons *made* money off Whitewater and lost nothing—surely not the $46,636 (amended) that they said.

"Even if the Clintons lost a small amount of money in the venture, which we adamantly do not believe they did," said Leach's staff memo, "they would have lost far more if federally insured deposits weren't transferred into Whitewater. No average citizen could have had potential losses so handily covered."

Leach's accounting of the Clintons' gains include:

1. $8,000 in real dollar gain from the interest deductions on Whitewater loans taken on their tax returns.
2. $20,000 in capital gains on the sale of Lot 13 and the model house, figured from a $28,000 sale and an $8,000 purchase.
3. $500 capital gain in the $1,000 sale of their White-water share to McDougal in December 1992 handled by Vincent Foster.
4. $35,000 (or more), which is the Clinton's share of infusions of capital that Madison Guaranty and its affiliated companies put into Whitewater, which

had the direct effect of reducing the Clintons' losses or out-of-pocket requirements. The $35,000 is figured by taking one-half of the $70,000 Jean Lewis estimates was diverted from Madison to Whitewater in just one six-month window. A two-year spread, says Ms. Lewis, would raise the Clinton half share to over $50,000.

5. $55,000, which is the Clintons' share of the $110,000 of Hale's $300,000 loan to Susan McDougal, which reportedly went into the Whitewater account to buy the International Paper land outside Little Rock.

6. Payments of $9,200 by Whitewater to reduce the principal of Hillary's Bank of Kingston loan and $4,811 and $7,322 in direct payments by Whitewa-ter on the Clintons' subsequent Security Bank of Paragould note in 1984 and 1985—a total of $21,333 related to Lot 13 that should be income to the Clintons.

(Leach had also included $26,000 for Madison's retainer to Rose, but we've omitted that.)

Using his figures, we come up with a gross gain to the Clintons from Whitewater of $139,833. Deducted from that is the Clinton claim of $46,636 in losses, leaving a *net gain of $93,193!*

The Associated Press took exception to Leach's $20,000 capital gains on Lot 13 and quoted a Mississippi real estate expert who believes that the Clinton figures on that are correct.

Baffling Transaction

That transaction, in which Hillary sold the land twice, is baffling to many experts. *If* the Clintons' capital gains figure of only $1,640 is correct, says one CPA, the Clintons did receive—as personal income—the $21,333 in payments by Whitewater to the banks holding the Clintons' loans for Lot 13. In any case, the profit on Lot 13 was at least $20,000, one way or another.

Giving the Clintons the benefit of the fact that it might be figured twice (2 and 6), this reduces their *profit* to $73,193.

(People are confused by the Clintons' claim that they had to be honest on Whitewater because they lost money. That's not sensible, accountingwise. The corporate operation could be a giant bust, as it was, and still have individuals involved make money because funds were put into or taken out of the corporation for their benefit.)

None of Leach's figures includes the giant slush funds of $400,000 recently revealed by banker Maurice Smith that Clinton received in the form of personal loans. We know that $50,000 of it was borrowed for the 1984 campaign and legitimately recorded with the secretary of state. Another $100,000 was borrowed by the Clinton campaign committee, half of it just days before the 1990 election. But the remaining money is in limbo and might well be personal income to the Clintons, totally unreported.

Even the $50,000 loan, part of which might have been paid back directly by Madison, may have tax ramifications. Some of it might be income for the Clintons, says Leach. If, as a result of the 1985 fund-raiser at the Madison Guaranty, funds that were not legitimate campaign contributions, were transferred to Clinton to pay off his loan, Madison could have a business deduction for that amount, now estimated at $12,000 (Duberstein v. Commissioner, 1960). But the Clintons could then be responsible for the same amount of personal income.

The whole question of the Clintons' taxes during this period is a swamp that would swallow up any rational person. *Money* magazine, though, has given it a try, dealing entirely with the tax forms as filed by the Clintons.

Giant Debt

They come up with a startling conclusion: *The First Couple may owe Uncle Sam as much as $99,858*, not counting Leach's points ($73,193) or the $250,000 in lobbying and unreported election campaign funds still in limbo.

In April 1993 *Money* examined their returns for the years 1980–1992 and quibbled with their charitable contributions. The Clintons took $40 for used running shoes, $15 for used long johns and $80 for a pair of used brown shoes. On personal expenses, the magazine explains that in addition to his $35,000 salary as Governor, Clinton received an additional $70,000 a year: $19,000 for work-related costs and $51,000 for meals and entertainment in the mansion.

Money quibbled here with a lot of items, including deductions for printing, travel, advertising and others. They also cut his car deduction and, most important, questioned the validity of several interest payments to McDougal and banks as being technically improper. All told, playing nasty, *Money* figures the Clintons owed $45,000 in bank taxes and interest.

Then, in November 1993, after the Clintons released their 1978–1979 tax forms (which had been held back because they didn't want anyone to see Hillary's enormous commodity gains), *Money* went back to work and raised the ante to a possible $99,858.

Of course, that's still penny ante to the Clintons, or at least to HRC, a millionaire lady who, with her husband, has a net worth of up to $1,620,000, according to the formal disclosure (Form SF 278) filed on May 16, 1994. It is a document of dozens of pages, with an impressive list of seventy-four assets, ranging from cash (up to $250,000), bonds, stocks, and a hedge fund now in a blind trust managed by Essex Investment Management in Boston.

Its portfolio for private investors, GAM Boston, according to *Money*, has an impressive record of a 214 percent gain over five years.

The Clinton fortune started with the amazing, not-according-to-Hoyle $99,000 profit from cattle futures that started Hillary on her financial road upwards, fueled by the excellent income from her part-time work at Rose Law Firm from 1977 to 1992, plus her directorships, all the rewards of political fame.

Rose Law Firm
During the last seventeen years, Rose has played an important role in the life of both Clintons, and it continued to do so during this crucial "Whitewater" spring of 1994. In fact, news about the Rose Law Firm itself kept popping up periodically.

One reason was the behavior of its former partners, who had become leading White House players. Some Arkansans, like Bruce Lindsey, the President's senior adviser, who was not a Rose man, escaped damage. But of the other four Arkansan males—Webb Hubbell, Vincent Foster, William Kennedy, and David Watkins—three were from Rose and none of the four would be left in power in the White House by May 1994.

Foster, of course, committed suicide in 1993. Hubbell, arguably the real boss of the Justice Department and Bill Clinton's favorite golfing partner, resigned in March 1994. Paradoxically, he was pushed out as a result of a complaint from Rose, his former firm, which was tired of the negative national attention.

According to the *Washington Post*, Rose was now investigating whether Hubbell had given favorable billing to relatives such as his father-in-law, Seth Ward, and whether he had overbilled the RTC, which was looking into Rose itself for conflict of interest.

Hubbell stoutly defended himself as innocent and was supported by Janet Reno and Bill Clinton. But he resigned to return to Little Rock to defend his name.

Just a week later, in March 1994, another former Rose partner in the higher echelons of the Clinton White House, William H. Kennedy III, was in trouble in the now-historic Nannygate department. Kennedy had paid his nanny's Social Security for 1992 with a check imprinted with his wife's former married name. But he had not paid his nanny tax for 1991 at all. Ironically, Kennedy had been in charge of background ethics checks for White House personnel. He paid the 1991 taxes but was taken off that job, and given an anonymous position.

The *Washington Post* commented: "This from the fellow who was in charge of judging whether other would-be jobholders have acceptable backgrounds for government service. . . ."

Of the "Famous Four" that once ran Rose, only

Hillary, the one with the best connections to the President, was left in power.

The Golf Game

The fourth Arkansan in trouble, David Watkins, a key White House administrator and also a player in Travelgate, had a grateful patron in Hillary Clinton, for whom he had turned $2,000 into $47,000 in the cellular phone coup. But he ran into a media buzz when he used one of the President's Marine heliocopters to take friends to a Maryland golf course. He claimed he was scouting the area for a future presidential golf trip, but the President was under pressure to fire him and did.

The White House still had a few Arkansans—notably Bruce Lindsey and Patsy Thomasson—left at the top, but it was beginning to show an alien face, which might actually be a happy accident for the Clintons.

The Rose Firm, spotlighted by Hillary's ascendancy, has been under investigation. Because of Rose's charges that Hubbell overbilled the RTC, that agency sent auditors to Rose to examine the $1.27 million in fees the firm has earned handling RTC cases. The results of that probe are not yet known.

Just a month before, in February 1994, Rose was investigated for conflict of interest. That went back to 1985, when the firm represented Madison before Arkansas S&L regulator Beverly Bassett and then, in a clever turnaround, represented the government (FDIC) in a lawsuit against Madison's accountants. In that $20 million suit, the government paid a large legal fee and recovered very little in an out-of-court settlement.

The question was whether Rose had disclosed its prior representation of Madison Guaranty. In February 1994 the FDIC cleared Rose of conflict of interest, offering the peculiar suggestion that Rose's disclosure of its earlier defense of Madison "may not be required."

(The clearance was given by FDIC's legal division, which had hired Rose in the first place.)

Claim of Whitewash

That didn't sit well with members of the Senate Banking Committee, especially Alfonse D'Amato of New York, who charged that it was a "whitewash." The evidence was an RTC report, which surprisingly revealed that "interviews of current and former Rose firm attorneys who may be knowledgeable on this subject were not conducted."

The acting FDIC chief, Andrew C. Hove, quickly agreed to reinvestigate and has turned the case over to the inspector general of the agency.

Rose continued to be in the public spotlight. In early March 1994, as Fiske paraded witnesses before the grand jury in Little Rock, a young courier for Rose testified that he had shredded several boxes of files marked with the initials VWF—Vincent W. Foster—at just about the time when Mr. Fiske was named as Special Counsel. The firm denies that any significant papers were shredded, except on a routine basis.

In any case, those who know the Little Rock scene are convinced that Rose's part in the Whitewater drama is far from over.

That spring of 1994 was a busy time for the intrigue of Whitewater and its tributaries. During the period, se-

crets, controversies, and subpoenas filled the Beltway air
as the "fourth-rate real estate venture" began to grasp the
attention of millions of Americans who now saw it as a
metaphor for an injured democracy.

The public anxiously awaited both the congressional
hearings and the report of Special Counsel Fiske or "Independent Counsel," as he preferred to call himself, which
might shed some light on this frustrating episode in presidential politics.

They didn't have long to wait.

Chapter Twelve

Whitewater Whitewash
The Hearings and the
Independent Counsel

The Fiske report was a grand disappointment.

No one expected it to be the end-all of Whitewater revelations. In fact, it was designed to cover only two aspects of the enormous story: the improper contacts, or "cover-up," between the Treasury Department and the White House and Vince Foster's suicide.

The rest would have to wait. The report was delivered on June 30, 1994, to great expectations, all of which were soon dashed. Not only wasn't it the end-all, it left some stunned by its seeming vapidness. On the suicide, Fiske concluded that the Deputy White House Counsel did indeed kill himself. Little unexpected there.

But what was unexpected, as we've seen, was that the FBI findings opened a forensic can of worms, which were left festering—like much in the strange tale of Whitewater. That only stimulated more conspiracy theories, including one that even if it were a suicide, which most now accept, the body might have been moved to its National Park location *after the fact.*

Fiske also tried to determine if Foster's suicide was in any way related to Whitewater. Here, the hard-headed former U.S. Attorney disappointed many by amateurishly entering the world of Freudian speculation.

Was Whitewater, or Bill Clinton, or Hillary Clinton on Foster's mind when he pulled the trigger on July 20, 1993? Janet Reno —who obviously was interested in uncoupling the two events—had also given Fiske that assignment.

No Thought of Whitewater
Fiske had a sure answer. No, he says, the suicide and Whitewater were not connected. "We found no evidence," he stated in his bound blue report, "that issues involving Whitewater, Madison Guaranty, CMS [Hale's company: Capital-Management Services], or other personal legal matters of the President and Mrs. Clinton were a factor in Foster's suicide."

Really? That's quite a psychiatric limb to walk out on, especially since we know so little about suicidal motivation. What was his evidence? Simple, he tells us. Foster *did not talk* about problems relating to Whitewater or the Clintons in the presuicide weeks when he was depressed.

Since when do suicide victims run about eloquently voicing their true fears? It's more complicated than that. Those who take their own lives are usually very depressed, as was Foster, and often secretive and nonverbal. Even psychiatrists find it hard to get them to level, and Foster had never seen a psychiatrist.

Foster could have been obsessing about Whitewater, the Clintons, Hillary, Madison Guaranty, McDougal, the Clintons' personal tax returns, his sex life, the heat in the Washington summer, or anything.

Just that day, Foster had received a phone call from David Lyons, author of the report on supposed Clinton losses in Whitewater. (Perhaps Foster knew better.) It was also the day the FBI invaded and searched the office of David Hale, the man who claims that President Clinton pressured him into making illegal loans.

But, Special Counsel Fiske assured us, Foster wasn't thinking of any of that when he pulled the trigger. Fiske's "evidence" had no judicial value, but he had made his adventure into pop psychiatry at public expense and expected to be taken seriously.

This one nonfinding set up early doubts about the accuracy of the whole report—as if Fiske had set out to give the administration a clean bill all around. That's probably not true, but the flimsy work, plus his friendly ties to Bernie Nussbaum, set up suspicions, grounded or not, that finally did him in.

The third disappointment was the clean bill of health so casually granted to *all* participants in the affair.

Fiske called it an investigation into the "series of meetings and other contacts between White House and Treasury Department officials from September 1993 through March 1994." His grand jury investigation, in which he paraded ten administration witnesses before the Federal District Court, covered "a total of more than twenty different contacts, either face-to-face or telephone conversations."

Lack of Guilt

His conclusion? A bland sanguinity. Again, Fiske found innocence everywhere. *No one*, but no one, he concluded, was guilty under Section 1505, U.S. Code, relating to obstruction of justice.

He first outlined the pertinent parts of the law:

"Whoever corruptly . . . influences, obstructs, or impedes or endeavors to influence, obstruct, or impede the due and proper administration of the law under which any pending proceeding is being had before any department or agency of the United States . . . shall be fined not more than $5,000 or imprisoned not more than five years, or both."

He made it clear that these interlopers didn't have to succeed to have committed a federal crime. Just "attempting" or "conspiring" to do so is criminal enough. Good law, and a rather broad net. But Fiske couldn't seem to find any evidence, or anyone, to fill it.

Mr. Fiske wrote in his report: "We have concluded that the evidence is insufficient to establish that anyone within the White House or the Department of Treasury acted with the intent to corruptly influence an RTC investigation."

Here Fiske entered swampy territory. It seems his report was incomplete, especially in light of the upcoming hearings.

Just a few days before they began on July 26, 1994, two bombshells were released by the congressional committees. One was a diary written by Josh Steiner, the 28-year-old chief of staff to Treasury Secretary Bentsen. (Celebrity-struck Washington pols love to write things down for posterity.) The diary had several revelations for the public, including the fact that the White House had really pressed down on Altman *not* to recuse himself. Said Steiner, the Samuel Pepys (or Liz Smith) of Whitewater: Altman was under "intense pressure" from the White House.

Altman Lambasted

When Altman did finally recuse himself, Steiner tells us that the President was furious. His anger compounded when he learned that Altman had made the move while on the phone to a newspaper editor! Soon after, Steiner's diary informs us, White House staffers George Stephanopoulos and Harold Ickes called Altman, lambasting him for recusing himself without first clearing his decision with the President.

Exasperated, Steiner finally became philosophical about the whole situation: "Every now and again you watch a disaster unfold and seem powerless to stop it."

Steiner's writings added a little color to the cover-up. "The biggest danger is that this meeting [February 2, 1994] will give the Republicans further ammunition in their call for Congressional hearings," he wrote to his girlfriend in New York. "These would be a real disaster for the administration. Yours truly might be in some trouble. Who knows, I might be back in New York sooner than we think."

The Steiner diary also reveals that "BC," as he called the President, was being briefed regularly on the affair, as was Hillary. Her eyes and ears was Margaret Williams, who was aggressive in protecting (or injuring?) the First Lady. At one White House–Treasury confab, Williams even asked Roger Altman to get Ellen Kulka, the general counsel of the

RTC, to brief the Clintons' personal attorney, David Kendall, on the criminal referrals.

According to one staffer's memo, Williams's instructions to Altman were something like, "You'd better do it quickly," a reflection of Hillary's growing panic. Altman rushed to do that bidding, but Kulka turned down the invitation as "inappropriate."

How to Make Friends

The other bombshell was the "scrapbook" (Beltway for "diary") of Roger Altman, another stab at literary satisfaction that would provide more grief than immortality. One selected page, revealed by the Congressional staff, shows him alienating four good friends—Hillary Clinton, Maggie Williams, Bill Clinton, and Lloyd Bentsen—in just four succinct paragraphs.

About Hillary and Maggie, Altman's "scrapbook" says: "On Whitewater, Maggie told me that HRC (Hillary Rodham Clinton) was 'paralyzed' by it. If we don't solve this 'within the next two days,' you don't have to worry about her schedule on health care."

On Hillary alone, he comments: "HRC doesn't want (the counsel) poking into twenty years of public life in Arkansas."

On Bill Clinton via Maggie: "Maggie's strong inference was that the W. H. (White House) was trying to negotiate the scope of the Independent Counsel with Reno and having some difficulty."

On Lloyd Bentsen: "LMB went to see George (Stephanopoulos) on Whitewater yesterday; to argue for 'lancing the boil.' "

This pre-hearing titillation made headlines, with the

morsels feeding the growing Whitewater appetite. Armed with new information, critics who were dissatisfied with Fiske's clean bill for all those involved in the affair, started to think "Whitewash."

Even the *New York Times* chimed in. Two days before the hearings, their editorial was critical of Fiske's findings—frustrated that criminality, as Fiske saw it, should be the only guide to political morality.

On July 24, 1994, the *Times* angrily stated in an editorial: "An action does not have to rise to the level of criminality to be labeled stupid, irresponsible and improper. That seems a fair description of the activities of sworn public servants who, at the least, were mucking around in government departments trying to control inquiries into the President's finances."

"Mucking around" sounds a lot like "influencing, impeding, and obstructing," don't you think?

The *Times* then commented on what it called "Whitewater Disinformation": "The White House insists there is no cover-up. Why quibble over words? Call it a failed effort to thwart a legitimate investigation."

Increased Doubt

Fiske is now gone, possibly a casualty of the hearings, which began on July 26, 1994, and ended on August 5, 1994. Though limited and sometimes bedeviled, they did compress a great deal into a short, sometimes explosive, period. They opened up more avenues of doubt and inquiry, which we'll later explore.

The first witness on the morning of July 26 before the House Banking Committee was Lloyd C. Cutler, the Presi-

dent's interim counsel, a white-haired seventy-six-year-old
veteran of Washington who proceeded to describe the
hanky-panky of the White House–Treasury contacts in the
most moral of tones. Before the day was over, he had overwhelmed the opposition, defending the White House so
brilliantly that he should be granted the title "Master of Disinformation."

Mr. Cutler cleverly represented himself as an impartial
observer with no mean partisan goals. "I am not here as a
special pleader for the President of the United States," he
said. Instead, he was an "investigator" who had just completed his work of plumbing the White House staff. He was
pleased to state that not only was there no criminal activity, as Fiske had confirmed, but there was not even an "ethical" violation. Cutler swore (he was under oath), there
were just some "errors of judgment."

He was referring to Bernie Nussbaum, a convenient
fall guy who had already left the White House under attack.
Nussbaum had been a touch remiss in dealing with Roger
Altman on the recusal issue, Cutler later said.

In his understated theatrical manner, Cutler even
called on the ghost of Joseph Welch, the hero of the Army-
McCarthy hearings. In a similar historic tone, he repeated
the classic comment, "Have you no decency?"

It was a playlet for the disingenuously handicapped.
Except for an occasional outburst by frustrated Republicans, Mr. Cutler got away with it. And when he was finally
reminded that he was, after all, the President's lawyer, Cutler drew himself up sharply. With clenched jaw, he displayed anger that anyone would challenge his integrity.
Lawyers, he said, have to trust one another.

There was silence rather than laughter, conclusive proof of my theory that Washington is suffering from mass mental instability.

(It's really a shame that President Clinton didn't handle the whole thing by himself—take it by the ears, shake it hard, and tell the simple truth. He should have called a press conference and told the nation that his young troupe had stepped "way out of line." They were going to be spanked, and good. He would have been a national hero, with a ten-point jump in his approval polls. Instead . . .)

Pure Partisanship

The House hearings opened with a display of rules calculated *not* to get at the truth, an ambience that would linger oppressively in the Rayburn hearing room throughout the week. The Chairman of the House Banking Committee, Henry Gonzalez of Texas, was refreshingly ridiculous and a prime model for the term limits movement.

He didn't even try to disguise his open partisanship, determined that no real hearing would take place in *his* hearing room that could injure *his* President.

The result, of course, was to increase the suspicion that hundreds of Washingtonians were trying to protect the President—but from what most of them had no idea.

(Events going back to Arkansas and up to today demonstrate that these suspicions stem not only from the revelations to date, but also from the First Family's strange syndrome of paranoia combined with the need to obfuscate—an ailment which is apparently contagious.)

In the House hearings, each member had only five minutes per witness, three of which were generally taken

up by answers. Virtually all Whitewater questions before
September 1993 were off grounds, preempted by the Fiske
investigation. And Sheriff Gonzalez was there to make sure
everyone obeyed the rules.

The following day in the House, July 27, the rehearsed
playlet continued. Bernard Nussbaum, former White House
Counsel, spent the entire morning outlining another unique
idea, one as startling as Cutler's claim of impartiality.

Washington has graduated from simple lack of candor, long a political staple of both parties, to creative hog-
wash. Cutler had first told us he was an "investigator," and
now Nussbaum topped him. (Both are $400-an-hour attor-
neys in private life.)

Threatening Press
The reason he went along with the Treasury-RTC meetings
on the criminal referrals, Nussbaum said in his peripatetic
New York style, was because of the press! There were *imminent* press queries, still not in print but threatening!
They had to break tradition by convening on the Whitewater criminal referrals.

This was really new. This argument had never been
used before in the nation's 218-year history. The media
were the real villains, forcing him to break the security attached to the RTC documents mentioning the Clintons,
Nussbaum told the committee with a straight face, if with
nervous body movements.

At that fateful September 29 meeting, the White House
was involved in *official business*, Nussbaum assured them.

What was the "official business" that had forced him
to violate the White House's own code of ethics (See *Con-*

clusion), which forbids transfers of nonpublic information to the White House? Haiti, or health care, or possible nuclear war with North Korea?

No, it was "imminent press inquiries" that the President might have to answer—apparently under unbearable pressures from reporters wanting to know what he had done in Little Rock when trying to corner a fast buck.

This was a new concept of government, one in which the press determined how federal officials should operate. Under this tyrannical rule of the fourth estate, and of press leaks that had not yet happened, the laws of the land had to be abruptly rewritten, on the spot, according to Nussbaum's edict.

Nothing could be private any longer. No information—IRS, FBI, RTC, Justice— could stay secret. Nothing was privileged. No information on passports (remember how the Bush administration had checked Clinton's travel visas) meant anything as long as the press called! The Privacy Act of 1974 had to be scrapped because Mr. Nussbaum, acting on behalf of a beleaguered White House, had invented a new governmental theory—and for less than $400 an hour.

Yielding to the press was not only "ethical" but "official business," he swore under oath.

In the time they had, the opposition could not break through Nussbaum's outrageous creativity and the banality of Chairman Gonzalez. The afternoon of the second day, *ten* members of the White House Staff—Stephanopoulos, Ickes, McLarty, Lindsey, Maggie Williams, Eggleston, et al.—sat at a long table and, like automatons, called out "no" when administration backers asked if they had done anything wrong.

House members would have only thirty seconds to query each witness, but the Republican opposition now bunched itself together for single questioners. Still Sheriff Gonzalez beat them back. It was an embarrassing playlet.

Enlightened Senators

The farce continued until the Senate hearings began on Friday, July 29. This quickly demonstrated the brilliance of the Founding Fathers when they orchestrated a bicameral legislature, with Senators elected (originally appointed) statewide. Here, the democratic system, unlike the parish stupidity of the House hearing, started to flourish. Chaired by Democrat Donald C. Riegle of Michigan, a comity was established that permitted a true hearing to begin, with appropriate results.

(And besides, Senators are in office for six years, longer than Presidents, the ranks of whom they see come and go.)

The first go-around was generally useless, focusing on the Foster suicide— except for statements by some Senators that they didn't believe the Special Counsel should have played Dr. Freud.

But the next two witnesses were pure paydirt.

Jean Hanson, the attractive blond General Counsel of the Treasury Department, and William Roelle, slow, soft-spoken former Senior Vice President of the RTC, re-created the beginnings of the Washington end of the story.

Roelle, a twenty-five-year career officer, told of receiving a call from the Kansas City RTC office informing him that nine new criminal referrals on Madison Guaranty were on their way to the Washington office of the RTC—before they were to be sent to the Justice Department. At least one of them mentioned President and Mrs. Clinton.

This was a unique special action, as witnesses later testified. In fact, of 1,200 criminal referrals that the agency had handled, *this was the first one ever sent to the Washington RTC office before going to Justice.* I wonder why?

Roelle got a one-sentence summary of each over the phone, with the names of the individuals involved. The Clintons were mentioned as "possible witnesses," and reportedly had been "possible beneficiaries" on a prior referral. He told this to Ms. Hanson at the instruction of Mr. Altman.

An Honest Witness
At the Senate hearing, Mr. Roelle emerged as the most direct of all the witnesses, adding a sense of normality to the proceedings. But, of course, he's no longer working for the government.

"Ms. Hanson asked if she could see the referrals," Roelle later testified, explaining that he discouraged her on that. Then he cautioned her not to tell *anyone* except Mr. Altman, the acting CEO of RTC, about them.

He added that it was "improper for anybody to know about a criminal referral from the RTC." In the case of the innocent, it was damaging. In the case of the guilty, it could compromise the case.

His advice was like chaff in the wind. Two days later, Ms. Hanson was at the White House talking to Bernie Nussbaum about another matter. Afterwards, she pulled him aside and told Nussbaum what she knew about the nine Madison Guaranty referrals, especially the one that included the Clintons.

Nussbaum listened, then called in Cliff Sloan, one of his attorneys. He asked Ms. Hanson to repeat her story.

The next day, September 30, Hanson wrote her famous memo to Roger Altman, explaining that she had spoken to Bernie Nussbaum and Cliff Sloan about the matter and had filled in Secretary of Treasury Bentsen as well. She ended with the cooperative fillip: "Is there anything else you think we should do?"

The memo was produced by a Senator at the hearing, who asked Hanson if it was hers as indicated.

Thus began the great theme of the whole week, a symptom of witness after witness, mostly young people, who seemed to be suffering from premature Alzheimer's and couldn't remember much about their busy lives, especially as they related to Madison-Whitewater. The syndrome has also been dubbed "selective amnesia" or "attention deficiency disorder."

Ms. Hanson improved on the burgeoning Washington lexicon when she said that she had no "specific recollection" of the memo but that it was her initials on the paper and it looked like "the kind of memo" she wrote.

Contradictory Testimony

But she stood behind her story. She claimed she had filled in her Treasury colleagues on her trip to the White House, despite what they later testified to —starting one of the continuing conflicts of the Whitewater hearings, one that could have grave legal ramifications.

In the case of Secretary Bentsen, Hanson stated that she had—as Treasury General Counsel—asked him in March to tell the Banking Committee that he had known of the secret meetings all along. But according to Hanson, he refused. In the case of Roger Altman, not only did he know about her White House trip, Hanson testified, but he had actually "tasked" her to do the deed.

(Washington's greatest injury to our nation might not be just fiscal bankruptcy but the ultimate destruction of the English language.)

On Tuesday morning, August 2, when the new witness, Josh Steiner of diary fame, appeared before the Senators, they were waiting.

Because modern American politics is increasingly driven by money, obfuscation, secrecy, even lying, extraordinary surprises are more commonplace. We saw that on the eve of the Whitewater hearings, when one surfaced that surprised veteran political observers, myself included.

Congressional investigators felt they had several pieces of powerful ammunition to prove a cover-up. There was Jean Hanson's memo, Jean Lewis's notes and tape, the "scrapbook" of Roger Altman, and Josh Steiner's diary, filled with solid statements of Treasury and White House vulnerability.

One of the prehearing revelations, as we've seen, was the Steiner diary, a lush, literate appetizer. In his writings, twenty-eight-year-old Josh Steiner, chief of staff to Lloyd Bentsen and a graduate of Andover, Yale, and Oxford—and simply "Josh" to some older Senators—had provided a rare insight into the operation.

There was no way the defenders of the cover-up could discredit that diary, right?

Wrong. Just before the hearings, Mr. Steiner announced that *he didn't mean what he wrote* about "intense pressure," "disaster," etc. *Incroyable!* (One is reminded of the man caught in bed with another woman, who shouts at his wife: "Who do you believe—me or your eyes?")

The recantation of one's own writing is the perfect symbol of Washington today, a new level of intellectual and moral distortion that is affecting the government scene at all levels. According to Steiner's lawyer, the diary was merely "impressionistic." One should not draw conclusions from what he *actually* wrote.

Washington Play

Without meaning to, the young man had achieved the ultimate in Beltway drama. He had taken the reality of our sometimes sordid capital and transmuted it into a fantasy, a Hollywood-on-the-Potomac.

When Steiner, who could have been the genuine star instead of the goat, appeared at the hearing, he was surprised that the Senators not only presented him with giant photo blowups of his diary entries but demanded that he read from them.

It became a painful, pitiful playlet. Steiner, looking as sheepish as a repentant serial murderer, stammered that his *written* emphasis was wrong. Painstakingly, he explained why he had not meant what the diary said. The "intense pressure" wasn't really "intense," he told the bemused Senators. In fact, it may not have been "pressure" at all, just advice. And Stephanopoulos hadn't been as forceful about firing the Republican investigator as he had noted in his diary.

If he had to do it all over again, he would have written

it differently, he told the Senators while everyone laughed.
When asked if he was still writing a diary—a six-year
habit—his voice quickened. "No."

It was heartrending. It's really a shame because
Steiner is such an attractive and apparently idealistic
young man. The diary was both sharp and fervid, a confirmation of the value of an education that would now cost
$250,000. Then poor Josh, stammering out his silly ex-
cuses, suddenly became an aged figure by denying his own
excellent creation. Had he possessed more guts, he could
have joined the pantheon of American heroes, a more substantial reward than being a political toady for the White
House today and then forgotten tomorrow.

Roger's Performance

The next witness was the star of the hearings, par excel-
lence—if in a defamatory sense. Roger Altman, personal
friend of Bill and Hillary, multimillionaire, former acting
CEO of the RTC, and Deputy Secretary of the Treasury,
came on at about 2 P.M. and stayed in the witness chair for
twelve hours, until 2 A.M.

It was a bravura performance of evasion, obfuscation,
"don't recall" responses that had nothing to do with the
questions, and a seeming desire to aggravate the Senators,
some of whom said he was "lying."

On the desk, Altman had put up a small sign for himself: "Slow and Calm." But he might have been too much so
as he bobbed and weaved at each inquiry.

Their annoyance with the man grew with the hours,
until at the end, several Senators called for his resignation.
(Altman finally heeded their call on August 17, 1994.) The

resentment of his evasion naturally started with the Republicans, but before it was over, some Democrats were annoyed as well.

Altman had talked himself into a box. First, he said he "didn't recall" telling, or "tasking," Ms. Hanson to go to the White House with the referral news. He didn't believe he knew she went there on September 29, 1993, to tip off the President through his minions. He didn't believe he had any knowledge of that meeting, or the October 14 meeting between the Treasury and the White House either, both of which were attended by Ms. Hanson.

That testimony was placed in doubt by Bill Roelle, who stated that on October 6, 1993, he was seated in Roger Altman's office. The conversation turned to Madison-Whitewater. Altman got Ms. Hanson on the phone and told her to "call Bernie" and several other White House people.

Secret Meetings
Altman even had problems with White House meetings he did attend. The first of those was on February 2, 1994, and the second was on February 3, both related to Whitewater.

As we've seen, on February 2, Altman went to the White House to meet with Bernard Nussbaum and others, to give them a "heads up" on the statute of limitations for RTC civil suits.

What had gone on there? Altman was asked by the Senators. He now testified that he had told the White House that he believed a lawsuit against the Clintons could be ready in time for the February 28 statute deadline—if the RTC decided there were grounds. Ellen Kulka had told him as much.

This was important information. If the case couldn't
be finished before the statute expired on February 28,
1994, then the Clintons were home free—at least on a civil
suit. But if the case could be ready by that date, as Altman
had indicated, they had to be prepared for real trouble.

Another participant at that meeting, Deputy Chief of
Staff Harold Ickes, remembers it differently. He testified
that he believed that Altman had said the work for such
an RTC lawsuit probably wouldn't be ready by the February 28 cutoff date. If this were so, then the Clintons could
rest much easier.

When requestioned by a Congressman, Ickes stuck to
his guns—sort of. He said he remembered it that way, but
he could be wrong. In fact, in one of the best hedges of a
hedge-happy hearing, he disclosed that he was totally deaf
in one ear!

Returning to Roger Altman's testimony, it became
even more heated when the Senators questioned him about
his fierce internal and external debate on whether to *recuse* himself from the entire Madison-Whitewater affair.
This question was vital because until March 30, 1994,
Altman was Acting Director of the RTC.

Disputed Recollections

No one except the participants knows *exactly* what happened at the February 2 meeting. We can assume there was
a touch of panic among the White House staffers when Altman told them he was leaving the Madison-Whitewater
matter. In their testimony, those in attendence say "no." Although several people admit that they encouraged Altman
not to recuse himself, they say there was no pressure.

Nussbaum, for example, ostensibly reminded him that the Ethics Officer of Treasury had ruled that there was no legal or ethical reason to recuse himself. Then why do it? Also, didn't Altman have a responsibility to his job?

Supposedly, they merely asked Altman to sleep on it.

It all sounds so pleasant, but there was a disturbing, conflicting word in the air. Young Josh Steiner spoke with Altman right after he returned from that meeting and put down his impressions of the conversation in his famed diary. As we know, he said that Altman had been put under "intense pressure" *not* to recuse himself. We also know that Altman ran to the White House the next morning to do their bidding.

Other witnesses who were there said Nussbaum was very excited as he made his points. (But as someone commented, Nussbaum gets excited when ordering dinner.) Nussbaum did know that with Altman gone, Jack Ryan and Ellen Kulka would make all the key decisions. He didn't know about Ryan, but Kulka apparently gave him the shakes. Joel Klein, Nussbaum's deputy at the time, testified at the hearings that "Ms. Kulka was someone he [Nussbaum] had known from a case . . . and he said, in words to this effect . . . she was a difficult person to deal with, she was unreasonable, she could be unfair."

At the congressional hearing on August 2, 1994, Senators, their voices politely muffling strong annoyance, went after Altman. They waved the four letters he had sent the committee between March 2 and March 21 to try to correct his February 24 testimony. They wanted to know why it took so long, and why it had been so incomplete. The chairman pointed out that they had even offered to reconvene the hearing after February 24 to have him explain better, but he had refused.

The first correction letter that Altman sent, on March 2, 1994, had described the two White House meetings he hadn't testified about as being related only to "press inquiries," the old Nussbaum saw. The Senators were not pleased.

Difficult Recall

Altman still said he could not "recall" knowing about those meetings and didn't think his other contacts with the White House were "substantive."

One Senator pointed out that Altman had never mentioned the recusal matter at all during his February 24 testimony. Why?

Altman bobbed, weaved, whispered, and obfuscated. After a while, his answers seemed more like inner discussions with his own psyche than outward responses to questions. The Senators were developing into a hanging jury. They became so accusatory as the night wore on that at one point, D'amato listed eight pieces of testimony by other Treasury or White House staffers that contradicted Altman's own statements—to which Altman eventually responded: "I did not lie to Congress."

D'Amato, the quintessential New Yorker, took to calling him "Roger the Dodger" and "gutless wonder." Said the expressive Senator: "Not responsible for anything. Not Roger the Dodger. This lawyer did it. That lawyer did it."

The most Altman would say about his plethora of "I don't recalls" was to confess that his testimony was "imperfect."

So miffed were the Senators, Republicans, and some Democrats alike, that they played back his February 24, 1994, testimony on video to check on inconsistencies. In one dramatic moment, after he told the committee that he had only one substantive contact with the White House on Whitewater (the number has now grown to four), he turned around and spoke briefly with Treasury counsel Jean Hanson, who was sitting right behind him.

On the video, you can see her move her head, but it's impossible to hear what she is saying. "I turned to her," Altman now told the Senators, "and she confirmed my answer."

As if in a television drama, one of the Senator's microphones was on at the time. As soon as the video was finished, you could hear his voice race across America, "He is going to try to lay it on her."

(Our young diarist, Josh Steiner, commenting on Altman's testimony, said he "gracefully ducked" the question of the number of contacts with the White House. The phrase is now part of Beltway lingo, which refers to evasion of a question as a "graceful duck.")

Was She "Tasked"?

There's no doubt that the testimony of Altman and Hanson is contradictory. She is definitive in saying that Altman "tasked" her to bring news of the Madison criminal referrals to the White House on September 29, 1993.

He was typically less definitive, abusing the term "believe," but he still denied the charge. "I do not believe that I suggested that the White House be informed on any facts relating to this referral," he testified, "I do not believe that to be the case."

Not only were the Senators peeved at Altman, Maggie Williams, honcho for chief honcho Hillary Clinton, was burning. In his "scrapbook" (Beltway for "diary"?), Altman had broken privacy by supposedly quoting Williams that Hillary was "paralyzed" by the Whitewater affair, something Williams later denied. When pieces of his "scrapbook" were released, Altman went to Williams's office on the second floor of the West Wing to apologize. He carried a note in a sealed envelope marked "Personal and Confidential" and handed it to her.

At the hearing, Williams testified that she went into her inner office and tossed the envelope, unopened, into the waste basket.

Altman seems to have alienated all his bases, whether at Treasury, the Congress, or 1600 Pennsylvania. He who had never visited the Ozarks and who much prefers the Hamptons to Arkansas, had been caught in Whitewater, whose rapids were apparently all engulfing.

One of the more titillating incidents of the hearings involved a memo touching on two delicate subjects: Hillary Clinton and the "redaction" of documents.

(In the new Washington lexicon, "redaction" takes the place of the English word "censored." Congressman Barney Frank gave us the best quip of the hearings when he said he was looking for a "redacted recusal".)

The memo was from Harold Ickes, deputy chief of staff, to the First Lady, dated March 1, 1994. At the hearing, a Congressman waved it in the air, its pages flapping. But of the twenty-five sheets, only the first page had anything on it. *The White House had provided the committee with twenty-four blank pages of paper!*

White House Counsel Cutler claimed the memo had been redacted because it was "not relevant to the committee's inquiries" and added that in his fifty years of practice, no other lawyer had ever questioned his skill at "redaction."

There's always a first time. Before the hearings were over, Mr. Cutler had reacted to the criticism over the blank pages and had produced the Ickes missive to the First Lady in full. It proved interesting.

The memo was written by counsel Neil Eggleston, then sent to Ickes, who sent it to "HRC," as the First Lady is known in the somewhat cowed White House. It included the following information:

1. After Altman had met with Bernie Nussbaum about the statute of limitations on February 2, 1994, the ethics officer of the Treasury Department ruled that Altman did not have to recuse himself from matters involving Madison-Whitewater.

2. Regarding a possible conflict of interest involving Hillary's old law firm in the Madison case (on which she had worked), the FDIC had decided that the record was not clear. If they found that Rose had not properly disclosed its prior representation of Madison, then the firm could be "permanently barred from any further work for the RTC and the FDIC."

3. The RTC was investigating whether it had a civil action to recover money from anyone involved in Madison Guaranty. "The RTC could also sue outsiders, *including the President and Mrs. Clinton* [italics mine], if the RTC found that outsiders

worked with insiders illegally to divert assets of
the savings and loan," the memo continued. "For
example, if the RTC believed that the Clinton
campaign knowingly received diverted Madison
assets at the April 1985 fundraiser or that the Clintons knowingly received other diverted Madison
Guaranty assets through Whitewater, it could
bring suit."

With apologies to Mr. Cutler, it surely seems like "relevant" material.

The morning following the Altman testimony at the
Senate hearing, the witness was Lloyd Bentsen, Secretary
of the Treasury and the grandest old man of American politics. The tall, craggy, handsome, articulate, rich seventy-
three-year-old Texan had served thirty years in public life,
mostly in Congress, reaching the position of Chairman of
the Senate Finance Committee. He was his party's 1988
candidate for Vice President—lending a little seasoned ma-
turity to Mike Dukakis's race.

(Bentsen is the one who reminded voters that Dan
Quayle was no Jack Kennedy, and there are those who believe he might have won at the head of the ticket.)

Grand Old Politician
Now, as he sat in the witness chair, you could almost hear
the deference in the room. Bentsen began by implying that
since he was appointed, he had little time to engage in the
gossip of Whitewater. Just in the last six months, the period under study, he had 130 meetings at the White House,
testified 11 times before Congress, made 60 speeches,

held 80 interviews and 25 press conferences, traveled to 6 countries and 10 states, and received 2,400 memos.

"I have turned the Treasury Department upside down. I have turned my memory inside out," he testified, "without finding one written briefing to me on these White House meetings." In fact, he pointed out, he had specifically told his staff not to bother him with any cases coming out of the RTC.

He flatly denied comments by Ms. Hanson that he had ever discussed the Madison-Whitewater criminal referrals or the meetings at the White House with her. Neither had he received any memo from her on the matter. He questioned the judgment of both Hanson and his chief subordinate, Deputy Treasury Secretary Altman.

Not only had he not attended any White House conferences on the subject, but until he read about the meetings in the paper in March 1994, he claimed he didn't know that those in September and October had ever taken place.

This was a direct contradiction of Jean Hanson's testimony that she had spoken to him about it twice. Once was on the day following her September 29 meeting at the White House. In fact, she had claimed that in March, she had suggested that he tell Congress about his prior knowledge of the meetings, an idea she says he rejected.

Each of the stories of the top Treasury Department officials—the Secretary, Deputy Secretary, and General Counsel—differed in some major way.

The natural result was tension at the Treasury. "It is very, very formal on the third [executive] floor right now," a Treasury spokesman commented. "The feeling is that there is a deep rift that simply cannot be healed."

Single Admission

Bentsen dismissed any possibility that he had been involved in such trashy affairs. His only admission to the
committee was that "it would have been better off if some
of these meetings had never taken place." He assured the
committee that he intended to restructure the department
so that it would never happen again.

One Senator mentioned that Roger Altman denied that
he had ever "tasked" Ms. Hanson to go to the White House
and inform them about the criminal referrals that mentioned the First Family. What did Bentsen think of that?
Could Ms. Hanson have gone to meet with Mr. Nussbaum
on her own?

Bentsen, who thinks carefully before he answers anything, contemplated. "She's a very confident woman. Yes,
that's possible."

Bentsen's name and a mention of Whitewater had
even come up in Roger Altman's famous scrapbook. A January 4, 1994, entry stated: "LMB went over to see George
[Stephanopoulos] on Whitewater yesterday, to argue for
'lancing the boil.' "

A Treasury spokesman confirmed that meeting but
pointed out that Secretary Bentsen had told the White
House to lay out all the details on Whitewater once and for
all and get rid of it. Obviously, his recommendation fell on
deaf ears.

The Treasury part of the case is complicated and still
not over. In fact, a brown envelope was recently found,
torn in half, in Jean Hanson's safe. In it was a two-page
memo of practice questions and answers for investigators.
One of them asked Ms. Hanson if she had told Mr. Altman

about the September 29 meeting at the White House. The answer was "no." Ms. Hanson describes these Q&As as "practice," not as a rendition of what actually happened.

Who are we to believe?

By the time Bentsen's testimony was over, it was clear—at least for now—who had won. The committee had not laid a finger on the impeccably tailored frame of the Grand Old Politician.

With the next day's witness, Bernard Nussbaum, it was quite another story. On Thursday evening, August 4, 1994, at 10:30 P.M., the hardworking Senate panel heard the testimony of the former White House counsel, who had gotten a free ride at the House the week before under the protective wing of Chairman Gonzalez.

But this time, the ambience was different, cooler, even somewhat hostile. In the interim between his first and second appearances, a lot had been learned, and Mr. Nussbaum received a comeuppance of sorts, a payback for his "The Press Dictates White House Policy" rationalization of the week before. And since that time, the testy subject of Roger Altman's recusal had also arisen.

In fact, Nussbaum was greeted with a rather unprecedented verbal assault.

"You crossed the line," a suddenly impassioned Chairman Donald Riegle of the Senate Banking Committee, a fellow Democrat, shouted at Nussbaum. "I think you had no right to inject yourself into Roger Altman's consideration of whether he should recuse himself." Riegle was warming up. "This is one time you should have bit your tongue if you had to bite it in half and not stick your nose in the decision."

Bi-partisanship

Despite the mangled metaphor, Riegle, who had been perfectly nonpartisan during the week, was now speaking for
several Senators on both sides of the aisle.

Nussbaum started the late session confident and smiling. But as the criticism was heaped on, it got to him. In his
defense, the peppery New Yorker attacked Altman in return, saying he had recused himself only because "he
couldn't take the heat." Altman should have stayed in the
fray, Nussbaum said, which was the "only principled thing
to do."

But the Senators had the last, angry word. Democratic
Senator John Kerry of Massachusetts, who had become increasingly annoyed by some of the administration's tactics,
asked Nussbaum if he still thought that Altman should not
have recused himself.

"Yes," answered the former White House official.

"Then I'm very happy you're not serving as the President's counsel," answered the irate Senator.

One of the last panels assembled, on the last day of
the hearings, Friday, August 5, was surprisingly in the
House, and called by Henry Gonzalez.

It was triggered by new information garnered by Congressman Jim Leach, who believes that there was a subtle,
or not-so-subtle, attempt to delay, or even sabotage, the
Madison criminal referrals somewhere in the bowels of
the RTC.

The panel consisted of all career, nonpolitical ap-
pointees. They included John E. (Jack) Ryan, now acting
CEO of the RTC, having replaced Roger Altman; Ellen
Kulka, General Counsel of the RTC; April Breslaw, the RTC

counsel from Washington who had been tape-recorded by
Jean Lewis; James Dudine, in charge of RTC criminal investigations; Stephen Katsanos, RTC public relations director; William Roelle, former Senior Vice President of the
RTC; and Thomas L. Hindes, an assistant general counsel
of the RTC.

Missing Witness
The committee had invited Jean Lewis, the whistle-blower,
but she had declined, saying she preferred to wait until the
scope of the hearings was broader—meaning it would
cover the Arkansas days.

The bone of contention at this hearing was twofold:
April Breslaw's talk with Jean Lewis in Kansas City and
Congressman Leach's charge that RTC was in no hurry to
get the referral mentioning the Clintons to the Department
of Justice for action.

Congressman Leach gave the impression that there
was a person or movement within the RTC hoping to keep
those referrals bottled up by first rerouting them unexpedi-
tiously to Washington from their usual route from Kansas
City to the U.S. Attorney in Little Rock.

In the process, they would be slowed down, perhaps
even killed.

Whether or not anyone in Washington or Kansas City
had such a motive, the criminal referrals were actually
"shortstopped" on their way. Some in the RTC, it seems,
thought the referral on Madison Guaranty was not necessary, or even valid. McDougal had already been tried and
acquitted. And there may have been strong sentiment to
protect the President—at virtually any cost.

260 THE GREAT WHITEWATER FIASCO

In any event, this referral was cherry-picked out and given special attention never afforded anyone else.

"I asked for those referrals to be sent to Washington instead of Justice," testified James Dudine, RTC Chief of Criminal Investigations.

When he was asked whether this had ever happened before, he thought.

It had happened one time since, but "this was the first time a referral had come to Washington before going to Justice."

Dudine explained that Kansas City had asked for a three-week delay, but the referral had been held up ten days. During that time, a kind of rebuttal—a "legal analysis" as he called it—had been written. Reportedly the analysis had argued against the referral on several grounds, including the fact that it would place McDougal in double jeopardy. Then there ensued a debate whether that analysis had also been sent to Justice. Dudine was unclear on the subject and no one seemed to know for sure. Moreover, it seemed to have disappeared, scooped up in Whitewater.

Jack Ryan, acting head of the RTC, was definitive in his statement. He had been surprised to learn that Jean Hanson had brought the Madison referral to the White House to share the news. He didn't think it should have been done.

Madison had been brought up three or four times in their weekly meetings, he said under oath, but he had never told April Breslaw what she said he had said.

Right now, he explained, things on the referral were moving ahead in three directions:

1. As a result of the extension of the statute of limitations, the RTC had reopened the investigation of
   Madison for a possible civil suit.
2. The Inspector General was continuing to investigate the Rose Law Firm's conflict of interest (including Hillary, we assume).
3. The RTC had continued to retain the law firm that
   employs Jay Stephens, the contested Republican,
   and that is conducting the investigation of Madison for possible civil suits.

Sage Warning

William Roelle, former senior vice president of the RTC, repeated his concern that the referrals should never have
been shown to anyone outside of the RTC, as he had
warned Jean Hanson. Steve Katsanos, RTC public relations
man, described how Treasury brass has twice tried to cen-
sor his "Early Bird" newsletter, once to delete the First
Lady's name in an item on the Rose Law Firm and the second time to delete a mention of Roger Altman, who was
then acting director of the RTC. Then Ellen Kulka denied,
under oath, that she had ever told April Breslaw to say
what she had said she said to Jean Lewis.

April Breslaw was the star witness, much as Altman
had been before her. But her testimony far surpassed even
his in indecision, unsureness, obfuscation, and a failure of
memory so deep that it sounded almost medical in nature.

Breslaw, an attractive dark-haired young woman attorney, had been with the FDIC, then the RTC, first in the
regional office in Dallas, then beginning in 1992, in Washington. She was part of the team handling the *civil* investi-

gation of Madison, just as Jean Lewis had been on the *criminal* side.

That fateful day, February 2, 1994, is strongly in her memory, *except* for what she said to Jean Lewis. There, she explained, her memory was "dim" and "vague." But strangely enough, it wasn't so dim that she didn't now think that she had been somehow lured into making the explosive statement that the "head people" would be "happy" if she took it easy on the President and the First Lady.

With a look that said "sincerity," she testified that she had "no recollection" of what she had said to Jean Lewis, nor could she explain why she had mentioned Ellen Kulka and Jack Ryan as those who wanted the soft report.

Not only that, but she thought that the "secret taping" of her remarks by Jean Lewis was not cricket. It had all happened so "casually," she said. The meeting was about over, and they were relaxing on the couch when the subject came up.

When did she first hear about the brouhaha over her remarks? It was when she heard herself attacked on the floor of the House by Congressman Leach on March 24, 1994. What was her response? Breslaw "categorically denied" that she had said any such thing.

Breslaw's surprise, and chagrin, on learning that she had been taped by Jean Lewis resulted in quick action. The very next day she recused herself from the Madison case.

Has she heard the tape since? a Congressman asked. Yes, part of it was played for her by the prosecutor at the grand jury hearings in Little Rock.

Was it her voice? Did she remember saying that?

Yes, it was her voice, but her recollection of that conference was "so dim" that she really couldn't say what she had said.

Josh Steiner saw his thoughts in writing and not only remembered but acknowledged that he had believed it at the time. But he didn't believe it anymore. Breslaw heard herself on tape, and though she believed it was herself talking at the time, she didn't remember having said it. And she didn't really believe she could have ever said it, even though she could hear it.

Whitewater, like Watergate, like the Army-McCarthy hearings, was producing acting performances that amateurs never imagined they could achieve. But in Whitewater, Mr. Fiske apparently believed them all. There is something about the American political scene that makes it at least a first cousin to the dramatic arts, a skill at which Americans excel.

Surprise! Surprise!

After the hearings concluded that Friday afternoon, August 5, one would think the Whitewater story would get a rest. But no. In a monumental surprise, the Justice Department that same afternoon announced that Special Counsel Fiske was out.

Back in January 1994, when the White House was resisting naming an investigator for Whitewater, Janet Reno may have made the sagest remark of her career. She said that no one would trust a Special Counsel named by herself and the President who was instructed to investigate the President. She was clairvoyant.

On June 30, the day Fiske's report was distributed,

Congress reinstated the old Independent Counsel law (a law, incidentally, which the Republicans had killed in 1992 because of anger at the seven-year probe of Iran-Contra!). The following day, Janet Reno petitioned the court to appoint Mr. Fiske to continue the Madison-Whitewater probe.

But complaints had come into the court from Republican members of the Senate Banking Committee. Senator Faircloth of North Carolina wrote the court that he didn't think Fiske had been tough enough and should be dismissed. Orrin Hatch of Utah thought the Fiske report was incomplete.

Others felt that Fiske had asked to narrow the scope of the hearings too much, and still others were annoyed because of the skimpiness of his report—with no facts to substantiate his decisions. Fiske answered that all evidence was secret because it involved grand jury testimony.

Thus full circle, and a bit Catch-22-ish.

The three judges named by Rehnquist to choose and direct the Independent Counsel were Judge David B. Sentelle, of the Court of Appeals for the District of Columbia, appointed by President Reagan, and who heads the panel; John D. Butzner, Jr., a senior judge on the United States Court of Appeals in Richmond, appointed by Lyndon Johnson; and Joseph T. Sneed, senior judge on the United States Court of Appeals in San Francisco, appointed by President Nixon.

A Matter of Appearance

On August 5, the panel decided not to hire Fiske, commenting that their ruling was no reflection on him personally.

They felt that since he had been appointed by Janet Reno, there might be the appearance of the administration investigating itself—a point made by Reno back in January.

The man chosen as new Independent Counsel is Kenneth Winston Starr, a forty-eight-year-old attorney in private practice in Washington and like Fiske, a Republican, if considerably more conservative. A former appeals court judge and Solicitor General of the United States, he, like Fiske, has a reputation for integrity.

"Replacing Mr. Fiske was a reasonable step," wrote the *New York Times*, which has been impartial during the entire Whitewater affair. They pointed out that Fiske had been recruited by Janet Reno, and that therefore, "his own appearance of impartiality was beclouded." In fact, the *Times* applauded the selection of former Solicitor General Starr, who they described as a man of integrity. Soon after taking office, Starr promised to be "fair and even-handed" in continuing the investigation.

Then, just two weeks after Starr's appointment, the *Times* asked that he resign for the very same reason—that "a cloud of political favoritism" now hung over him that would "undermine public confidence." The *Times* was speaking of the meeting of the head of the three man judicial panel, Judge David Sentelle, with Senators Lauch Faircloth and Jesse Helms—both outspoken opponents of Fiske—in the Senate dining room at a time when Sentelle was considering the new appointment for Independent Counsel.

For the sake of appearance, the same reason that Fiske was taken off the case, the *Times* believes that Starr's appointment now looked terrible. It was his "duty" to resign, they commented, adding that the Chief Justice should appoint a replacement for Judge Sentelle so that a new Independent Counsel would be free of any appearance of partiality.

Now that the hearings—at least this first phase—are over, there are lingering questions that Mr. Starr will have to answer, lest he repeat the performance of Mr. Fiske.

So tell me, Mr. Starr:

Was Mr. Fiske's conclusion that none of the parties involved was guilty of obstructing justice, or attempting to obstruct justice, under Section 1505—which includes lying to Congress (the same statute used to indict Oliver North)—accurate, or does it need revisiting now that you are in charge of the investigation?

The Independent Counsel by current law is *not* charged with determining unethical behavior, which is quite frustrating to concerned Americans. As we've seen, the investigative agencies, from the IGs to the Office of Government Ethics, are bureaucratically unable to come to the obvious and commonsense conclusion that there was unethical behavior by numerous people at the White House and in the Treasury. That's the nature of self-protective bureaucracy.

Therefore the law should be changed to give the Independent Counsel full powers in this area by setting up an ethical standard for the entire government and granting him the power to judge with dismissal and loss of benefits as the *minimum penalty.*

Diminished Democracy
Everyone says Whitewater is still not Watergate, I'm not so sure. It's true that it does not have (yet?) an overt act of

presidential obstruction like the eighteen-minute missing tape in the Nixon case. Instead, as much of the hearings demonstrated, it is a slow, torturous atrophying of the *process* of democracy, both in Arkansas and in Washington.

As a result of the case thus far, there has been an inevitable impact on the careers of several of the characters involved.

Roger Altman has resigned as Deputy Secretary of the Treasury, as has Jean Hanson, chief counsel of the Treasury Department. Surprisingly, L. Jean Lewis, her supervisor, Richard Iorio, and their boss, Lee Ansen, have been suspended with pay, pending an internal review.

We have witnessed and will continue to witness as the story further unravels in the months (and years?) to come a wanton disregard of the rules and a display of hubris by the First Family and a clique of self-important whipper-snappers—and gray hairs as well—in the White House.

That's only the symptom of the underlying weakness of the behavior of this and several prior presidential administrations. There is a looseness of discipline in the White House, one stimulated by an exaggerated sense of power by people who forget that they were appointed to serve, not to glory in their own narcissism.

In a democracy, as we've said before, there are no goals—only a process that maintains freedom. Once the rules are abrogated, as has consistently happened in Whitewater and its tributaries, then the rule of the people vanishes.

What can we do to stop this assault?

Read on.

Conclusion

The Lessons of Whitewater

How to Clean Up the
Money–Conflict–Politics Mess

The story of Whitewater, from its beginnings in Arkansas up through the congressional hearings in the summer of 1994, plus several post-hearing developments, is not just a dramatic tale somewhat touched by tragedy. It is, as promised, an instructive one as well.

And as each additional step it takes in Washington entangles it even more, Whitewater has not only become a paradigm of what is wrong in American politics but a key to how and why.

The events in Arkansas demonstrate the solid damage done to democracy by money, distortions due to political influence, and numerous conflicts of interest. In Washington, the attempt by the Clinton administration to minimize Whitewater by failing to be frank has backfired. It has only compounded the error, as often happens in the nearly paranoid atmosphere of the capital.

And now, there's a new side to the story. That's the government's internal "oversight," the work of agencies asked to investigate and separate fact from fiction in the conflicting tales of what happened in the White House–Treasury–RTC contacts. As Congressman Leach reminds us, that's only 5 percent of the continuing Whitewater story, but it was the full subject of the recent hearings.

These watchdog groups and individuals include the ethics investigation by Lloyd Cutler, interim White House Counsel; the work of so-called "Independent Counsel" Robert Fiske; the Treasury Department Inspector General; and the Office of Government Ethics. Their job was to evaluate the possible breaches of ethics in an impartial way or, in the case of Fiske, search for criminality.

Did they do their work well? Hardly. The results to date fail to pass the commonsense test. Nor do they conform to the facts as they've come out in the Senate testimony. (The House hearings, as we've seen, were a carefully staged farce.)

What did the oversight investigations find? Fiske found no criminality. Cutler discovered no ethical problems, just some cases of "bad judgment." The Inspector General (IG) of Treasury decided that everything was fine, and the Office of Government Ethics found no ethical violations, just some "troubling" activity. Collectively they provided no light and demonstrated only a tendency for political protection—intended or not.

In fact, the Office of Government Ethics report has been distorted by those pleading innocence. First, the OGE did *no* investigation on its own. It merely analyzed the report of the Treasury IG. *Second, it excluded evaluation of any members of the White House staff!* Third, it admitted that its judgment fell short by definition—that "conduct that some may perceive as 'unethical' does not necessarily violate the standards of conduct" of the OGE.

In fact, the OGE admits that only "some personal financial or other interest in the undertaking" would violate their standards. No wonder no savvy observer took their evaluation seriously.

It may be unethical, they're saying, but they'll call it ethical. That's Washington at its best!

Any intelligent person who has followed the story knows that all these probes failed to get at the truth in this latest chapter of Whitewater. Despite their verdicts, there has been—from a commonsense point of view—a massive disregard of ethics and decent governmental behavior.

We don't need a lawyer to understand what really happened this past year:

1. The Kansas City office of the Resolution Trust Corporation (RTC) called and told Bill Roelle that there were nine new criminal referrals on their way to Washington. At least one of them mentioned the President and Hillary Clinton.

2. Roelle told this to Roger Altman, acting head of the RTC, and to Jean Hanson, General Counsel of the Treasury.

3. This information is private, privileged, and secret and, according to RTC rules, is to be shown to no unauthorized personnel, with no exceptions.

4. Ms. Hanson—with or without the knowledge of Roger Altman—brought news of the criminal referrals to the White House.

5. The White House justified receipt of the details of the criminal referrals on the grounds that press leaks were "imminent." But, of course, press leaks are always "imminent" in Washington.

6. Roger Altman, who was going to recuse (or excuse) himself from the case because of his personal friendship with the President, went to the White House to tell them that. But they convinced him otherwise because of fear that professional RTC people might not be as kind to the Clintons as Altman if a suit was actually filed against the First Family.

7. The White House, which was in receipt of the absolutely privileged criminal referral news they should never have heard about, passed it on to the President and Mrs. Clinton, who were possible "beneficiaries" and "witnesses." The receipt of the information could warn them, and others in Arkansas, weakening any possible case, civil or criminal.

8. Some official in the RTC "shortstopped" the actual referrals on their way from Kansas City to the U.S. Attorney in Little Rock. In an unprecedented action, they were sent to Washington for a "legal analysis" which delayed, and could have quashed, the referrals.

There were other actions, several of which were quite unethical to citizen observers—such as George Stephanopoulos talking about "finding a way to fire" Jay Stephens, an outside RTC counsel handling the civil case against Madison Guaranty and thus Whitewater.

This, not the whitewash by the watchdog groups—all

delivered *before* the Senate hearings—is what we now know actually happened in the latest chapter of Whitewater. Almost everyone involved in oversight duty failed in their responsibility.

So far, only two things in the unraveling of Whitewater seem to be working properly: Jean Lewis's exhibition of courage in sticking to her guns and one-half of the congressional oversight, that of the U.S. Senate.

What is there to do? A great deal.

There are three basic problems that evolve from Whitewater: MONEY, CONFLICT OF INTEREST, AND FAILED GOVERNMENT WATCHDOG ACTION.

We'll look at all three, then offer almost a score of reforms that should help make America a better democracy—so that Whitewater will not have happened in vain.

First, we'll examine the excessive role that money plays in electing our public officials, whether in Arkansas or in the Bronx. Every time we approach Election Day, for mayoralty, state legislature, gubernatorial, or presidential races, the call comes, loud and lamenting, from American politicians for more and more money.

Money and politics are married, if uncomfortably, in America. Each year, the tally of cash spent in the name of democracy rises, until today it is equivalent to an industry. In 1992, we spent $1.3 *billion* electing our public officials. (Of which we have too many: There are 86,000 governmental units in the United States, but that's another story.)

Of that amount, over $1 billion was spent in the campaigns of federal officials, from the House through the Senate, and, finally, the presidency. The presidential race approaching in 1996 will be another record breaker. Last time, in the contest between Bush, Clinton, and Perot, plus the dozen or so in the primaries, the tab was $300 million in both private and federal expenditures.

According to the Federal Elections Commission (FEC), the taxpayers, through their checkoff on Form 1040, spent $42 million for the presidential primaries, then $11 million for each of the two gala national conventions, which generally decide nothing. Few Americans realize that we underwrite the *entire* cost of these spectacles, which usually nominate on the first ballot after the primaries.

(We don't pay for liquor and parties, but we do pick up the tab for noisemakers and balloons.)

Right after the conventions, the FEC handed each of the two survivors a check for $55 million, which they could spend any way they wished. Unfortunately, much of it went for political television advertising, which can be as polluting, intellectually and morally, as cigarettes are for our lungs. And to get the matching funds in the primaries, presidential candidates must press for contributions. Just in the presidential primaries of 1992, $127 million was spent, part of an ever-escalating activity.

On the congressional level and in races for the state-houses, there are no matching funds, so it's grubbing all the way, with large campaign chests needed to win. Mr. Clinton was an expert, raising over $10 million in his political career in that small state, according to an estimate by a Pulaski County official. There were many political debts to pay for that money, which is true of thousands of politicians around the country.

The raising and spending of money is the basic cause of corruption, financial and philosophical, in our political system. It starts with contributions and ends with excessive outside influence and power. The election and campaigning laws need to be changed drastically, if we are to make democracy work better.

Here are some ideas on how to make money much less important in our election system:

I. DRASTICALLY REDUCE THE SIZE OF POLITICAL CONTRIBUTIONS.

This is especially needed on the state level, where there is no public funding. Arkansas, for example, had a $1,500 limit on contributions, which has now been scaled down to $1,000—a small step forward.

The danger of large contributions is obvious: One big favor deserves another, and still another contribution the next year, and then another favor. Eventually it can lead to dangerously unethical behavior by state legislators and governors.

The simplest way to reduce the power of special interests in our state campaigns is: *Make $100 the maximum contribution for all state races, from the legislature to the governor's seat.* Only the simplest-minded of politicians can be bought for $100.

II. PROHIBIT SPECIAL INTERESTS FROM CONTRIBUTING TO POLITICAL CAMPAIGNS.

Special interests—trade and professional associations, banks, utilities, corporations, etc.—gain their power through the campaign pocketbook. That was especially true in Arkansas, where $1,500 gifts from such organizations went a long way. Many states permit the same, encouraging large gifts of money, with favors after election as the quid pro quo.

The solution is simple: *only individual citizens should be able to contribute to a political campaign, to a maximum of $100.*

That will cut off most of the power now exercised by lobbies and special groups on a state basis. (We'll deal with federal election campaigns in a moment.)

III. LIMIT CANDIDATES' CONTRIBUTIONS TO THEIR OWN CAMPAIGN.

The present system favors either wealthy people or those like Governor Clinton, who have easy access to banks and the ability to raise small fortunes on their own. (Remember Marlin Jackson's statement that Clinton borrowed $400,000 on his name for his campaigns and lobby slush funds.) Clinton's $50,000 contribution to his 1984 race, made with borrowed money, is legal in Arkansas and everywhere else.

To correct this abuse, legislation should be passed in all states prohibiting candidates from contributing any more than anyone else—$100—to their own campaigns.

The only leeway should be the right of a candidate to lend his campaign fund up to perhaps $5,000 as primary seed money, to be paid back *before* election time.

IV. NO MORE END RUNS.

The famed "end run" that Clinton accomplished with his giant slush fund should be made illegal in all states. Legislation should be passed, where it does not now exist, stating that money borrowed by a politician for lobbying purposes, and paid back by others, should be considered as personal income reportable to the Internal Revenue

Service. Candidates and officeholders *must be bound by campaign contribution laws at all times.*

V. ELIMINATE ALL CAMPAIGN CONTRIBUTIONS TO POLITICIANS FROM BANKS AND S&Ls.

These institutions are both regulated and insured by the government and should be off-limits to campaign chests. Their political action committees (PACs) should be excluded from contributing as well.

The Keating Five scandal should have taught us a lesson, as should the Madison Guaranty's influence with the former Governor of Arkansas.

Political contributions from this source, or from their executives, to either state officials or members of Congress are a potential invitation to corruption. They should be prohibited by law.

VI. ELIMINATE ALL TELEVISION POLITICAL ADVERTISING.

We've seen the case of Bill Clinton, who borrowed and spent feverishly to air television commercials in the last days of his campaigns. He is not unique. These ads have become a national obsession among politicians. The result is that the majority of money contributed to many campaigns is spent on television advertising, much of it of a nasty, negative, even false cast.

Remember, the airwaves are owned by the people and administered by Congress through the Federal Communications Commission (FCC), which licenses stations for a period of time, subject to renewal.

Congress has already exercised its constitutional

power over television advertising by *totally banning* both liquor and tobacco advertising. It's now time to do the same for political ads. Congress should instruct the FCC to eliminate political advertising on television and radio as a product that too often distorts the truth.

Is such an action constitutional? Of course it is.

Those who defend broadcasting's First Amendment rights are plain wrong. The First Amendment prohibits *any* legislation that would curb freedom of the press. But Congress has already restricted certain advertising on television, and is considering controlling television violence, which it can legally do. The same is true of political advertising. Since the First Amendment has already been ruled not applicable to *some* TV advertising, it could hardly protect political ads.

By taking political ads off the air (we can't do that in newspapers because of the First Amendment), we'll dramatically cut down the need for campaign funds. In its place, Congress should require stations to give free air time to all legitimate candidates for office.

This might be the greatest advance for democracy in our television-controlled generation.

VII. CHANGE FEDERAL ELECTIONS LAWS FOR CONGRESS WITH A FIVE-POINT PROGRAM.

Reforming federal elections laws is actually the easiest thing to do because it is centered in one place—Congress—rather than in fifty state capitals. And Congress desperately needs reform.

In 1992, congressional candidates spent $678 million to get elected. This is an obscene reflection on our democracy. To bring it into line, the amount of money spent must be cut by two-thirds or more.

Several pieces of legislation on congressional campaign reform are now in various stages in the House and Senate. Unfortunately, they're all shallow and basically worthless even if passed. In Senate races, for example, they would reduce a typical $4 million campaign chest down to $3 million and help challengers—who are outspent eight to one—by only a smidgen.

The real reform of congressional campaign finance is simple:

1. All PACs should be eliminated.
2. There should be no bundling, or grouping, of individual contributions by organizations. That destroys the sense of individuals, not special interests, giving to their candidates.
3. Out-of-state contributions should be prohibited for congressional candidates, making the elections truer to the wishes of local voters. One Connecticut Senator, for example, receives the *majority* of his campaign funds from out of state. That should be halted immediately. Wealthy Hollywood individuals should not be permitted to influence elections by remote control.
4. The maximum individual contribution for congressional elections, which is now $1,000 per person, should be reduced to $250. And that should be the *sole* source of income for the campaign. That amount should be allowed for adults only. Right now, a family with eight children

could contribute $10,000, which violates the spirit of the law.

5. We should consider a matching-fund method for congressional campaigns ($250 maximum) similar to the one now in place for the presidential race.

The second obstacle to democracy highlighted by the Whitewater fiasco is conflict of interest, which, with the problem of money, plagues us at every level of government. The separation of the private individual from the government individual can never be total, but that must be the goal of our system.

Here are some ways we can start to solve the gnawing problem of politicians seeking personal gain because of their public personas.

VIII. ELIMINATE UNSECURED BANK LOANS FOR POLITICIANS.

Candidates and officeholders often have easier access to banks, which are flattered to help out a winning officeholder. Remember that governors and state legislators regulate many banks and S&Ls in their states. They can also issue charters for both to open. Bankers seeking to curry favor often close an eye, or two, when politicians apply for loans for themselves or their campaigns. Politicians and bankers then become a dangerous combination, as we've seen in Arkansas.

(Years ago, a young man I know, running for the state legislature, was "grateful" that a "generous" local bank gave him a gift of its new public stock issue.)

Governor Clinton was of course expert at borrowing

money without putting up collateral. These loans may appear to be private, but they're really not. The deposits lent out are insured, and if the bank goes belly up, as did Madison, the taxpayers pick up the default, not the politician.

The best safeguard is legislation stipulating that those running for office, or in office, *cannot* receive loans without collateral. And that includes cosigners, who would represent an "end run" around such a prohibition.

The $3.5 million that Clinton borrowed from the friendly Worthen Bank in Little Rock for the 1992 presidential campaign is a stunning case in point. With reform legislation, that loan would not have been permitted because there was no solid collateral, merely a pledge of future matching funds.

IX. WHY WE NEED THE WHITEWATER CLAUSE.

Governor Clinton's pain over Whitewater began with his poor judgment call of going into partnership in a land deal with a banker, James McDougal.

He should have realized that this could have developed into a conflict of interest, but he didn't. To prevent it from happening to others in the future, legislation should be passed making it not only unethical but illegal for any public officeholder to have business dealings with any organization— or major executives of those organizations— regulated by that branch of government.

In most states, this would include banks and utilities, and today would extend to businesses under major environmental regulation by the state. When greed and hubris raise their heads, good legislation such as this can dampen it—and save reputations.

X. "NOT A CUP OF COFFEE" LAW.

Personal favors from special interests and big contributors to elected officials must be stopped. The Clintons (as do other state and federal officeholders) enjoyed living it high up on the Tyson and Lasater jets, for example. Changing that could be accomplished by one piece of legislation in Congress and all fifty states.

In my prior book, *A Call for Revolution: How Washington Is Strangling America*, I suggested legislation that would make it illegal for any officeholder to personally take even a cup of coffee—let alone a plane ride, or a golf trip, or a vacation, or a television set, or cash—from a lobbyist, or from any citizen or organization.

This law should apply to all members of Congress, all state and municipal officeholders, and all members of state legislatures. And in the new political environment, *to their spouses as well*.

Unknown to the public, such bribery, on a rather grand scale, is now quite legal for congressmen in Washington. Members of both the House and Senate can now *ethically* take up to $250 a year, in cash or gifts, from *each* lobbyist, *each* year. Even more ridiculous is the fact that House and Senate ethics rules exempt gifts of $100 or less, in unlimited number, from counting toward the $250! Ingenious members of Congress could take in $100,000 and never have to disclose it.

Somewhat as a result of my suggestion, activists in Washington State have placed a "Not a Cup of Coffee" law on the ballot in November 1994 as part of a voter initiative. That will stop *all* gift giving to politicians, which is just a legal form of bribery.

(Incidentally, the Initiative—the placing of new laws
on the ballot through citizen petitions and follow-up public
votes—should be law in all fifty states. But in only twenty-
three states do voters have that right, a strange anomaly in
our democracy. Politicians, of course, are in no hurry to
cut off their own personal pork, or power.)

XI. RESTRAIN APPOINTMENT OF CRONIES TO TOP POLITICAL JOBS.

This is not an easy one, but it's important. Not only
was this a symptom of bad government in Arkansas—
where Clinton's banker became Highway Commissioner
and friends were appointed to regulatory agencies—it is a
nationwide problem.

It seems natural to put old friends into high positions
of government, but experience proves that this often
works out poorly. Witness the debacle of Clinton cronies
from Arkansas in potent Washington slots.

This is a difficult problem to solve, but it must be examined.

One possibility is for all commissioners, deputy commissioners, and key appointments at the state level to be
confirmed by their state senates (except in Nebraska,
where it'll have to be done by the unicameral body).

On a federal level, the answer is simpler. Right now,
none of the President's staff, for example—including the
group that became privy to the RTC criminal referrals—are
confirmed by the U.S. Senate. Senate confirmation should be
extended to all top presidential staff. It might make them re-
flect that they have a responsibility to the American people,
not just to the White House and the President.

If George Stephanopoulos, for example, had been investigated and then confirmed by the U.S. Senate, he might have been less apt to entertain ideas on how to fire an independent agency investigator. They might also be less comfortable with discussing such privileged information as happened in the Madison-Whitewater case.

There's a great deal of talent out there. Elected officials should have the grace to search for it and not take the cheap, often fatal, step of relying on cronies.

XII. BOND BROKERAGE FAVORITISM MUST BE STOPPED.

Every once in a while, an exposé hits the papers in which politicians are shown to be getting kickbacks from brokerage firms that handle state and municipal bond business.

In Governor Clinton's case, he helped build Lasater's Arkansas bond operation and was rewarded with large contributions and fund-raising help— even with a debt of his brother's being paid off. Later, with Lasater out of that business, Clinton shifted allegiance to the Stephens people. His final reward, skeptics believe, was the $3.5 million 1992 campaign loan from the Worthen Bank, which is partially owned by Stephens.

Bond brokerage business, at every level of government, should be awarded by an impartial group, perhaps a panel of retired state supreme court justices appointed by the governor and confirmed by the state senate.

Otherwise, it's an avenue for possible kickbacks or for large campaign contributions.

XIII. STOP CASHING IN ON POLITICAL CELEBRITY.

As we've seen, at least two federal officials (and there are surely others) have cashed in on their celebrity by accepting Initial Public Offerings—IPOs. Brokerage firms sometimes know which new public issues will be instant market stars, even on their very first day out in the market.

Federal legislation should be passed making it illegal for members of Congress, *and their spouses*, to accept such IPOs. State governments should do the same.

The spousehood route to fortune through political celebrity is a relatively new phenomenon, and Hillary Rodham Clinton is the perfect exponent. She built a personal fortune by cashing in as the wife of the Governor of Arkansas—through directorships, full pay for part-time legal work, a too-easy $99,000 gain from cattle future trades she didn't make herself, and more. Next, we'll look at the whole problem of spouses in modern political society.

XIV. ELIMINATE SPOUSES' CONFLICTED ROLE IN GOVERNMENT.

This is a relatively new concern in American political life and one we had better face up to — quickly.

The paradigm is, of course, Hillary Clinton, who has invented a new concept—"political partnership"—an idea not mentioned in the Constitution or in any congressional legislation.

In Little Rock she mastered the art of conflict, whether in her partnership at the Rose Law Firm, in her activities as a criminal lawyer, as the attorney for clients who were major contributors to her husband's campaigns, or as an attorney pleading before a state regulatory chief named by her husband. She was unique in the political history of Arkansas, or any other state.

Now she has transferred her energies and style to the national level.

What does that consist of? First, she is—and isn't—a federal worker. When she held secret health insurance meetings, a federal judge ruled that she was ex officio, a government employee. In her dual capacity of wife and public executive, she has a full-time staff of thirteen and an office in the Executive West Wing.

Her expenditure of taxpayer money is perhaps $2 million, with millions more for her health-care lobbying, with no such appropriations from Congress. White House costs are handled by the Treasury Subcommittee of the House Appropriations Committee, which has informed me that "there is no appropriation for Mrs. Clinton."

Margaret Williams is her chief of staff, which is an invented job. To legalize the cover, Ms. Williams is budgeted as an "Assistant to the President," but she works mainly for Mrs. Clinton.

The attempt to mix the two, to have a spouse (whether wife or husband) who is not elected by the people or officially appointed by the President working in the White House's Executive West Wing, is a dangerous precedent. In our system, accountability, not just the desire to do "good," is the hallmark of democracy. No one can fire or impeach Mrs. Clinton, nor would Congress force her to come as a witness to account for her acts. This makes her tenure in the present situation untenable.

She is not sensitive to any of this. As her life shows, she is imbued with the righteousness of her actions and the importance of her "goals." In such a view, the *process* of democracy is less important than the *goals*. But there are no specific goals in a democracy, only the maintenance of freedom. *Democracy is solely the process of a free people.*

Hillary has crossed the line from spouse to politico, and in doing so may be violating several federal laws. One is the nepotism act, Title 5, Section 3110, which was written after John Kennedy named his brother Bobby as Attorney General.

The law lays out the prohibition against hiring blood relatives or spouses and has a tortuous legal phrase about the "penalty." It states:

"An individual appointed, employed, promoted or advanced *in violation* [italics mine] of this section is not entitled to pay, and may not be paid from the Treasury. . . ."

Hillary, who has been ruled a de facto federal employee by the courts, is in obvious violation. And the "penalty," for gosh sakes, is she can't be paid. That's of little concern to a woman who has over a million dollars in liquid assets.

The second law she may be violating is the Anti-Deficiency Act, last amended in 1974, and listed as U.S. Code, Title 31, Sections 1341, 1342, and 1517. Basically, it says that no one working for the federal government may obligate it by the expenditure of funds not authorized by Congress.

Neither Hillary nor her job, nor her travel, nor her phone bills, nor her staff, is in the federal budget, except as expenditures of the President, who doesn't have the power to shift them to Hillary.

What to do? Simple. The nepotism law should be

amended to make its violation a criminal offense. Then spouses could not serve as Hillary now does. Second, if Hillary wants to join the real political world, she should run for office.

But what about our tradition of supporting the spouse of the President? That's a good tradition, but Hillary has stepped over the line. Spouses, who are not mentioned in the Constitution, should finally be institutionalized by law. An appropriation—just for them—should be passed by Congress.

That legislation should include a prohibition on direct political activity such as lobbying Congress. These restraints were not necessary before, but the changes in women's roles have made them necessary. Since Hillary's role in the Clinton administration is basically nonfeminist (based on marriage, not true appointment or election), it should be handled by new regulations.

An equitable appropriation from Congress would be a staff of three for the First Lady, with offices not in the West Wing but in the White House residence. Along with that a stated allowance for travel, etc. None of her staff should be permitted to attend any White House meetings involving the governance of the nation, as Hillary's staff now does. For the Second Lady, a staff of two, with office space in the Vice President's mansion on the Naval Observatory grounds. Period.

The spouse problem is not restricted to Hillary Clinton. Heather Foley, wife of Tom Foley, Speaker of the House, is chief of staff to the Speaker. Like Hillary, Mrs. Foley gets around her violation of the nepotism act by not getting paid. (She can afford it as well. The Speaker makes $171,500 a year, the same as the Vice President.) She has a

staff of twenty and spends millions of dollars of the taxpayers' money each year.

What to do? Simple, again. The nepotism law should
be amended to make that totally illegal, and Mrs. Foley, a
very able woman—who now holds major national power—
should leave and do what she wants *outside* the government. Or, of course, run for office.

If that's politically incorrect heresy, so be it.

XV. STOP UNETHICAL CONTACTS BETWEEN GOVERNMENT AGENCIES.

The lamebrain excuse that secret information from
the RTC could be "ethically" released to the White House
because of "press inquiries" illustrates a frightening deteri-
oration in the privacy of restricted information.

As we know, these criminal referrals also mention
other people whose privacy has now been tampered with,
and whose lives possibly injured. Simultaneously, it allows
those who may be guilty to escape prosecution.

To prevent such abuse—and subsequent whitewashes—
from happening again, new legislation should be passed to
make illegal the transfer of any information on law enforcement, or potential law enforcement, from Justice, the FBI, the
RTC, or other such agencies, to the White House or other
agencies without investigative or enforcement duties.

The penalties should be criminal in all such cases.

The Privacy Act of 1974, which has "records management rules," and criminal penalties under U.S. Code, Title 5,
Section 552a, should be amended to provide such criminal
penalties to protect the innocent and, simultaneously, to protect the ability of the government to act against the guilty.

The third lesson Whitewater teaches us is that the watch-dog role of federal organizations is just not working. Everyone involved in the recent chapter of the Whitewater fiasco has received a virtually clean bill of health. This does not jibe with what we know and have heard in the Senate hearings.

Their verdicts also seem infected with Alice in Wonderland semantics. The "troubling" matters and those of "poor judgment" and "meetings that shouldn't have happened" in the White House–RTC–Whitewater affair should have been ruled as what they are—plainly unethical, and, perhaps worse, actions by a host of public officials.

Here, then, are suggestions on how to make investigations of Washington behavior more accurate and stronger:

XVI. NO MORE FALSE "INDEPENDENT COUNSELS."

The idea that a Special Counsel can be named by the President's own Justice Department to investigate him or anyone close to him is laughable. Yet that is exactly what Mr. Fiske, an appointee of Janet Reno, was claiming to do. That practice should be discontinued immediately.

All major investigations involving administration personnel should be conducted outside the Justice Department by a *truly* Independent Counsel. That position has been reinstated by Congress as of June 30, 1994. Under that legislation a panel of federal judges has chosen a new Independent Counsel in the Madison–Whitewater case, who will report back to them rather than to the Attorney General or the President.

But we have to go further. Now, the Independent Counsel goes into action only when the President requests it. Clean government requires that *either* the President or the Congress, by a majority vote in both Houses, can *automatically* trigger such an appointment to investigate any potential scandal.

And as I've indicated in the prior chapter, we have to give the Independent Counsel power to judge unethical behavior of federal employees according to a single standard, then punish the offenders.

Not only are the last two points effective actions for discovery, but they are also strong deterrents against hubris and arrogance by political appointees of the President, of which we've already seen too much in the past fifty years.

XVII. ELIMINATE FALSE INTERNAL "INVESTIGATIONS."

The idea of a political appointee "investigating" his friends and cronies is ridiculous. Yet that is what Lloyd Cutler, counsel to the President, claimed to do.

On the first day of the House hearings, Cutler, with his courtly demeanor, announced that he had "investigated" the matter. Naturally, nothing unethical took place. His conclusion was hardly shocking, except that it was seriously entertained by some Congressmen!

What would we expect him to say? The concept of "investigating" one's friends and cronies is not logical and should never be countenanced by voters interested in good government. In fact, legislation should be passed making it illegal.

If Mr. Cutler had just followed the White House's own ethical regulations, he would have had to come in with a different verdict. Subtitled "PROHIBITED CONTACTS WITH AGEN-

CIES," and dated February 22, 1993 (George Washington's birthday!), it states simply that "these restrictions apply with particular force where agencies have an adjudicative, investigative, enforcement, intelligence, or procurement function."

That surely covers the RTC. What are the restrictions? There are several, but they all say the same: that "no member of the White House staff should contact" or have "involvement" with any such agency with respect to any pending matter. It adds: "White House staff members should avoid even the mere appearance of interest or influence."

The penalty? "Violations of these restrictions may result not only in significant embarrassment to the individual involved and the White House, but in legal sanctions against the individual as well."

Were any "legal sanctions" applied against the White House staff?

Hardly. In fact, quite the opposite. Everyone has been as cleared.

If we want clean government, then all executive branch investigations must be *external* or, if handled internally, conducted only by totally independent agencies, not by people who work for the President.

XVIII. MAKE THE INSPECTOR GENERALS (IGs) TOTALLY INDEPENDENT.

They could handle a proper oversight role *if* they were granted real power. Right now, the IGs of the executive branches are too often disguised tools of the administration they work for.

The recent example of the Treasury Department Inspector General's Office, which also cleared everyone in that agency, is a case in point. The report was issued prior to the Senate hearing and makes *no mention* of several serious contradictions in testimony by Treasury executives Jean Hanson, Roger Altman, and Secretary Bentsen, for example.

If the IGs want to become effective and not just pick on clerks who steal stamps while absolving the political brass, they'll need a total overhaul.

IGs should have the right of subpoena. They should be *totally separated* from their agency and change from an arm of the executive, as they now are, into congressionally authorized and supported ombudsman organizations, as exist in the Scandinavian countries.

That type of watchdog would surely have come up with a different view of the whole operation.

XIX. THE OFFICE OF GOVERNMENT ETHICS (OGE) MUST BE REORGANIZED.

This agency is somewhat more independent than the IGs and has a director appointed for five years who often crosses administrations. But it, too, is insufficient, as witnessed by its double-talk and obfuscations.

On July 30, 1994, the OGE issued its report on the White House–Treasury contacts on Whitewater (also completed before the revealing hearings), stating that none of them were unethical, though some were "troubling."

This has created a new category of ethics. What, pray, is the difference between "troubling" and "unethical"? Washington, which has been teeter-tottering on the brink of instability, has now gone over the top. In fact, what they call "troubling" is exactly what the White House protocols call "unethical"!

This group and others have also engaged in the new

Washington fantasy: that the threat of "press exposure" changes a nonpublic, secret document such as a criminal referral into a public document. That, of course, is the height of political insanity.

The timing of the OGE report was quite premature. It was released before the major Senate hearings in which testimony considerably altered the view of events. And like the other watchdogs, they seem to know nothing about the seriously conflicting stories, and the possibility that someone may have committed perjury, or withheld evidence, even though they evaluated depositions from the very same witnesses.

The OGE report was obviously published hastily at the end of July to beat out the appearance of the Treasury witnesses before Congress, thus making things look better than they were.

And, as we've seen, their judgment was far more conditional and restricted by technical mumbo-jumbo than we had been led to believe. The OGE did *no* investigation of its own. It excluded any judgement of the White House staff, and it admitted that behavior could be seen as unethical without violating the OGE's standards of conduct.

Government ethics at the highest levels can be determined only by an *external* body. The creation of such a group would require bipartisan membership, a setup similar to the Ethics Committees of the Congress, or the operating principles of the Federal Elections Commission, which has a board of six—made up of three Democrats and three Republicans.

Whatever we end up doing, the present system of weighing the ethics of politicians in the executive branch is just no good. If we had any more of this supposed "impartiality," we'd have to close down the whole federal government.

XX. CURB THE USE OF CASH IN CAMPAIGNS

As our last item in the list of important reforms needed in American politics, we return to the subject of money. On August 20, 1994, it was revealed that an Arkansas bank handling Governor Clinton's 1990 gubernatorial campaign may have violated the Bank Secrecy Act (requiring the reporting of the withdrawal of cash) which can be a criminal offense. Clinton's campaign may also have violated these rules.

The *New York Times* uncovered the fact that, during that campaign, $52,500 was converted into $50 and $100 bills to be used for various purposes, some unknown. Federal regulations require any bank withdrawal, or private payment, of $10,000 or more be reported by the bank to the IRS, and also holds individuals responsible (U.S. Code, Title 31, Section 5322), if they are in collusion with the bank. In the 1990 campaign, Bruce Lindsey, now senior advisor to the President and then treasurer of Clinton's $2.8 million effort, signed checks for large "cash withdrawals." Lindsey says the money was used for a get-out-the-vote effort.

The first cash withdrawal for $30,000 was initially broken up into four $7,500 bank checks, which looks suspiciously like an attempt to circumvent the $10,000 IRS reporting requirement. Not until four years later, in 1994, apparently when it was learned that the Special Counsel was looking into it, did an attorney for the campaign's bank claim that the bank had "overlooked" the federal regulation and finally filed with the IRS. (That's still another tax error, or worse, in the Whitewater case.)

The reform is obvious. First, the criminal penalties for not disclosing the use of over-the-limit cash in political campaigns should be *doubled* and *enforced*. Second, the $10,000 limit on cash disclosure should be changed to $1,000 in all state and congressional campaigns to dry up the use of greenbacks in elections, an old Tammany Hall standby.

Whether in Arkansas or elsewhere, cash in politics is a dangerous instrument that can pay for pizzas in after-hours work, but it can also secretly buy votes and influence.

(After the 1990 Clinton campaign books were closed, $35,000 of the remaining money was put into a special account for "politically related expenses" for the Governor. By some extension of logic, $29,000 of this slush fund is reportedly still there, even though the Governor is now President!)

The saga of Whitewater continues, but it is far from over. As I promised, it holds lessons for us all. Some are technical, others quite simple, and all are vital if we're to avoid the collapse of our political system through loss of faith in public officials.

Cicero warned us of the hubris of politicians, the sin that destroys all civilizations. It infects the political class like a flu bug in an epidemic and can be restrained only by *strictness and humility* in public life.

Government is a sacred trust, not an opportunity for politicians and bureaucrats to glorify or enrich themselves. It must be treated as such if democracy is to survive as more than a brilliant, but disappearing, comet in the history of man.

The Whitewater experience has not been a good one for the nation, and it is far from over. There will be further reports from the new Independent Counsel, and additional congressional hearings.

We have survived other scandals, from Teapot Dome to Watergate, and we will survive Whitewater. But we will grow stronger only if we take its lessons to heart.

Documents

The following documents relating to the recent Whitewater hearings were supplied by a member of the House Banking Committee.

DEPARTMENT OF THE TREASURY
WASHINGTON

4.1

GENERAL COUNSEL

September 30, 1993

MEMORANDUM FOR ROGER C. ALTMAN
DEPUTY SECRETARY

FROM: JEAN E. HANSON

SUBJECT: The Rose Law Firm

Steve Katsanos has talked with Sue Schmidt (See attached RTC
Early Bird).

I have spoken with the Secretary and also with Bernie
Nussbaum and Cliff Sloan.

I have asked Bill Roelle to keep me informed. Is there
anything else you think we should be doing?

Attachment

149

*A memo from Treasury Chief Counsel Jean Hanson to Roger Altman, Act-
ing Director of the Resolution Trust Corporation, dated September 30,
1993, the day after her meeting at the White House on the Madison criminal referrals that mentioned the Clintons. Hanson says that she spoke
about it with Treasury Secretary Lloyd Bentsen, Bernard Nussbaum, then
counsel to the President, and Cliff Sloan, a White House attorney. She asks,
"Is there anything else you think we should be doing?" (Both Roger Altman
and Jean Hanson have since resigned.)*

fyle: Whitewr

X001049

MEMORANDUM

To: File

From: Bruce R. Lindsey

Date: October 20, 1993

Re: Whitewater Development Corporation

On Thursday, October 14, 1993, Bernie Nussbaum, Neil Eggleston, and Cliff Sloan of the White House Counsel's office, Mark Gearan and I met with Jack DeVore, Josh Steiner, and Jean Hanson of the Treasury Department. The purpose of the meeting was to discuss a telephone call that Jack had received the day before from Jeff Gerth of *The New York Times*.

Gerth informed DeVore that he is aware that a number of criminal referrals involving Jim McDougal and Madison Guaranty had been forwarded from RTC's Kansas City field office to its Washington office. (Apparently, the "normal" procedure is for a criminal referral to be sent from a field office directly to the appropriate U.S. Attorney's office. DeVore did not know why these referrals came to Washington instead.) Gerth stated that, to his knowledge, President Clinton was not a target of the referrals, although Governor Jim Guy Tucker might be.

One of the referrals, however, involved four cashiers checks -- each for $3,000, two made payable to the Clinton for Governor Campaign and two made payable to Bill Clinton. The checks were dated April 4 or 5, 1985. All four checks were deposited in the Bank of Cherry Valley. Gerth wanted DeVore to find out who had endorsed the checks. (A check of our campaign records turned up three cashiers checks for $3,000 each from J. W. Fulbright, Ken Peacock, and Dean Landrum, and a personal check for $3,000 from Jim McDougal, signed by Susan McDougal.)

1

wwd.mcm
102093.1

A memo from Bruce R. Lindsey, senior advisor to the President, dated October 20, 1993, in which he summarizes the Whitewater situation, including news of four possibly incriminating checks for $3,000 each that "turned up" in "our campaign records," referring to the 1984 gubernatorial race now under investigation by the Independent Counsel.

X001050

DeVore confirmed with the RTC that the referrals had been received in the Washington office, but had already been forwarded on to the Little Rock U.S. Attorney's office. DeVore wanted to make it clear to Gerth that the referrals had been sent to Little Rock **before** his call. DeVore's inclination was also to confirm to Gerth the fact of the referrals. He indicated that such confirmation was normal procedure. We suggested that instead of confirming the referrals, DeVore should indicate "off the record" that whatever had been received in Washington had been forwarded to the U.S. Attorney's office prior to Gerth's call.

The RTC believes that the funds for the cashiers checks came from a loan from Madison Guaranty to a Republican, but supposedly the Republican was unaware that some of the loan funds had been diverted.

cc: Maggie Williams
      Bill Kennedy
      Mark Gearan

2

102093.1

DIARY

- on Whitewater, Maggie told me that HRC was "paralyzed" by it.
- if we don't solve this "within the next two days" — you don't have to worry about her schedule on health care
- WMB went over to see George on Whitewater yesterday; to argue for "lancing the boil"
- Maggie's strong inference was that the W.H. was trying to negotiate the scope of an independent counsel with Reno and having enormous difficulty
- HRC "doesn't want (the counsel) poking into 20 years of public life in Arkansas"
- ~~[redacted]~~
-
-

2987

A page from the "scrapbook," or diary, of Roger Altman, dated January 4, 1994 in which he talks about Mrs. Clinton being "paralyzed" by Whitewater and the comment that "HRC doesn't want (the counsel) poking into 20 years of public life in Arkansas."

D R A F T -- March 7, 1994

Q. When did you find out about the meetings?

A. [When I heard about them in the media.] *Incorrect*

See Insert 18A.
Others? I know he learned about the two fall meetings prior to learning about them in the media.

A page from a draft of Q&A's prepared for Lloyd Bentsen prior to a House Appropriations Committee meeting. The handwritten comments were made by his counsel, Jean Hanson, who says that Bentsen knew about the White House fall meetings—which Bentsen denied under oath during the Whitewater hearings

THE DEPUTY SECRETARY OF THE TREASURY
WASHINGTON

Mack/Harold

Roger - Vintage Altman - you are truly one of our country's finest - [initials]

DEAR MR. PRESIDENT,

I WANTED TO EXPLAIN MY DECISION ON THE RTC RECUSAL AND TO ASSURE YOU THAT I TRIED TO ACT WITH THE ADMINISTRATION'S BEST INTERESTS IN MIND.

THE DECISION TO HAVE THAT MEETING WITH YOUR STAFF WAS DUMB. I TAKE FULL RESPONSIBILITY FOR IT. MY INTENTION WAS O.K. – EXPLAIN THE PROCEDURES THE RTC WOULD BE FOLLOWING (NO DISCUSSION OF THE SUBSTANCE OF THE CASE) – BUT THE APPEARANCES ESCAPED ME AND NEVER SHOULD HAVE.

RELATIVE TO RECUSAL, IT HAD BEEN UNDER CONSIDERATION FOR SEVERAL WEEKS. SECRETARY BENTSEN, TREASURY GENERAL COUNSEL AND THE RTC COUNSEL HAD URGED IT IN THE STRONGEST TERMS.

NEVERTHELESS, I HAD THOUGHT IT SUPERFLUOUS AND HAD DECLINED TO TAKE THAT STEP. MY APPOINTMENT WAS SCHEDULED TO EXPIRE ON MARCH 30. AND, MY INSTRUCTIONS TO RTC STAFF HAD BEEN TO HANDLE THIS MATTER IN IDENTICAL FASHION TO ANY OTHER CASE. THIS WAS TO ENSURE AN IMPARTIAL PROCESS.

BUT, AFTER MY TESTIMONY ON THURSDAY, IT BECAME CLEAR THAT APPEARANCES OF A CONFLICT WERE TAKING HOLD. I WAS ADVISED THAT THE ADMINISTRATION COULD BE HAMMERED OVER THIS FOR SOME TIME.

I CONCLUDED, THEN, THAT SUCH ONGOING CRITICISM WOULD BE MORE HARMFUL THAN ANY BENEFITS

299[illegible]

A letter from Roger Altman to President Clinton dated March 9, 1994, in which Altman explains why he recused himself from the Madison-Whitewater case. He says the "the decision to have that meeting with your staff was dumb," then adds, "I apologize for the embarrassment this has caused." A comment at the top of the letter appears to be scribbled by the President :"Roger—vintage Altman—you are truly one of our country's finest."

ASSOCIATED WITH MY REMAINING UNRECUSED FOR FOUR MORE WEEKS.

HAVING RESISTED THE INITIAL ADVICE, THIS WAS A HARD DECISION TO MAKE. I HOPE YOU UNDERSTAND MY MOTIVATIONS. I APOLOGIZE FOR THE EMBARRASSMENT THIS HAS CAUSED.

SINCERELY,

2993

I. 12/2/93 - 1/9/94, lines 1-3: Whitewater
(Clinton's real estate investments) and Madison S&L dominate the
news. Clear lesson: release everything right away.

II. 1/24-2/12/94, lines 1 forward: Two extremes: In
DC spent long hours w/ RA going over how he should handle the
RTC's investigation of Whitewater. The statute of limitations on
Madison Guaranty cases was supposed to expire 2/28. Should RA
recuse himself or should he stay involved. The hurdle was so
high (fraud) that it seemed unlikely the RTC would bring suit or
seek a tolling agreement from BC/HRC, but the chance existed. RA
originally decided to recuse himself but under intense pressure
from the White House, he said he would make the final
determination based on a recommendation from Ellen Kulka, the GC.
The GOP through D'Amato began a countdown to the 28th which was
particularly ironic since he had voted against extending the
statute during the RTC reauthorization period. As it turns out,
RA's problem will probably pass when the Congress decides to
extend the statute once again. Pressure on RA will certainly
mount next week when Congress holds hearings on the RTC given
that Ricki Tiegert the FDIC nominee declared that she would
recuse herself from all Madison related issues due to her
friendship w/ the Clintons. The WSJ also got into the act w/ a
scathing attack on RA and Gene Ludwig.

III. and IV. 2/13-2/27/94, line 7 forward: Every now
and again you watch a disaster unfold and seem powerless to stop
it. For weeks we have been battling over how RA should handle
the RTC investigation of Madison Guaranty S&L. Initially, we all
felt that he should recuse himself to prevent even the appearance
of a conflict. At a fateful WH mtg w/ Nussbaum, Ickes and
Williams, however, the WH staff told RA that it was unacceptable.
RA had gone to brief them on the impending statute of limitations
deadline and also to tell them of his recusal decision. They
reacted very negatively to the recusal and RA backed down the
next day and agreed to a defacto recusal where the RTC would
handle this case like any other and RA would have no involvement.
We are very concerned that at the RTC oversight hearings the GOP
would hammer away at the recusal issue so we renewed discussions
w/ the WH about what RA would do when his term expired on March
30. Once again they were very concerned about him turning the
RTC people they didn't know so RA did not formally commit himself
to stepping down (he could stay on if we had formally nominated a
successor). At the hearing, the recusal amazingly did not come
up. The GOP did hammer away at whether RA had had any mtgs. w/
the WH. He admitted to having had one to brief them on the
statute deadline. They also asked if staff had met, but RA
gracefully ducked the question and did not refer to phone calls
he had had. The next day, the NYT ran a front page story on the
mtg. The heat was on. We spent a tortured day trying to decide
if he should recuse himself. I spoke w/ Podesta to let him know

*Excerpts from the diary of Joshua L. Steiner, youthful chief of staff to
Treasury Secretary Lloyd Bentsen, from December 2, 1993 through February 27, 1994. The entries reveal a number of unknown facts about the
Treasury–White House contacts on Madison-Whitewater. The last entry is
poignant: "Such an incredible city. Been battling w/ the RTC/Madison.
Wrote two pages about what's been going on, suddenly realized that I could
be subpoenaed . . . So on that subject, nothing."*

of our deliberations. Very frustrating that he was the chosen
point of contact since he clearly was not in the complete
confidence of George and Harold. After Howell Rains from the NYT
called to say that they were going to write a brutal editorial,
RA decided to recuse himself. Harold and George then called to
say that BC was furious. They also asked how Jay Stephens, the
former USA, had been hired to be outside counsel on this case.
Simply outrageous that RTC had hired him, but even more amazing
when George then suggested to me that we needed to find a way to
get rid of him. Persuaded George that firing him would be
incredibly stupid and improper. The NYT ran a very mean
editorial which referred to the "bone headed conclave convened by
RA." Lessons: Do what you think is the right thing early
(recuse); remember that everything might eventually be asked
about under oath; don't let the WH get involved in any way.

V. 2/13-27/94: Such an incredible city. Been
battling w/ the RTC/Madison. Wrote two pages about what's been
going on, suddenly realized that I could be subpoenaed like
Packwoods and the most innocuous comments could be taken out of
context. So on that subject, nothing.

ABOUT THE AUTHOR

The Great Whitewater Fiasco is the sixth nonfiction work of author, editor, and educator Martin L. Gross.

It follows directly after the publication of his phenomenal bestsellers *The Government Racket: Washington Waste from A to Z*, and *A Call for Revolution* which triggered a national debate on the subject of government spending, inefficiency, and the need for true change.

Both books were *New York Times* bestsellers for more than thirty weeks and *The Government Racket* reached the No. 1 position on the *Washington Post* list.

Mr. Gross has appeared on a host of national television shows including "Larry King Live," "Good Morning America," "20/20," "CBS This Morning," "Prime Time Live," "The Tom Snyder Show," CNN, and C-Span to share his investigative research.

The author testified before the Senate Governmental Affairs Committee on the subject of Washington waste and inefficiency, spoke to the staff of the House Budget Committee, and received thanks from the Vice President's office for his revelations, several of which were used in the *National Performance Review*. Recently, he testified before the House "A to Z" hearings, offering detailed budget cuts in the billions.

Ross Perot has called his work a "handbook for cleaning out the stables" of federal government. He has also been praised by former Senator William Proxmire and many other public figures.

The former editor of *Book Digest* magazine, Mr. Gross is an experienced reporter who covered Washington for many years for national publications. His syndicated column, "The Social Critic," appeared in newspapers throughout the country, including the *Los Angeles Times*, *Newsday*, and the *Chicago Sun-Times*. His articles have been published in a variety of magazines, from *Life* to *The New Republic*.

The author's prior nonfiction works were selections of major book clubs and aroused significant controversy.

His first, *The Brain Watchers*, was a critique of psychological testing. Called the "bunkraker" by *Time* magazine, Mr. Gross was a leading witness at Congressional hearings, resulting in legislation curtailing their use in federal employment.

His second work, *The Doctors*, an indictment of poor medical care, received strong support from academic physicians, including the director of the prestigious Massachusetts General Hospital. The author was attacked by the AMA, whose organization has since followed most of his recommendations to improve the quality of medicine in America.

The author's third work, *The Psychological Society*, was a critique of American psychiatry. Mr. Gross was the leading witness at a U.S. Senate hearing, which resulted in legislation that followed his recommendations for increased research into mental illness.

Mr. Gross served on the faculty of the New School for Social Research for many years and has been Adjunct Associate Professor of Social Science at New York University.